SPMG

CW01594072

HEINEMANN MATHEMATICS 2

Teacher's Notes

For **Level 2** of the National Curriculum (England and Wales, and Northern Ireland) and for **Level A**/towards **Level B** of Mathematics 5–14 (Scotland).

HEINEMANN EDUCATIONAL

Heinemann Educational,
a division of Heinemann Publishers (Oxford) Ltd,
Halley Court, Jordan Hill, Oxford OX2 8EJ

OXFORD LONDON EDINBURGH
MADRID ATHENS BOLOGNA PARIS
MELBOURNE SYDNEY AUCKLAND SINGAPORE TOKYO
IBADAN NAIROBI HARARE GABORONE
PORTSMOUTH NH (USA)

First published 1992
Reprinted 1992
93 94 95 10 9 8 7 6 5 4 3 2

Writing team

Ian K Clark
Peter S Henderson
Archie MacCallum
David McCulloch
John Mackinlay
Myra A Pearson
Catherine D J Preston

Designed by Miller, Craig & Cocking
Produced by Oxprint Ltd

Printed in the UK by Scotprint Ltd, Edinburgh.

ISBN 0 435 02113 3

Preface

Heinemann Mathematics is a new course which offers continuous development from nursery through the infant and junior stages to secondary level. It has been created by the Scottish Primary Mathematics Group, augmented by experienced nursery, primary and secondary teachers. The new material draws on feedback from practising teachers and experience gained from years of classroom use of the original SPMG course, 'Primary Mathematics – a development through activity'.

The course is based on the belief that mathematics is best learned through practical activities, discussion and teaching by the teacher. There is an emphasis on problem solving, pattern and investigative work. Mathematics is presented 'in context' wherever possible so that it can be seen to be related to the world outside the classroom and the world of the child's imagination. The course aims to help children to apply mathematics in a variety of situations. Calculators are used at appropriate points to introduce concepts and to solve problems.

This approach is in tune with the guidelines provided by the National Curriculum (England and Wales), Mathematics 5–14 (Scotland) and mathematics in the Northern Ireland Curriculum. Heinemann Mathematics has been designed to provide teachers with resources and a structure to meet the requirements of each curriculum. Assessment material linked to attainment targets is included.

Teachers will wish to select from the materials provided as part of a broader strategy of teaching, where resources are matched to individual needs and abilities. A variety of formats such as workbooks, cards, textbooks and photocopiable masters is employed so that the course materials can be used flexibly in ways which suit particular teachers and children.

Contents

Heinemann Mathematics 2: Comparison Chart

AT	Programme of Study	Teacher's Notes	Workbooks	Workcar
1/2	• selecting the materials and the mathematics to use for a practical task. • describing work and checking results. • asking and responding to the question: 'What would happen if...?'	for all workbook chapters	**2** pp. 1–6, 13, 14 **3** pp. 2–6, 17, 18 **4** pp. 1–6, 10–18, 23 **Measure** pp. 1–12, 16–18, 21, 22 **Shape** pp. 1–10	
2/2a	• knowing and using addition and subtraction facts up to 10.	pp. 12–34, 44–7	**1** pp. 1–23 **2** pp. 1–6, 20–23	
	• reading, writing and ordering numbers to at least 100 and using the knowledge that the tens digit indicates the number of tens.	pp. 34–44, 51–71	**2** pp. 7–19 **3** pp. 2–15, 17, 18, 19	Place value 1
2/2b	• solving whole number problems involving addition and subtraction, including money.	pp. 12–34, 44–7, 66–9, 71–3, 77–92	**1** pp. 1–23 **2** pp. 1–6, 20–23 **3** pp. 16, 21–3 **4** pp. 1–12, 19, 20	Calculators 1-
	• comparing two numbers to find the difference.	pp. 25, 45–7	**1** pp. 21–3 **2** pp. 22,23	
	• using coins in simple contexts	pp. 30–4, 45, 46, 59, 71–3, 81, 92	**2** pp. 1–6, 22 **3** pp. 21–3 **4** pp. 6, 19	
2/2c	• understanding the meaning of 'a half' and 'a quarter'.	pp. 93–5	**4** pp. 21–3	
2/2d	• using non-standard measures in length, area, capacity, 'weight' and time, comparing objects and recognising the need for standard units. • learning and using the language for common units in length, capacity, 'weight' and time.	pp. 97–111, 116, 117, 119, 120	**Measure** pp. 1–12, 16–18, 21, 22, *for pp. 13–15: Ma 2/3e*	Length **1–5**
3/2a	• exploring and using patterns in addition and subtraction facts to 10.	pp. 12–17, 19, 21	**1** pp. 1, 3, 5–7, 9	
	• distinguishing odd and even numbers.	pp. 70, 87	**3** p. 20 **4** pp. 11, 12	
3/2b	• understanding the use of a symbol to stand for an unknown number.	pp. 44, 45, 69	**2** pp. 20, 21	Calculators 1–
4/2a	• recognising squares, rectangles, circles, triangles, hexagons, pentagons, cubes, rectangular boxes (cuboids), cylinders and spheres and describing them.	pp. 122–32, 143	**Shape** pp. 1–10 **Handling data** pp. 5, 6	Shape **1–6**
	• recognising right-angled corners in 2D and 3D shapes.	pp. 133–5	**Shape** pp. 11–12	
4/2b	• recognising types of movement: straight (translation), turning (rotation).	pp. 135, 138–9	**Shape** pp. 9, 15	
	• understanding angles as a measurement of turn.	pp. 135–6	**Shape** pp. 13, 14	
	• understanding turning through right angles.	pp. 135–6	**Shape** pp. 13, 14	
	• understanding conservation of length, capacity and 'weight'.	See 2/2d		
5/2a	• choosing criteria to sort and classify objects; recording results or outcomes of events.	pp. 141–3, 145–51	**Handling data** pp. 3, 4, 9, 10	
	• designing a data collection sheet, recording data leading to a frequency table.	pp. 141–3, 145–50	**Handling data** pp. 9, 10	
	• constructing and interpreting frequency tables and block graphs for discrete data.	pp. 141–3, 148–50	**Handling data** pp. 1–6, 11–13	
	• using diagrams to represent the result of classification using two different criteria.	pp. 150–1	**Handling data** p. 14	
5/2b	• recognising that there is a degree of uncertainty about the outcomes of some events and that other events are certain or impossible.	p. 152	**Handling data** p. 15	

for National Curriculum, Level 2

Check-ups	Assessment in Context	Contexts (Number of activities in brackets)	Problem Solving Activities	Resource Cards
	At the fair, Q3, 13, 21, 25, 26, 28 Treasure Island, Q32, 33	The street: 1–5 Islands: 2, 4, 6, 7	All activities	**24, 25** (Shape jigsaws)
for Workbook **1** pp. 1–4 for Workbook **2** pp. 1, 4 for Workbook **4** p.1: *Ma 2/3a: Workbook **4** pp. 1–4*	At the fair, Q7, 11, 12, 21, 22	The street: 2, 3, 7 Islands: 1–3, 6, 7	3 (Money banks) 8 (Papers) 10 (Pocket money)	**1, 2** (Subtraction picture) **12, 13** (Island pictures) **14, 15, 16, 17** (Island game)
for Workbook **2** pp. 2, 3 for Workbook **3** pp. 1, 2	At the fair, Q1, 2, 16–18 Treasure Island, Q2, 7, 11, 24, 25, 32 *at Level 3: Q3, 5, 12, 16, 21, 22*	The street: 2–5, 7 Islands: 3, 5–7	1 (Tens and units) 4 (The race) 6 (Number pairs) *at Level 1: 12 (Dominoes)*	**7** (Notation cards) **8, 9** (Fancy dress) **10, 11** (Three stories)
for Workbook **1** pp. 1–4 for Workbook **2** pp. 1, 4 for Workbook **4** p. 4	At the fair, Q13, 20, 21 Treasure Island, Q9, 15	The street: 3 Islands: 2, 3, 5–7	3 (Money banks) *at Level 1:* *10 (Pocket money)*	
for Workbook **1** p. 4 for Workbook **2** p. 4	At the fair, Q19 Treasure Island, Q27	The street: 3		
for Workbook **2** p. 1, 4 for Workbook **3** p. 4	At the fair, Q22 Treasure Island, Q15	The street: 3, 5 Islands: 2, 3, 5–7	3 (Money banks) 8 (Papers) 10 (Pocket Money)	**3, 6** (Fair game)
for Workbook **4** p. 4	Treasure Island, Q10		5 (Fish)	
for **Measure** pp. 1–3; *for p. 4: Ma 2/3e*	At the fair, Q15, 25 Treasure Island, Q1, 6, 13, 14, 20 *Ma 2/3d: Q5*	The street: 1–5, 7 Islands: 1, 3, 6, 7	5 (Fish) 13 (Fruit)	**18, 19** (Area puzzles)
for Workbook **3** p. 1 *Ma 3/3a: Workbook **3** pp. 1,3*	Treasure Island, Q19, 31	Islands: 5, 7	*Ma 3/1a: 7 (Flags)*	**10, 11** (Three stories)
for Workbook **3** p. 1	Treasure Island, Q17	Islands: 5	6 (Number pairs)	
for Workbook **1** p. 3 for Workbook **2** p. 1, 4	Treasure Island, Q12, 26, 31	The street: 2 Islands: 4		
for **Shape** pp. 1–4	At the fair, Q4, 6, 10, 27, 28 Treasure Island, Q4, 18, 33	The street: 1, 3, 4, 5 Islands: 2, 3, 5–7		**24, 25** (Shape jigsaws)
for **Shape** pp. 2, 3				
			2 (Shape puzzles)	
for **Shape** p. 3				
for **Shape** p. 3	Treasure Island, Q23	The street: 3, 4, 7	11 (Snail trails) *(also Ma 3/1a)*	**26, 27, 28** (Find the gold)
	At the fair, Q23, 24	The street: 2–4, 6 Islands: 1–3, 6		**29, 30** (Pets)
for **Handling data** p. 2	Treasure Island, Q28	The street: 2–4, 6 Islands: 1, 3, 6		**7** Notation cards
for **Handling data** pp. 1, 3	Treasure Island, Q29	The street: 2–4, 6 Islands: 1, 3, 6	13 (Fruit)	
	At the fair, Q24 Treasure Island, Q30	Islands: 6		**31, 32** (Pirates)
	At the fair, Q14			

Heinemann Mathematics 2: Comparison Chart

	Strand	Level	Teacher's Notes	Workbooks	Workcards	Check-ups
INFORMATION HANDLING	(C)	A	pp. 141–3			
		B	pp. 141–50	**Handling data** pp. 1–6, 9–13		
	(O)	A	pp. 141–3, 145–51	**Handling data** pp. 1–6, 14		
		B	pp. 141–50	**Handling data** pp. 1–6, 9–13		for **Handling data** p. 2
	(D)	A	pp. 141–3	**Handling data** pp. 5–6		
		B	pp. 141–51	**Handling data** pp. 1–8, 12–14		for **Handling data** pp. 1, 3, 4
	(I)	A				for **Handling data** p. 1
		B	pp. 141–50	**Handling data** pp. 5–6, 9–13		
NUMBER, MONEY AND MEASUREMENT	(RTN)	A	pp. 34–45, 50–51, 93–4	**2** pp. 7–21 **3** p. 1 **4** pp. 21–22	Number/place value **1–6**	for Workbook **2** pp. 2,3 for Workbook **4** p. 4
		B	pp. 51–71, 94–5	**3** pp. 2–15, 17–18, 23		for Workbook **3** pp. 1–3
	(M)	A	pp. 30–4, 45–6, 77–8	**2** pp. 1–6, 22 **4** pp. 1–2		for Workbook **2** p. 1
		B	pp. 71–3	**3** pp. 11–12, 21–3		for Workbook **3** p. 4
	(AS)	A	pp. 14–27, 30–34, 45–7	**1** pp. 1–23 **2** pp. 1–6, 22–3 **4** p. 20		for Workbook **1** pp. 1–4 for Workbook **2** pp. 1, 4
		B	pp. 43, 66–7, 69–92	**3** pp. 16, 19, 21–23 **4** pp. 1–2	Calculators **1–9**	for Workbook **4** pp. 1–4
	(PS)	A	pp. 14–22	**1** pp. 1–10		for **Shape** p. 4
		B	pp. 57–8, 67–70, 125–9	**3** pp. 9–10, 17–18, 20 **4** pp. 10–12 **Shape** pp. 1–6		for Workbook **3** p. 3 for **Shape** p. 2
	(FE)	A				
		B	pp. 44–5	**2** pp. 20–21	Calculators **1–9**	for Workbook **1** p. 3 for Workbook **2** p. 4
	(ME)	A	pp. 98–111, 120	**Measure** pp. 1–12, 21–22	Length **1–5**	for **Measure** pp. 1–3
		B	p. 119	**Measure** pp. 19–20		
	(T)	A	pp. 113–17	**Measure** pp. 13–15, 17–18		for **Measure** p. 4
		B	pp. 113–17	**Measure** pp. 13–16		
SHAPE, POSITION AND MOVEMENT	(RS)	A	pp. 124–32	**Shape** pp. 1–6	Shape **1–6**	for **Shape** pp. 1–4
		B	pp. 124–6, 132 (Level D: pp. 130–32)	**Shape** pp. 1–4, 9–12 (Level D: **Shape** pp. 7–10)		for **Shape** pp. 1, 4 (Level D: **Shape** pp. 2, 3)
	(PM)	A	pp. 88–90, 135–6	**Shape** pp. 13–14		
		B	pp. 135–6	**Shape** pp. 13–14		for **Shape** p. 3
PROBLEM SOLVING & ENQUIRY	PSE		pp. 16–24, 31–2, 65–71, 79–92, 98–101, 110–11, 120, 126–32	**1** pp. 1–6, 13–19 **2** pp. 1–5 **3** pp. 17–18 **4** pp. 3–18 **Measure** 1–4, 10–12, 21–22 **Shape** 1–4, 9–10	Length **1–5** Shape **6**	

Strands (C) Collect (O) Organise (D) Display (I) Interpret
(PS) Patterns and Sequences (FE) Functions and Equations (ME) Measure and Estimate (T) Time

or Mathematics 5–14, Levels A and B

ssessment in ntext	Contexts (Section numbers)	Problem Solving Activities	Resource Cards
	The street: 4, 6 Islands: 6 The street: 4, 6 Islands: 6		
the fair, Q23, 24 easure Island, Q28	The street: 2 Islands: 1, 3 The street: 2 Islands: 2, 6		**29**, **30** (Pets) **31**, **32** (Pirates) **7** (Notation cards)
the fair, Q24 the fair, Q9 easure Island, Q29, 30	The street: 2, 3, 6 The street: 4, 6 Islands: 1, 3, 6		**31**, **32** (Pirates)
  easure Island, Q27	The street: 3 The street: 6 Islands: 3, 6	13 (Fruit)	
the fair, Q1, 16, 17 easure Island, Q8 easure Island, Q7, 10, 11, 24, 25, 32	The street: 2–5, 7 Islands: 1, 6, 7 The street: 2 Islands: 3, 5, 6, 7	6 (Number pairs) 1 (Tens and units) 4 (The race)	**8**, **9** (Fancy dress) **7** (Notation cards) **10**, **11** (Three stories)
the fair, Q22 easure Island, Q15	The street: 3–5 Islands: 2, 3, 6, 7 Islands, 6, 7	3 (Money banks) 10 (Pocket money)	**3–6** (Fair game)
the fair, Q7, 11–13, 19–21 the fair, Q18 easure Island, Q2, 3, 9, 12, , 21, 22	The street: 2, 3 Islands: 2, 3, 6, 7 The street: 2 Islands: 1, 3–7	8 (Papers)	**1**, **2** (Subtraction picture) **12**, **13** (Islands picture) **14**–**17** (Islands game)
the fair, Q8 easure Island, Q19 easure Island, Q11, 17, 31	The street: 5 Islands: 4, 5, 6	7 (Flags) 12 (Dominoes)	**10**, **11** (Three stories)
easure Island, Q26	The street: 2 Islands: 4, 6		
the fair, Q15, 25, 26 easure Island, Q1, 6, 14	The street: 1–5, 7 Islands: 1, 3, 6, 7	5 (Fish) 9 (Sausage and egg) 13 (Fruit)	**18**, **19** (Area puzzles)
the fair, Q5 easure Island, Q5	The street: 3 Islands: 2, 6 The street: 3 Islands: 2, 6, 7		**20–23** (Opening and closing times) **20–23** (Opening and closing times)
the fair, Q4, 6, 10, 27 evel D: Q28) easure Island, Q33 evel D: Q4)	The street: 1, 3–5 Islands: 2, 3, 6, 7 The street: 5 Islands: 6	2 (Shape puzzles)	
  easure Island, Q18, 23	The street: 1, 3, 4, 7 Islands: 7 The street: 5	11 (Snail trails)	**26**, **27**, **28** (Find the gold)
the fair, Q3, 13, 21, 25, 26, 28 easure Island, Q15, 31–3	The street: 2, 3, 5 Islands: 4, 6, 7	All activities	**24**, **25** (Shape jigsaws)

(RTN) Range and Type of Number (M) Money (AS) Add and Subtract

(RS) Range of Shapes (PM) Position and Movement [PSE] Problem Solving and Enquiry

Heinemann Mathematics 2: Comparison Chart fo

AT	Statement of Attainment	Teacher's Notes	Workbooks	Workcar
P/2	• select, with help, the materials required for a task. • describe the current work. • respond to questions such as, "What would happen if…?"	for all workbook chapters	**2** pp. 1–6, 13, 14 **3** pp. 2–6, 17, 18 **4** pp. 1–6, 10–18, 23 **Measure** pp. 1–12, 16–18, 21, 22 **Shape** pp. 1–10	
N/2a	• read, write and order whole numbers to at least 100; use the knowledge that the tens-digit indicates the number of tens.	pp. 34–44, 51–71	**2** pp. 7–19 **3** pp. 2–15, 17–19	Place value 1
N/2b	• understand the meaning of 'a half' and 'a quarter'.	pp. 93–5	**4** pp. 21–3	
N/2c	• have quick recall and be able to use addition and subtraction facts to 10.	pp. 12–34, 44–7	**1** pp. 1–23 **2** pp. 1–6, 20–23	
N/2d	• solve whole number problems involving addition and subtraction, including money.	pp. 12–34, 44–7, 66–9, 71–3, 77–92	**1** pp. 1–3 **2** pp. 1–6, 20–23 **3** pp. 16, 21–3 **4** pp. 1–12, 19, 20	Calculators 1
N/2e	• make a sensible estimate of a number of objects up to 20.	pp. 50–54	**3** p. 1	Estimation 1-
A/2a	• explore and use the patterns in addition and subtraction facts to 10.	pp. 12–17, 19, 21	**1** pp. 1, 3, 5–7, 9	
A/2b	• understand the commutative property of addition.	*See* Heinemann Mathematics 1, Workbook 5		
A/2c	• understand the relationship between addition and subtraction.	pp. 21–3, 79–92	**1** pp. 13–18 **4** pp. 3–20	
A/2d	• distinguish between odd and even numbers.	p. 70, 87	**3** p. 20 **4** pp. 11, 12	
A/2e	• understand the use of a symbol to stand for an unknown number.	pp. 44, 45, 69	**2** pp. 20, 21	Calculators 1
M/2a	• use non-standard measures in length, area, volume, capacity, 'weight' and time to compare objects and recognize the need to use standard units.	pp. 97–111, 116, 117, 119, 120	**Measure** pp. 1–12, 16–18, 21, 22 M/3a: **Measure** pp. 13–15	Length **1–5**
M/2b	• know how to use coins in simple contexts.	pp. 30–4, 45, 46, 59, 71–3, 81, 92	**2** pp. 1–6, 22 **3** pp. 21–3 **4** pp. 6, 19	
M/2c	• know the most commonly used units in length, capacity, 'weight' and time, and what they are used for.	pp. 97–111, 116, 117, 119, 120	**Measure** pp. 1–12, 16–18, 21, 22	Length **1–5**
S/2a	• sort 2-D and 3-D shapes in different ways and give reasons for each method of sorting.	pp. 128–9 S/3a: pp. 122–32, 143	**Shape** p. 1 S/3a: **Shape** pp. 1–10 **Handling data** pp. 5, 6	S/3a: **Shape:**
S/2b	• understand the notion of angle in the context of turning.	pp. 135–6 S/3b: pp. 133–5	**Shape** pp. 13, 14 S/3b: **Shape** pp. 11–12	
S/2c	• give and understand instructions for turning through right-angles.	pp. 135–6	**Shape** pp. 13, 14	
S/2d	• recognize in practical situations different types of movement: straight, turning, turning over.	pp. 138–9	**Shape** p. 15	
D/2a	• choose criteria to sort and classify objects; record results of observations or outcomes of events.	pp. 141–3, 145–51	**Handling data** pp. 3, 4, 9, 10	
D/2b	• help to design a data collection sheet and use it to record a set of data leading to a frequency table.	pp. 141–3, 145–50	**Handling data** pp. 9, 10	
D/2c	• construct, read and interpret block graphs and frequency tables.	pp. 141–3, 148–50	**Handling data** pp. 1–6, 11–13	
D/2d	• represent the result of classifying real objects using two different criteria.	pp. 150–1	**Handling data** p. 14	
D/2e	• understand possible outcomes of simple random events.	p. 152	**Handling data** p. 15	
D/2f	• understand that there is a degree of uncertainty about the outcome of some events and others are certain or impossible.	p. 152	**Handling data** p. 15	

lathematics in the Northern Ireland Curriculum, Level 2

ieck-ups	Assessment in Context	Contexts	Problem Solving Activities	Resource Cards
	At the fair, Q3, 13, 21, 25–8 Treasure Island, Q32, 33	The street: 1–5 Islands: 2, 4, 6, 7	All activities	**24, 25** (Shape jigsaws)
r Workbook **2** pp. 2, 3 r Workbook **3** pp. 1, 2	At the fair, Q1, 2, 16–18 Treasure Island, Q2, 7, 11, 24, 25, 32	The street: 2–5, 7 N/1a: 5 N/3a: 2 Islands: 3, 5–7 N/1a: 1	1 (Tens and units) 4 (The race) 6 (Number pairs) N/1a: 12 (Dominoes)	**7** (Notation cards) **8, 9** (Fancy dress) **10, 11** (Three stories)
r Workbook **4** p.4	Treasure Island, Q10		5 (Fish)	
r Workbook **1** pp. 1–4 r Workbook **2** pp. 1, 4 r Workbook **4** p. 1	At the fair, Q7, 11, 12, 21, 22	The street: 2, 3, 7 Islands: 1–3, 6, 7	3 (Money banks) 8 (Papers) 10 (Pocket money)	**1, 2** (Subtraction picture) **12, 13** (Island pictures) **14–17** (Islands game)
r Workbook **1** pp. 1–4 r Workbook **2** pp. 1, 4 r Workbook **4** p. 4 N/3d: Workbook **4** pp. 1–4	At the fair, Q13, 20, 21 Treasure Island, Q9, 15 N/3d: Q3, 16, 21, 22	The street: 3 Islands: 2, 3, 5–7 N/3d: 1, 4–7	3 (Money banks) N/1d: 10 (Pocket money)	N/3d: **12, 13** (Island pictures) **14, 17** (Islands game)
	Treasure Island, Q8	Islands: 6, 7		
r Workbook **3** p. 1 A/3a: Workbook **3** p.3	Treasure Island, Q19, 31	Islands: 5, 7	A/1a: 7 (Flags)	**10, 11** (Three stories)
r Workbook **1** p. 3 r Workbook **4** p. 1	Treasure Island, Q21, 22			
r Workbook **3** p. 1	Treasure Island, Q17	Islands: 5	6 (Number pairs)	
r Workbook **1** p. 3 r Workbook **2** pp. 1, 4	Treasure Island, Q12, 26, 31	The street: 2 Islands: 4		
r **Measure** pp. 1–3 M/3a: for **Measure** p. 4	At the fair, Q15, 25 Treasure Island, Q1, 6, 13, 14, 20 M/3a: Q5	The street: 1–5, 7 Islands: 1, 3, 6, 7	5 (Fish) 13 (Fruit) M/1a: 9 (Sausage and egg)	**18, 19** (Area puzzles)
r Workbook **2** pp. 1, 4 r Workbook **3** p. 4	At the fair, Q22 Treasure Island, Q15	The street: 3, 5 Islands: 2, 3, 5–7	3 (Money banks) 8 (Papers) 10 (Pocket money)	**3, 6** (Fair game)
r **Measure** pp. 1–3 M/3b: **Measure** p. 4	At the fair, Q15, 25 Treasure Island, Q1, 6, 13, 14, 20 M/3b: Q5	The street: 1–5, 7 Islands: 1, 3, 6, 7	5 (Fish) 13 (Fruit) M/1a: 9 (Sausage and egg)	**18, 19** (Area puzzles) M/3b: 20–23 (Opening and closing times)
r **Shape** p. 1 S/3a: for **Shape** pp. 1–4	S/3a: At the fair, Q4, 6, 10, 27, 28 S/3a: Treasure Island, Q4, 18, 33	S/3a: The street: 1, 3, 4, 5 S/3a: Islands: 2, 3, 5–7		S/3a: **24, 25** (Shape jigsaws)
r **Shape** p. 3 S/3b: for **Shape** pp. 2, 3				
r **Shape** p. 3	Treasure Island, Q23	The street: 3, 4, 7	11 (Snail trails)	**26–8** (Find the gold)
			2 (Shape puzzles)	
	At the fair, Q23, 24	The street: 2–4, 6 Islands: 1–3, 6		**29, 30** (Pets)
r **Handling data** p. 2	Treasure Island, Q28	The street: 2–4, 6 Islands: 1, 3, 6		**7** Notation cards
r **Handling data** pp. 1, 3 D/1c: **Handling data** p. 4	At the fair, D/1c: Q9 Treasure Island, Q29	The street: 2–4, 6 D/1c: 6 Islands: 1, 3, 6	13 (Fruit)	
	At the fair, Q24 Treasure Island, Q30	Islands: 6		**31, 32** (Pirates)
	At the fair, Q14			
	At the fair, Q14			

Introduction

Heinemann Mathematics 2 is intended for use with infants working towards Level 2 of the National Curriculum (England and Wales, and Northern Ireland) and for those completing Level A of Mathematics 5–14 (Scotland). It also introduces some aspects of Level B work.

The Heinemann Mathematics 2 materials consist of:

- Teacher's Notes
- Workbooks
- Workcards
- Assessment and Resources Pack.

Workbooks Workcards	Teacher's Notes	Assessment and Resources Pack

Workbooks

Workbooks are included as they help young children with recording and are the best way to present some activities for this age group. It is also felt that their convenience of use and value as a record of work will be helpful to teachers.

Seven workbooks are included, four of which provide a sequence in number, including money. There is one workbook dealing with various aspects of measure, one on shape and one on handling data.

Throughout the workbooks headings ('Extension', 'Problem solving' and 'Investigation') have been included to indicate that a page, or part of a page, involves a particular type of work. These pages are also referenced at the beginning of the appropriate chapter in the *Teacher's Notes*. A symbol  has been included to indicate that use of a calculator may be appropriate.

Workbook 4 can be used alongside the 'Islands' Context provided in the *Assessment and Resources Pack* (see page 76). A large coloured picture is included in the Pack, to be used as part of the 'Islands' theme associated with pages 1–18 of Workbook 4.

Workbook 1	Addition and subtraction to 10
Workbook 2	Money to 10p Place value to 20 Further aspects of subtraction
Workbook 3	Estimation Place value to 100 Money to 50p
Workbook 4	Addition and subtraction to 13 Halves and quarters

Measure Workbook
Length Weight Capacity Area Time

Shape Workbook
3D shape 2D shape

Handling data Workbook

A chart showing the mathematical content of the workbooks and cards of Heinemann Mathematics 2 is given on pages 2 and 3.

Content of Workbooks and Workcards for Heinemann Mathematics 2

Workbook 1	Subtraction to 10 Money within 10p Addition and subtraction to 10 Subtraction: comparison	Subtraction stories of 7, 8, 9 and 10 Subtraction within 10p (1p coins) Linking addition and subtraction facts Word problems Vertical setting *How much more? How many more?*
Workbook 2	Money to 10p Number sequence to 20 Calculator work Counting to 20 Place value to 20	Counting and making up amounts to 10p using 1p, 2p and 5p coins Introducing the 10p coin Change from 5p and 10p The sequence of numbers to 20 *Number before, number after* Reading and writing numbers from 11 to 20 Introductory activities Counting or putting out sets of 11 to 20 objects Number names eleven to twenty For example, $13 = 10 + 3$ and $10 + 3 = 13$ Also, $15 = 1$ ten + ____ units
Place value Cards 1 to 6	Place value to 20 Counting on Aspects of subtraction	Practical activities Number line to 20 Complementary addition *Difference in price* *Difference between*
Estimation Cards 1 to 5	Estimation to 20	Practical activities
Workbook 3	Estimation to 20 Number to 100 Place value to 99 Counting on Number patterns to 100	Practice examples Recognising and writing numbers to 100 Calculator work Ordering numbers to 100 Counting activities to 50 Counting in tens Laying out tens and units Place value structure to 99 Number line to 100 Patterns and puzzles Adding on 10 Odd and even numbers
Calculator Cards 1 to 9	Calculator work Money to 50p	Addition and subtraction within 20 Counting and laying out coins Introducing the 20p coin

Workbook 4	Addition and subtraction to 20	Practical activities: Islands context
	Addition and subtraction to 13	Practical activities and recording for addition and subtraction stories of 11, 12 and 13
	Money to 13p	Applying addition and subtraction facts to 13
	Calculator work	Addition and subtraction to 20
	Fractions	Introducing halves and quarters
Measure	Length 1	Measuring lengths in non-standard units
	Weight	Weighing in non-standard units
Length Cards 1 to 5	Capacity	Pouring, filling and packing using non-standard units
	Area	Concept and language of area; finding areas in non-standard units
	Time	Telling the time from analogue and digital clocks: half past
		Months of the year; days of the week
	Commonly used units	hours, minutes, seconds, litres, pints, pounds, metres, miles
	Length 2	Group investigation
Shape Cards 1 to 6	3D shape models	Sweet factory theme: making models using cubes, cuboids, spheres, cones, pyramids, cylinders
Shape	3D shape names and patterns	Recognising 3D shapes Reading and writing names
	2D shape names and patterns	Revision of squares, rectangles, circles and triangles Recognising and naming pentagons and hexagons
	Right angles	Finding right angles Turning through right angles
	Transformations	Moving along, turning round and flipping over 2D shapes
Handling data	Block graphs	Drawing graphs Horizontal display
	Relationships	Mapping diagrams
	Collecting and interpreting data	Tick charts, frequency tables, block graphs
	Carroll diagrams	Two-attribute sorting
	Probability	Impossible, certain, uncertain

Workcards

Workcards are used to provide further practical activities involving number, measure and shape. Thirty-one single-sided cards are included. These are divided into five groups of cards related to specific mathematical topics. Each group is colour-coded to make the subject content of the cards easier to identify. The cards are referenced from workbook pages.

Some of the workcards can also be used to stimulate and support activities suggested in the *Contexts*. (See page 5.)

		Referenced from
Place value	**Cards 1 to 6**	Workbook 2, Page 18
Estimation	**Cards 1 to 5**	Workbook 3, Page 1
Calculators	**Cards 1 to 9**	Workbook 3, Page 19
Length	**Cards 1 to 5**	Measure Workbook, Page 4
3D Shape	**Cards 1 to 6**	Shape Workbook, Page 1

Teacher's Notes

The *Teacher's Notes* are the central element of the course. They make suggestions about teaching methods, mathematical content and assessment. They also indicate how the workbooks, workcards and *Assessment and Resources Pack* can contribute to a balanced, well-integrated course covering the attainment targets in the curriculum followed by your school.

The *Teacher's Notes* are divided into seven chapters, centred on the seven workbooks. The introductory two pages for each chapter provide useful summaries under the following headings:

Overview **Key words and phrases** **Resources**

Summary of the aims and mathematical content of each workbook together with its associated cards and teaching notes.

Workbook pages which contain 'extension' or problem solving or investigative activities are highlighted.

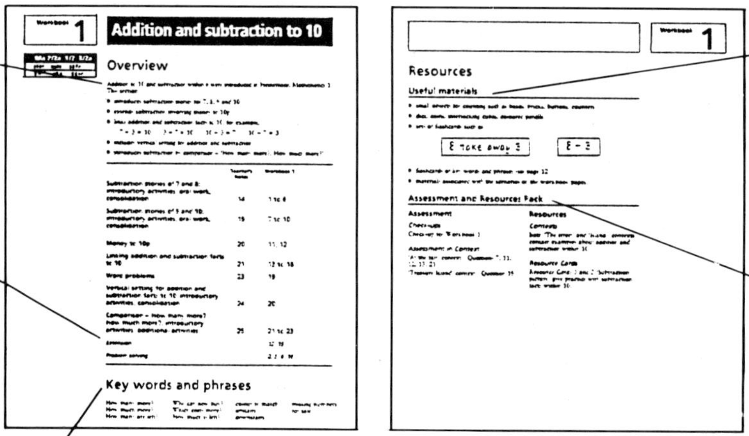

List of materials useful for workbook pages, cards and introductory teaching activities.

Specific references to appropriate items from the *Assessment and Resources Pack*.

Important language associated with the teaching activities, workbook pages and cards.

The introductory pages are followed by the Teaching Notes which give

- a variety of practical activities from which the teacher can *select* to introduce each new section of the work. These activities generally begin with situations in which the teacher is involved with a group of children but also include practical activities for individual children
- brief notes for groups of workbook pages or cards which follow up each new topic
- specific suggestions for oral work and consolidation
- additional activities to provide further practice or extension
- references to attainment targets.

Assessment and Resources Pack

The Pack contains booklets, pictures, photocopiable masters and resource cards, including photocopiable record sheets. The teacher should select assessment and resource materials from the Pack to suit the needs of particular children.

Assessment

There are two types of assessment in the Pack: *Check-ups* and *Assessment in Context* booklets.

Check-ups

The *Check-ups* booklet contains seven check-ups, each linked to the mathematical content of one of the workbooks. The booklet contains notes for teachers and photocopiable sheets for use with children.

Assessment in Context

The *Assessment in Context* booklet contains teacher's notes and photocopiable sheets for two contexts:

At the fair **Treasure Island.**

A large coloured picture for each context is supplied in the Pack. The pictures are intended to introduce the contexts. Some questions, particularly those asked orally, are directly related to the pictures.

Each assessment context contains a variety of questions related to the same theme and covering a range of attainment targets. It is suggested that no more than a few questions from any assessment context should be used at any one time. To help teachers relate the mathematics assessed within each context to individual workbooks, references to specific questions within the *Assessment in Context* are made at the beginning of each workbook chapter in the *Teacher's Notes*. It is not suggested, however, that the *Assessment in Context* material be used immediately after completion of a particular workbook.

Resources

There are three further items supplied in the Pack as resources for use in conjunction with the *Teacher's Notes*, workbooks and workcards. These are: *Contexts* and *Problem Solving Activities* booklets and *Resource Cards*. The teacher can select from this material to suit particular needs. No attempt should be made to use all of it with any class or child.

Contexts

The *Contexts* booklet contains suggestions for teachers for a wealth of mathematical activities related to two extended contexts or themes:

The street **Islands.**

The activities cover a wide range of mathematics and include problem solving and investigative activities, practical work and extension ideas. Relevant activities are referenced at the beginning of the appropriate chapter in the *Teacher's Notes*. However, it is envisaged that the *Contexts* will be used as part of an extended topic rather than as a 'dip-in' resource.

A large coloured picture is supplied in the Pack for use with the 'Islands' context.

Problem Solving Activities

The *Problem Solving Activities* booklet contains thirteen activities in the form of photocopiable sheets for children and notes for the teacher. The problems are intended to supplement the problem solving and investigative activities in the workbooks.

Resource Cards

The *Resource Cards* contain games, self-correcting activities and teaching aids linked to the activities in the *Teacher's Notes*, workbooks and workcards. A set of notes for teachers is provided to give details about preparing and using the cards.

Eight cards are provided as extra practice in addition and subtraction. Language such as 'difference', 'total', 'sum' and 'how many more' is included. Some of the examples involve money.

Photocopiable cards provide simple checklists to indicate curriculum coverage for each child/group.

References to attainment targets

- Detailed references to attainment targets for the National Curriculum (England and Wales, Mathematics 5–14 (Scotland) and Mathematics in the Northern Ireland Curriculum are included in the *Teacher's Notes* and in the *Assessment and Resources Pack*. These references are provided as an aid to planning and recording. There is no intention to suggest that teaching should follow targets in a slavish way.

For Scotland, references to strands have been coded as follows:

Collect	C	Fractions, Percentages and Ratio	FPR
Organise	O	Patterns and Sequences	PS
Display	D	Functions and Equations	FE
Interpret	I	Measure and Estimate	ME
Range and Type of Numbers	RTN	Time	T
Money	M	Range of Shapes	RS
Add and Subtract	AS	Position and Movement	PM
Multiply and Divide	MD	Angle	A
Round Numbers	RN	Problem Solving and Enquiry	PSE

For Northern Ireland, references to Attainment Targets have been coded as follows:

Processes in Mathematics	P
Number	N
Algebra	A
Measures	M
Shape and Space	S
Handling Data	D

- Charts which show how all the materials of Heinemann Mathematics 2 relate to attainment targets for each curriculum are included on pages vi–xi as well as in the Overview for the *Assessment and Resources Pack*.
- The statements of attainment and strands covered by each chapter in the *Teacher's Notes* appear at the start of the chapter beside the Overview section. For example, for Workbook 1, the targets are:

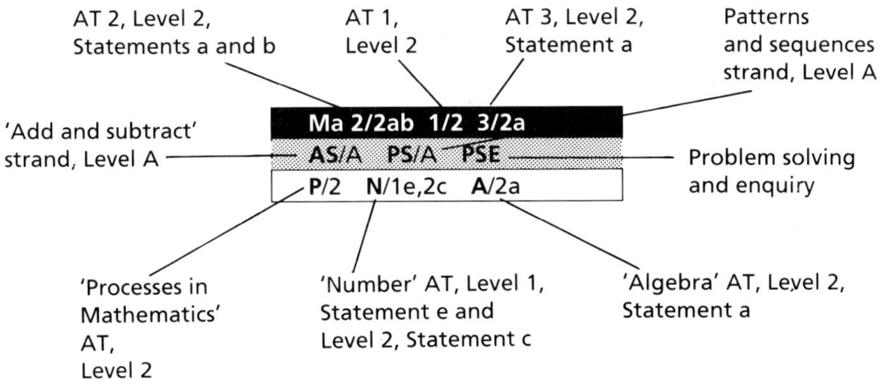

- Opportunities to develop and assess the skills covered by AT 1 are provided by many of the activities in Heinemann Mathematics 2. Statements of attainment, however, have not been referenced for this attainment target as the particular Statement of Attainment being addressed will depend largely on the way the activities are organised, implemented and discussed in the classroom.
- Specific attainment targets for introducing teaching activities, as well as for workbook pages and workcards, are shown in the margins in the Teaching Notes. Targets are given for introductory teaching suggestions as well as for workbook pages and workcards.
- The teacher's notes in the *Assessment and Resources Pack* for the *Check-ups*, *Assessment in Context*, *Contexts* and *Problem Solving Activities* booklets and for the *Resource Cards* each contain charts indicating relevant attainment targets.
- The *Check-ups* are intended to help teachers to check children's progress against attainment targets. These targets are given at the top of each check-up page. Each question in the *Assessment in Context* booklet is referenced to appropriate targets.

Using the Course

THE IMPORTANCE OF TEACHING

Heinemann Mathematics 2 is a package of materials intended to help teachers following any of the nationally recognised curricula (see pages vi–xi) to implement a balanced course in mathematics for their children at either Level 2 (England and Wales, Northern Ireland) or Level A/B (Scotland). A number of features built into the design of Heinemann Mathematics 2 influence the ways in which it is best used by teachers. For example:

- The teaching model on which the course is based is one where new ideas are introduced through the involvement of the teacher and children in **practical activities and discussion.** This is usually followed by further practical activities for the children to do by themselves. Written work involving the use of workbooks and cards is only attempted after sufficient practical work and discussion have taken place.
- Given this model, the *Teacher's Notes* is a crucial component of Heinemann Mathematics 2 as it provides suggestions for practical teaching activities and comments on the use of the other materials.
- **Teaching by the teacher is essential** and cannot be replaced by the use of workbooks, cards and photocopiable sheets. The function of such materials is to check up on what has already been taught, to provide a record of work done and to set new challenges where children apply what they have learned, often in problem solving and investigative situations.

> The workbooks and workcards are not designed to teach new concepts to children working through them on their own without prior teaching and discussion.

- Heinemann Mathematics 2 contains many more teaching suggestions and more pages and cards for children than should be tackled by any class, group or individual. **The teacher should select** from the available materials and, where necessary, supplement them or replace them by ideas from other sources to ensure a mathematical experience suited to the particular children in the class.

PLANNING PROGRAMMES OF STUDY

- The *Teacher's Notes* for Heinemann Mathematics 2 can help teachers to plan programmes of study as they suggest teaching sequences for developing topics in a structured way to meet curriculum requirements. They also contain references to attainment targets for the activities suggested and for the follow-up work in workbooks and workcards. In addition the course includes work which goes beyond these minimum targets.
- When planning activities to suit programmes of study the teacher should be selective by not trying to use all of the activities with all the children. There should also be flexibility about the order in which materials are to be used. For example, not all of the number work should be done before introducing measure, shape and data handling activities. There should be a balance of activities across these areas. Workbook activities should certainly not be planned on the basis of 'a page a day'. The guiding principles should be choice and flexibility to suit the needs of the

children. **When planning a new section of work the teacher should read the *Teacher's Notes* first.**

- The planning of differentiated work for groups of children is helped by reference to
  - suggestions for *additional activities* and *oral and mental work* in the Teaching Notes
  - 'extension', problem solving and investigative work referenced in the workbooks and in the Overview for each workbook chapter; and *Problem Solving Activities* in the *Assessment and Resources Pack*
  - the *Resource Cards* in the *Assessment and Resources Pack*
  - other ideas and resources beyond Heinemann Mathematics 2.
- The index on page 154 indicates where, in the *Teacher's Notes*, particular mathematics topics can be found.

PROVIDING A CONTEXT

- An important consideration in planning is the use of contexts to teach and learn mathematics. Many of the teaching ideas in the *Teacher's Notes* suggest short, simple contexts, often involving the use of materials. The workbook pages also use scenarios to contextualise the mathematics. Indeed, the first eighteen pages of Workbook 4 are based on a theme about 'Islands'. These scenarios can be developed and linked to other cross-curricular work going on in the classroom. It is also useful to consider how best to use the local environment, radio and television programmes and appropriate computer software.
- The *Contexts* booklet in the *Assessment and Resources Pack* provides suggestions for two extended contexts: 'The street' and 'Islands'. These contexts provide suggestions for mathematical activities which are referenced to attainment targets and can be incorporated in extended themes involving other curricular areas.

  Some of the activities in 'The street' context are related to the Length workcards (referenced from the Measure Workbook). The cards could offer a stimulus for starting the context, or could be incorporated as part of an extended 'street' theme.

  Pages 1 to 18 of Workbook 4 are based on an 'Islands' theme which could be extended and developed using the 'Islands' context in the *Contexts* booklet of the *Assessment and Resources Pack*. A large coloured poster showing the islands is provided in the Pack and could be used with Workbook 4 or the 'Islands' context.
- The *SPMG Infant Pictures* can also be used with Heinemann Mathematics 2 to provide scenarios to promote the use of mathematical language.
- The Heinemann Mathematics 1 *Assessment and Resources Pack* contains five extended contexts which could easily be adapted to suit the content of Heinemann Mathematics 2.

ORGANISING AND IMPLEMENTING

There will be times when the teacher will wish to work with the whole class or with individual children. For most activities, however, working with groups of children will be appropriate to allow the teacher to teach and to differentiate work. The teaching suggestions in the *Teacher's Notes* contain activities for group teaching which might on a few occasions be adapted for use with a whole class, at the teacher's discretion. The practical activities for children in the Introductory Activities sections of the notes are intended to be flexible enough to use with groups or individuals. The introductory activities contain more suggestions than are appropriate to be used with any one group or class. The intention is that teachers select some of the given activities and use other ideas of their own.

As stated earlier, the children should not attempt to use workbook pages or workcards without prior teaching and sufficient practical experience. **Workbook pages and cards themselves require introduction** and to be read and 'talked over' with the teacher so that it is clear to the children what they have to do, where they can find the necessary resources and how they should record their work.

- A balance of number, measure, shape and information handling is required. This will mean that sections of the Measure, Shape and Handling Data workbooks and associated cards are used throughout the school year by interspersing them with the number work.
- The five batches of workcards should be separated and, perhaps, kept in wall pockets so that the children can use and replace them for themselves. Some batches are referenced from the tops of workbook pages and indicate introductory practical activities coming *before* the use of the workbook pages.
- The teacher should miss out pages and cards which are not appropriate to particular children. Most problem solving and investigative activities are not intended only for more able children but some 'extension' activities are likely to be used in that way.
- The *Resource Cards* can be used to give supplementary activities to individuals or small groups. The notes with the cards describe how to use them and how they relate to the workbooks.
- The *Problem Solving Activities* booklet provides 'stand alone' problems for use with individuals or small groups. They can be used at any time, perhaps long after the mathematics involved is known to the children as they are concerned with developing simple strategies and mathematical thinking skills.
- Some of the work in the *Contexts*, *Problem Solving Activities*, workbook pages and workcards requires the children to **record their own work** without the help of a fill-in format.

ASSESSING AND RECORDING

Assessment

- Much of the assessment in a primary classroom is continuous. Information is gathered through talking to the children, observing them working and noting how successful they are when recording responses. This sort of information is very important as it can be used to identify particular strengths and weaknesses so that future teaching can be more effective.
- The *Assessment and Resources Pack*, which forms part of the Heinemann Mathematics 2 materials, provides the teacher with a useful tool for checking and formally recording children's progress.
- The *Check-ups* in the *Assessment and Resources Pack* can be used after a unit of work has been completed to monitor understanding of mathematical ideas and plan remedial action or new pieces of work. Each check-up assesses the type of work in one of the workbooks and its associated workcards. Some involve practical work. Each check-up should supplement teacher observation of children's work on activities from the workbook and its associated *Teacher's Notes* and workcards.
- The *Assessment in Context* booklet, also in the *Assessment and Resources Pack*, can be used to test children's ability to apply mathematics. The questions in each context range over several attainment targets and contain some problem solving items.

- For each workbook, questions relevant to the mathematics content of the particular chapter are listed at the front of the chapter in the *Teacher's Notes*. To help teachers relate the mathematics assessed within each context to individual workbooks, references to specific questions within the *Assessment in Context* are made at the beginning of each workbook chapter in the *Teacher's Notes*. It is not suggested, however, that the *Assessment in Context* material be used immediately after completion of a particular workbook.

Recording

Simple photocopiable checklists of statements of attainment are also included (within the *Resource Cards*) for Level 2 (England and Wales, and Northern Ireland) and Levels A and B (Scotland). For children working at Level 1, the checklist provided with the Heinemann Mathematics 1 materials could be used. Children at Level 3 will require the checklist provided with Heinemann Mathematics 3 materials.

Workbook 1

Addition and subtraction to 10

Ma 2/2ab 1/2 3/2a
AS/A PS/A PSE
P/2 N/1e,2c A/2a

Overview

Addition to 10 and subtraction within 6 were introduced in Heinemann Mathematics 1. This section

- introduces subtraction stories for 7, 8, 9 and 10
- extends subtraction involving money to 10p
- links addition and subtraction facts to 10, for example,

  $7 + 3 = 10 \quad 3 + 7 = 10 \quad 10 - 3 = 7 \quad 10 - 7 = 3$
- includes vertical setting for addition and subtraction
- introduces subtraction by comparison – 'How many more?, How much more?'

Key words and phrases

How many more?
How much more?
How many are left?
Who can now buy?
Which costs more?
How much is left?
colour to match
upstairs
downstairs
missing numbers
for sale

Resources

Useful materials

- small objects for counting such as beads, bricks, buttons, counters
- dice, coins, interlocking cubes, coloured pencils
- sets of flashcards such as

8 take away 3	$8 - 3$

- flashcards of key words and phrases (see page 12)
- materials associated with the scenarios on the workbook pages.

Assessment and Resources Pack

Assessment

Check-ups

Check-up for Workbook 1

Assessment in Context

'At the fair' context: Questions 7, 11, 12, 13, 21

'Treasure Island' context: Question 19

Resources

Contexts

Both 'The street' and 'Islands' contexts contain examples about addition and subtraction within 10.

Resource Cards

Resource Cards 1 and *2* (Subtraction picture) give practice with subtraction facts within 10. *Resource Cards 33–36* provide further practice examples.

Workbook **1**

Teaching notes

SUBTRACTION STORIES OF 7 AND 8
Introductory activities

Ma 2/2ab 1/2 3/2a		
AS/A	PS/A	
N/1e,2c	P/2	A/2a

1 Revision

Some oral revision of subtraction within 6, introduced in Heinemann Mathematics 1, will be required. Possible activities are:

- 'Put out 6 cubes. Take away 3. How many are left?'

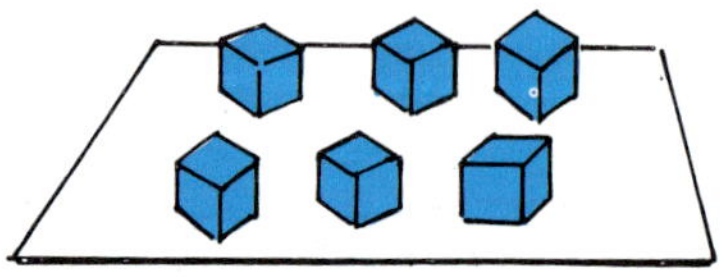

- 'Pick 3 flowers. How many are left?'

Such work can also be done by crossing out or rubbing out drawings.

- 'Hide 3 cats. How many are left?'

Practical activities where children can discover facts for themselves can be used to introduce subtraction stories for 7 and 8 and encourage the children to memorise facts. Alternative suggestions which can be adapted for any story are given below.

2 Trees

Use a scene with 7 card trees which can be 'chopped down' to illustrate facts for 7. For example,

Illustrate all the number stories for 7:

7 − 0 = 7
7 − 1 = 6
7 − 2 = 5

. . . and so on up to

7 − 7 = 0

This situation is similar to the work on Workbook 1, Page 1. Alternatively a group of seven children could stand like trees and then sit down when 'chopped'.

3 Mice

7 − 4 = 3

Using two pieces of card, one marked with seven mice, the other showing a mouse hole, the mice can be hidden in the mouse hole and the children asked

'How many are left?'

Mice also appear on Workbook 1, Page 2.

4 Crates on a lorry

Ask the children to put 8 crates (represented by cubes) on a toy lorry and then unload some.

'8 crates. Take off 2. There are 6 left.'

8 − 2 = 6

Repeat the loading and unloading procedure for other facts and then rearrange them to form a pattern.

$8 - 0 = 8$
$8 - 1 = 7$
$8 - 2 = 6$

. . . and so on up to

$8 - 8 = 0$

Workbook 1, Page 3 involves a lorry with 8 sacks.

5 Skittles

'How many are standing?'

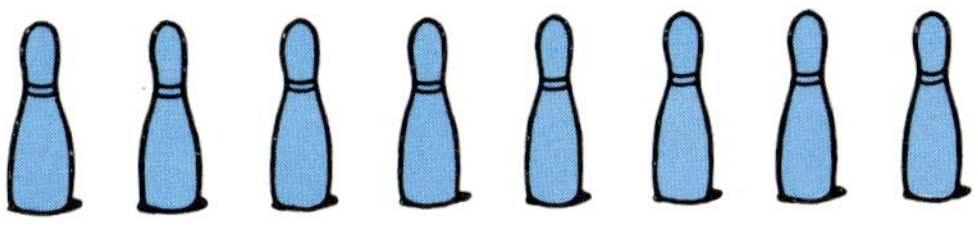

'3 fall down. How many are left standing?'

8 − 3 = 5

6 Individual activities

Each child should use materials to discover subtraction stories and, as they gradually memorise them, to check answers.

Beads

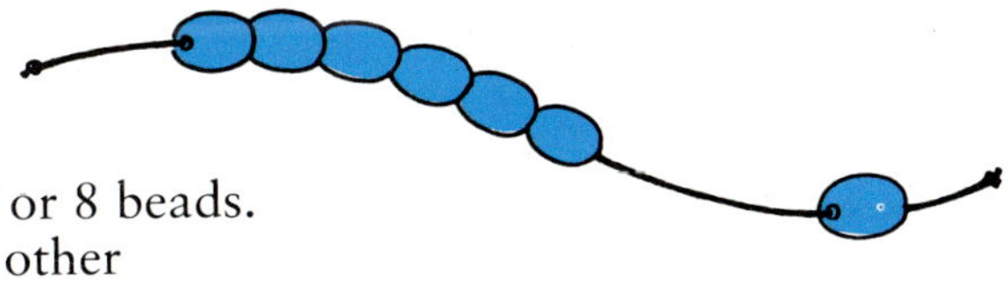

Provide a small string of either 7 or 8 beads. The child can move beads to the other end of the string to show 7 − 1. Repeat for 7 − 2, etc.

7 − 1 = 6

Cubes

Provide 7 or 8 small cubes.
The child covers some of the cubes with an inverted box to show, for example, 7 − 2.
The process can be repeated for other subtraction facts.

7 − 2 = 5

Holidays

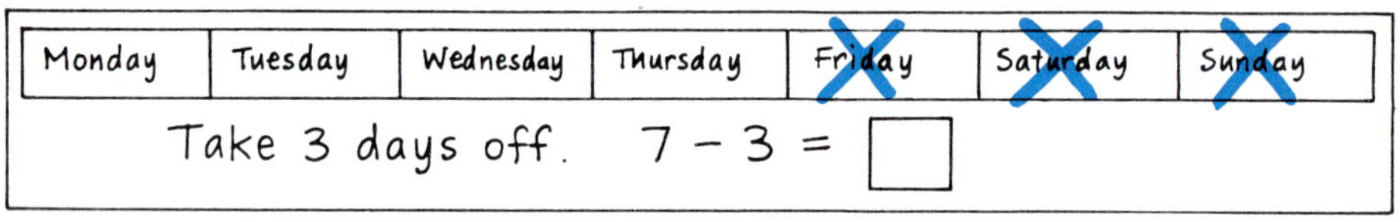

Provide a number of paper strips showing the days of the week on which the child can score off days. This can be repeated for other numbers of days off.

SUBTRACTION FACTS FOR 7 AND 8
Oral work

Ma 2/2ab 1/2 3/2a
AS/A PS/A PSE
N/1e,2c P/2 A/2a

The use of materials allows children to explore and discover subtraction stories which can be built up as a pattern, for example,

7 − 0 = 7
7 − 1 = 6
7 − 2 = 5
7 − 3 = 4
7 − 4 = 3
7 − 5 = 2
7 − 6 = 1
7 − 7 = 0

Children should also be helped to memorise individual facts by regular oral work with the teacher. Some activities are suggested below.

1 Teddies

Line up a set of 7 soft toys.
A child chooses a card from a pack and shows it to the group. For example,

4 go to sleep.
How many are awake?

All the children in the group can answer.

An oral answer 'three' can be checked by the child who picked the card by putting 4 teddies to sleep. Repeat for other cards such as

5 hide under the table.
How many are left?

. . . and so on.

2 How many in the box?

Ask children to count 7 cubes or other items to put in a box. Hold the box up high so that they cannot see the cubes inside.

'I am going to take out 2 cubes.'

'How many cubes are left in the box?'

The box can then be lowered so that the children can check to see if their answer was correct.

Workbook 1

Workbook Pages 1 to 6 *Subtraction stories of 7 and 8*

Page 2 has a problem solving element as children have to try to get the mice to their holes. They have to realise that a mouse which does not have a hole gets caught by the cat. Even if they find the mouse the cat catches first, they should still do the other examples.

On Page 5, the answers to the subtraction from 7 problems will depend on what appears on the dice. Children should be encouraged to find different numbers to take away from 7. The subtractions from 6 do not require a dice. The children should continue the sequence with 6 − 2 = 4 and 6 − 1 = 5.

The bottom part of Page 6 also continues a sequence where 8 − 3, 8 − 4, 8 − 5 are followed by 8 − 6 and 8 − 7.

Ma 2/2ab 1/2 3/2a
AS/A PS/A PSE
N/1e,2c P/2a A/2a

Problem solving

Problem solving

SUBTRACTION TO 8
Consolidation

1 Butterflies

Provide cards which can be matched to produce complete butterflies with correct subtraction facts and matching patterns. For example,

Ma 2/2ab 1/2 3/2a
AS/A PS/A PSE
N/1e,2c P/2 A/2a

2 Boxes

Provide boxes with subtraction facts on them. The children have to write the complete story before opening the box to check their answers by counting the cubes inside.

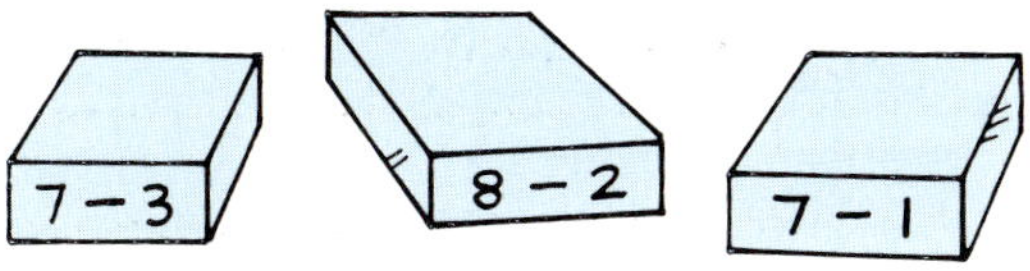

3 Lucky dip

Sets of flashcards with mixed facts from the stories of 3, 4, 5, 6, 7 and 8 could be placed in a box. The child picks the card and gives the answer.

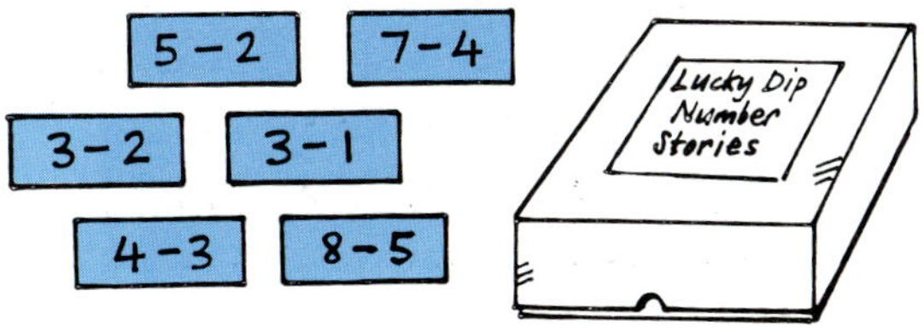

An alternative use of the cards is to find all the cards that give the same answer.

Answer 3	**Answer 4**
5 − 2	8 − 4
6 − 3	7 − 3
7 − 4	6 − 2

4 Tractors and trailers

Provide tractor cards with number stories on them and trailer cards with answers, which the children have to match. For example,

5 Boats and sails

Provide cardboard boats with number stories on them and sails with answers on to give another context for matching subtraction facts.

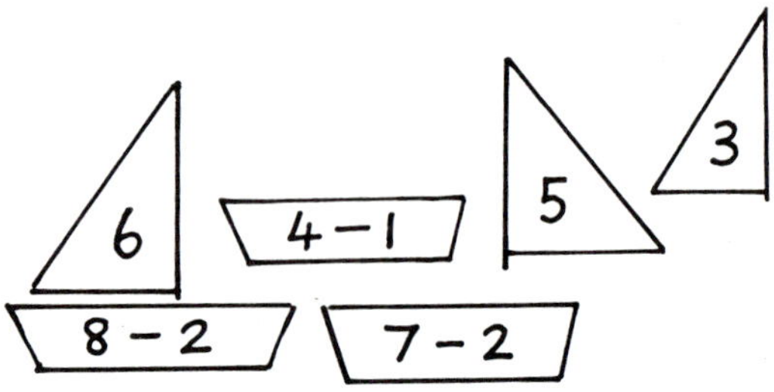

6 Birds and nests

Cardboard birds and nests will provide another scenario.

7 Jigsaw picture

Prepare a number story board and a picture board to match which can be cut up into eight answer cards. Write the answers 0 to 7 on the backs of the answer cards to correspond to the number stories on the board.

The children place the answer cards on top of the board and then turn them over to show the picture. If the answer card is in the wrong position then the picture will not be correctly arranged.

Board

7 − 2	7 − 4
7 − 3	7 − 5
7 − 1	7 − 0
7 − 6	7 − 7

8 Track game *(for up to 3 players)*

The flashcards provided for Activity 3 above can be used as a means of progressing along a track. The cards are placed in a pile, face down. Each child selects the top card in turn, works out the answer and then moves the appropriate number of spaces along the track. The first to reach 'home' wins.

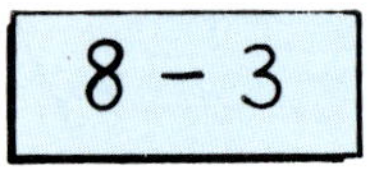

SUBTRACTION STORIES OF 9 AND 10
Introductory activities

Workbook **1**

Ma 2/2ab 1/2 3/2a
AS/A PS/A PSE
N/1e,2c P/2 A/2a

The activities suggested for the subtraction stories of 7 and 8 could be adapted to suit the stories of 9 and 10. Some further possibilities are given below.

1 Flags on a castle

'One flag is taken down. How many are left?'

$9 - 1 = 8$
$9 - 2 = 7$, and so on to build up the stories of 9.

2 People on a bus

Ask the children to draw pictures of ten people (on cards) and place them at the windows of a cardboard bus. Take off one person at a time to build up the subtraction story of 10.

$10 - 1 = 9$
$10 - 2 = 8$, etc.

3 Individual activities

Some of the activities suggested for the stories of 7 and 8 can be extended to suit 9 and 10. Ensure that counting material is available for children working on their own who require it.

4 Oral work

The suggestions made on pages 16 and 17 of these notes can be adapted to suit subtraction from 9 and 10. It is important that children have regular oral practice with these facts as an important aid to memorising them.

Ma 2/2ab 3/2a
AS/A PS/A
N/1e,2c A/2a

Workbook Pages 7 to 10 *Subtraction stories of 9 and 10*

The fruits on Page 7 can be scored out to help find answers for subtraction from 9. On Page 9, the ten people illustrated on the bus can be covered to subtract 1, 2 and so on to find answers for subtraction facts involving 10.

At the foot of Page 10, children should be made aware of the need to colour two balloons, *one on either side of the bus*, to show a subtraction and the appropriate answer. Discuss the example $9 - 3 = 6$ to establish the idea.

SUBTRACTION TO 10
Consolidation

Ma 2/2ab
AS/A
N/1e,2c

Further activities which can be used to consolidate subtraction facts for 7, 8, 9 and 10 are given below.

1 Buses

Prepare bus cards which the children can match to complete a bus. For example,

2 Answers

Prepare answer sheets as shown below. Ask the children to sort out flashcards and place them on the sheets to match the answers.

Assessment and Resources Pack

3 Resource cards

Resource Cards 1 and 2 from the *Assessment and Resources Pack* provide further practice with subtraction facts to 10 in the form of a subtraction picture.

MONEY TO 10p
Introductory activities

Ma 2/2ab 1/2
AS/A PSE
N/1e,2d P/2

The 1p coin was introduced in Heinemann Mathematics 1 and used for addition to 10p and subtraction within 6p. In this workbook, subtraction involving 1p coins is extended to 10p.

1 Class shop

Children can be given a certain number of 1p coins in a bag or purse. They go to the class shop to buy an article. Provide a worksheet on which they can record 'How much is left' by counting the remaining coins.

2 Shopping cards

Similar work can be done using shopping cards which have pictures of items priced up to 10p. Coins can be placed on top of the card to pay for the item and the children can count how much is left in the purse as a check.
They can then record 10p − 7p = 3p

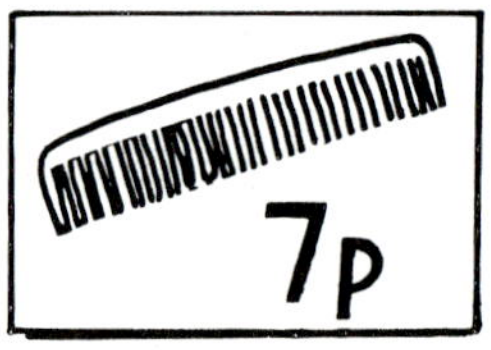

3 Shop sale

Price the items in the shop from 7p to 1
prices are reduced by, for example, 4p.
day.

Workbook Pages 11 and 1

1p coins should be available to help

On Page 11, it is important to stress

Page 12 is extension work which no
difficulty of spending and then spenc
earlier ones. For example, Abe start
After the first purchase he has 6p le
possible answers for the final questi

partitioning
comparison
complement of a set
counting back/reducing
inverse of addition
(what must be added to 3 to
make 12)

…book 1

b

on

LINKING ADDITION AND SUBTRACTION FACTS TO 10
Introductory activities

Ma 2/2ab	1/2	3/2a
AS/A	PS/A	PSE
N/2c	P/2	A/2a

This section consolidates earlier work by linking addition and subtraction facts for a particular total, often by partitioning a set. For example,

4 + 3 = 7
3 + 4 = 7
7 − 3 = 4
7 − 4 = 3

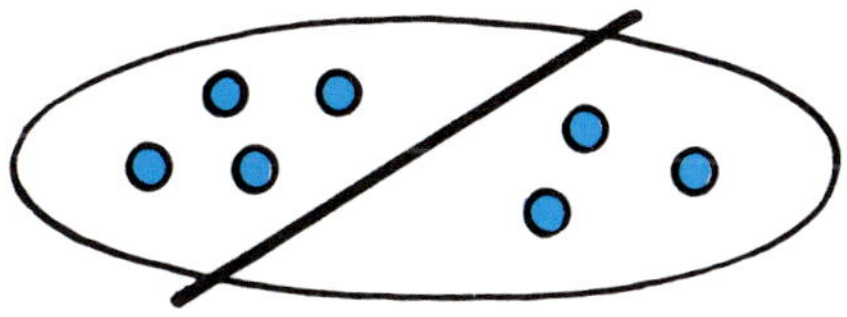

Teachers may wish to structure this work by considering

- the number stories for 3, 4, 5, then using Workbook Page 13
- the number stories for 6, 7, then using Workbook Page 14
- the number stories for 8, then using Workbook Pages 15 and 16
- the number stories for 9, 10, then using Workbook Pages 17 and 18.

A selection of activities which can be used to link facts is given below. Each activity can be adapted to suit other stories.

1 Ducks in a pond

Prepare a pond shape, using blue card, with a bridge over the middle. Put out 4 ducks as shown.

Show how the stories evolve.

3 + 1 = 4
1 + 3 = 4
4 − 1 = 3 (hide 1 duck on the right)
4 − 3 = 1 (hide 3 ducks)

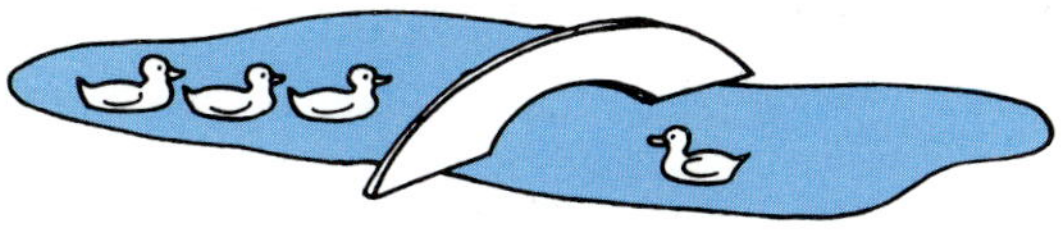

Repeat for other placings, for example,

2 + 2 = 4
4 − 2 = 2

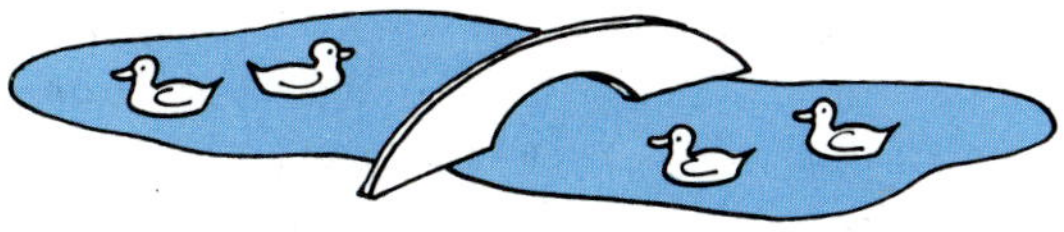

2 Birds on a tree

Arrange the birds in the tree to show different stories. This one shows

$3 + 2 = 5$
$2 + 3 = 5$
$5 - 2 = 3$ (hide 2)
$5 - 3 = 2$ (hide 3)

3 Fish in a tank

Use a blue paper tank and cut-out fish.

This placing shows $4 + 2 = 6$
$2 + 4 = 6$

and by hiding fish $6 - 2 = 4$
$6 - 4 = 2$

4 Eggs in an egg-box

Plasticine eggs or cubes of two colours can be used to find stories for 6.

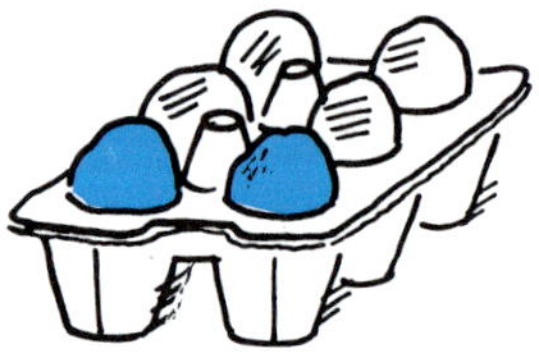

5 Cake cases

Use cake cases and plasticine cakes for this activity. Position the cakes on a partitioned tray to show

	$3 + 5 = 8$
Turn tray round for:	$5 + 3 = 8$
Hide 3 for:	$8 - 3 = 5$
Hide 5 for:	$8 - 5 = 3$

6 Car park

Use a large piece of card to represent a car park for toy cars. Park cars on it to show examples such as $3 + 6 = 9$

Turn the car park round:	$6 + 3 = 9$
Drive away the 6 cars on the right:	$9 - 6 = 3$
Remove the 3 cars on the left:	$9 - 3 = 6$

It is important that each child is given the opportunity to find his/her own stories for any particular number.

7 Individual activities

Cubes, counters, beads on a string can be used by the child. For example, give each child 7 cubes and ask them to find stories by placing a ruler at different positions.

$5 + 2 = 7$
$2 + 5 = 7$
$7 - 2 = 5$
$7 - 5 = 2$

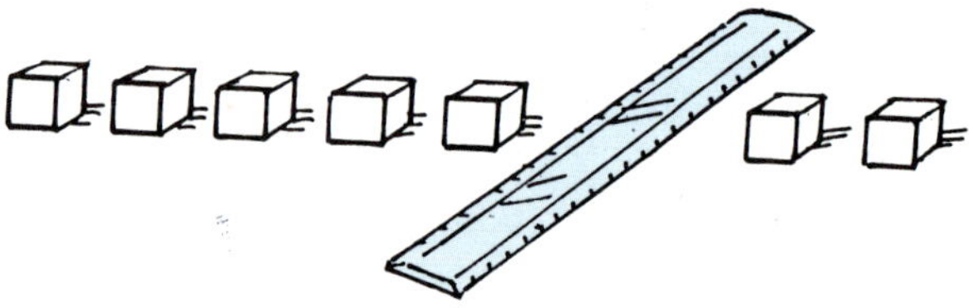

Workbook Pages 13 to 18 *Linking + and – facts for 3, 4, . . . , 10*

Ma 2/2ab 1/2
AS/A PSE
N/2c P/2

These pages should be interspersed with practical work and teacher/child discussion. For specific organisational suggestions, see *Teacher's Notes* page 21.

Pages 13 to 18 deal with linked facts for totals 3 to 10. The last example on Page 15 is labelled 'extension' and may cause some difficulty as it is a two-part question. On Page 16, the children should match lambs to sheep to find the sheep without a lamb. As this is intended as a problem solving exercise, allow the children to find their own way of tackling the problem.

Extension/ Problem solving

WORD PROBLEMS
Introductory activities

Ma 2/2ab 1/2
AS/A PSE
N/2cd P/2

In this section, addition and subtraction situations are illustrated with a diagram and are also stated in words. The children are invited to write a number story to describe each situation. Many children will find reading and interpretation of such problems difficult. Some preliminary activities related to Workbook Page 19 are suggested below.

1 People on a bus

Place a flashcard and allow the children to read it.

10 people on a bus.

Place 10 cubes on the bus to represent people.

3 get off.

'How could I write this?' Write 10 – 3

How many are left? Write 10 – 3 = 7

Repeat for other numbers on the bus, and getting off the bus.

2 Hamsters

2 hamsters in the sand.

3 more are put in.

'How could I write this?' Write 2 + 3

How many altogether? Write 2 + 3 = 5

3 On the wall

10 birds on the wall.

Put 10 objects to represent birds on top of a wall of interlocking cubes.

4 fly away.

Discuss what happens and how to record as a subtraction, 10 – 4

How many are left? Write 10 – 4 = 6

In all these activities the use of language is what is important, to help children interpret different situations.

Ma 2/2ab 1/2
AS/A PSE
N/2cd P/2

Workbook Page 19 *Word problems*

Discussion and teaching as indicated above should take place before the children try this page. Some children may need to have the words read to them. It is also important that they realise that they should write a number story complete with answer for each word problem.

VERTICAL SETTING FOR ADDITION AND SUBTRACTION FACTS TO 10
Introductory activities

Ma 2/2ab 1/2
AS/A
N/1e,2cd P/2

This section deals with addition and subtraction facts to 10, written in a vertical setting.

1 Upstairs and downstairs

In a house

Put two cardboard boxes one on top of the other to make a house. Put people (represented by cubes) upstairs and downstairs to generate sums.

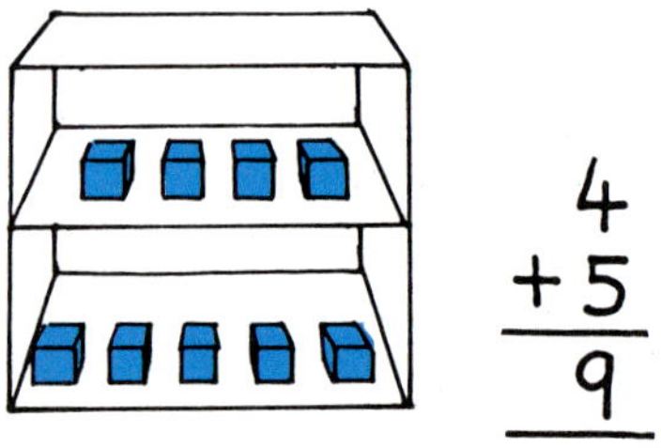

Do various examples. The children could write the sums on a chalkboard or a large sheet of paper.

In a bus

This could be done with a drawing of a double decker bus and using counters to represent passengers upstairs and downstairs.

2 Going out

Use a box to represent a top floor flat.

'5 people are in the flat. 3 go out. How many are left?'

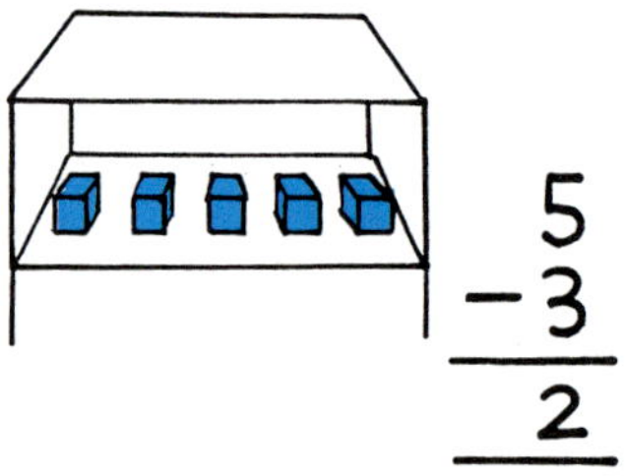

3 Cubes and beads

Use cubes and beads, arranged vertically, to illustrate addition, with the numerals opposite the appropriate colour.

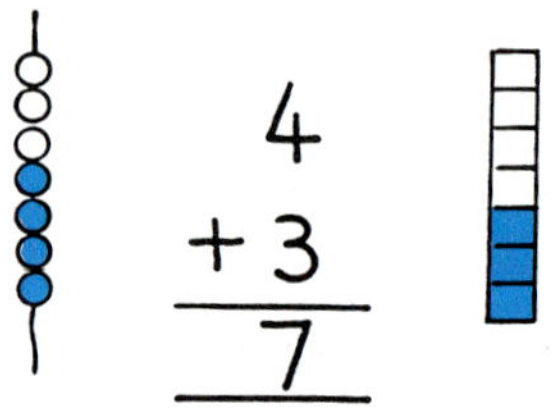

Ma 2/2ab
AS/A
N/2cd

Workbook Page 20 *Vertical setting*

This page can be introduced using the upstairs, downstairs activities described above.

ADDITION AND SUBTRACTION FACTS TO 10
Consolidation

Ma 2/2ab 1/2
AS/A
N/2cd P/2

1 Track game *(for up to 3 players)*

A track game, similar to the one on page 18 of these notes, can be used. A mixture of addition and subtraction facts are presented on flashcards. The cards are placed face down in a pile. A child chooses a card, answers the question and progresses that number of squares on the board. The first to reach home is the winner.

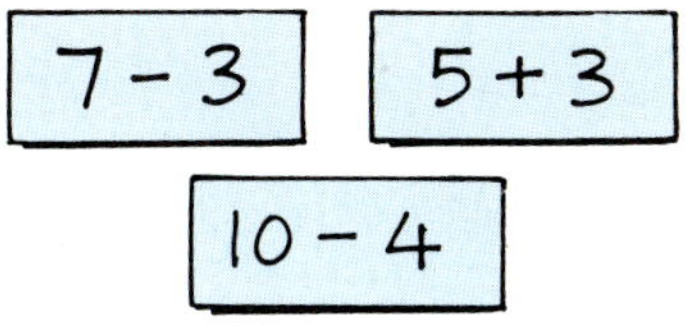

2 Matching

Prepare fact cards and answer cards in different colours. These can be matched. For example,

Yellow cards	3 + 1	7 − 2	5 − 3	10 − 4	5 + 3	1 + 6	-----
Blue cards	4	5	2	6	8	7	-----

3 Envelopes

Provide a set of picture cards such as these:

The children place each card in its correct numbered envelope.

4 Resource cards

Resource Cards 1 and *2* (Subtraction picture) from the *Assessment and Resources Pack* can be used to consolidate subtraction facts.

Assessment and Resources Pack

COMPARISON – How many more? How much more?
Introductory activities

Ma 2/2ab 1/2
AS/A
N/1e,2d P/2

Previous work concentrated on the physical removal aspect of subtraction. Here the comparative idea of subtraction involving language such as 'How many more?' and 'How much more?' is introduced. Its association with the '−' sign is emphasised. Practical activities similar to those which are described below should be carried out with the children to introduce the new idea.

1 Badges

Make some large badges. Give them to two children to wear and ask

'Who has more?'
'How many more?'

Take off the badges and match them:

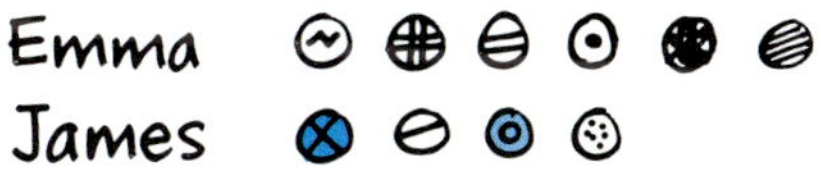

Emma has two more badges than James. $6 - 4 = 2$

Badges might be large card circles with a 'sticky' patch. For example,

2 Matching sets

The children can find the answer to 'How many more?' by matching sets of objects, such as cubes representing sweets. For example,

'Give Tom 8 sweets and Ruth 3 sweets.
How many more has Tom?'

Line up the sweets to match them.

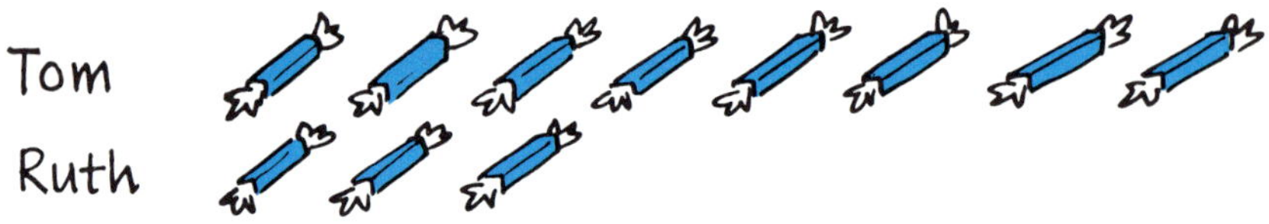

'Tom has 5 more.'

Stress that the answer can be found by *subtracting*. Record as 8 − 3 = 5.

3 Comparing costs

To compare the cost of two articles, 1p coins can be laid out to match the price of each item, and the coins matched as shown.

Ask 'How much more does the car cost?'
Write 8 − 5 = 3
Say 'The car costs 3p more.'

Ma 2/2ab
AS/A
N/2cd

Workbook Pages 21 to 23 *Subtraction: comparing*

On Page 21, all the items are lined up to make the comparison easy. Children are expected to use 1p coins for Page 22. The artwork at the top of Page 23 provides all the prices and children must realise that they have to look there each time for information. Children having difficulty with this page should continue to use coins. At times, the smaller number is given first. The children should realise that when they subtract they start with the larger number.

COMPARISON
Additional activities

Ma 2/2ab 1/2
AS/A
N/1e,2d

1 Shopping cards

Prepare shopping cards like those used on page 20.
The children choose two cards. Ask

'How much more does the hat cost?'

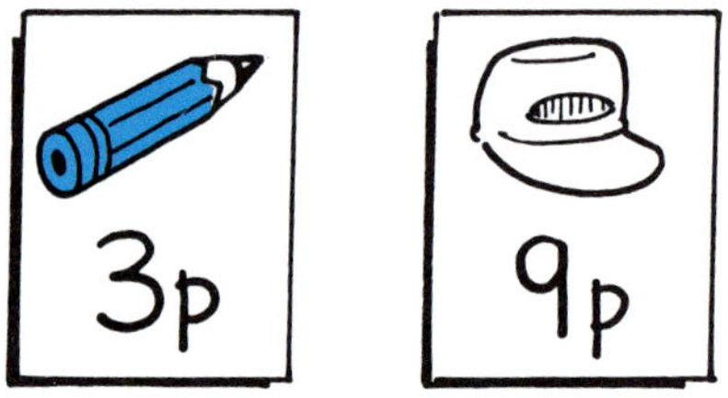

2 Dice

Two children throw a dice each.

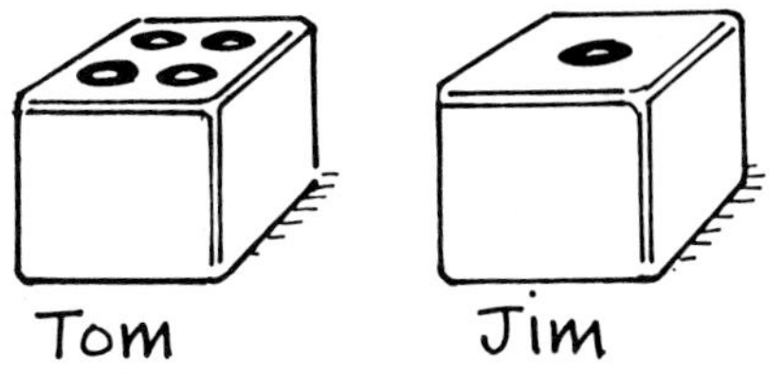

'Who scored more?'
'How many more did Tom score?'

The children can put out counters to match each score and then compare.

Blank dice could be marked with the numbers 5, 6, 7, 8, 9 and 10. This would give further variety in the numbers to be compared.

Workbook 2

Money to 10p Place value to 20 Further aspects of subtraction

Ma 1/2	2/2ab	3/2b	
RTN/A	M/A	FE/B	PSE
P/2	N/1e,2acd	A/2e	M/2b

Overview

This section

- contains activities to introduce the 2p, 5p and 10p coins and considers change from 5p and 10p
- extends the number sequence and counting to 20: introduces place value
- introduces the calculator
- uses a number line to 20 for 'counting on'
- introduces other aspects of subtraction, namely complementary addition and difference.

	Teacher's Notes	Workbook 2	Workcards
The 2p and 5p coins	30	1 to 3	
The 10p coin	32	4, 5	
Money – 1p, 2p, 5p and 10p coins: additional activities	33		
Change from 5p and 10p	33	6	
Number sequence to 20	34	7, 8	
The calculator: introductory activities	36		
Counting to 20: introductory activities, additional activities	36	9, 10	
Number names to twenty	38	11, 12	
Towards place value: Numbers to 20	39	13 to 15	
Place value to 20	41	16, 17	
Place value to 20: consolidation activities	42	18	Number/ Place value 1 to 6
The number line to 20: Counting on	43	19	
Complementary addition	44	20, 21	
Difference in price	45	22	
Difference between	46	23	
Problem solving		*1, 2, 3, 4, 5*	

Key words and phrases

coins
buy
number after/before
clear
look for a pattern
how many more to make
number and what makes ten
number + □ = 10
can be changed for
change
calculator
one more
tens
number line
subtracting
has the same value as
number names eleven to twenty
enter
count out/on
units
difference in price
difference between

Resources

Useful materials

- 1p, 2p, 5p and 10p coins
- gummed coins or coin stamps
- a number strip and/or a number line; calculators
- small objects for counting such as beads, bricks, buttons, counters
- interlocking cubes
- pegs and pegboard for counting and related activities
- flashcards of key words and phrases (see above); notation cards (see page 41).

Assessment and Resources Pack

Assessment

Check-ups

Check-up for Workbook 2

Assessment in Context

'At the fair' context: Questions 1, 2, 16, 17, 18, 19, 20, 22

'Treasure Island' context: Questions 26, 27

Resources

Contexts

'The street' context contains activities about money to 10p, number sequence to 20, place value to 20.

Problem Solving Activities

3 Banks (Money to 10p)
10 Pocket money (Money to 10p)

Resource Cards

Resource Cards 3 to *6* (Fair game) involve money to 10p, with *Cards 33–40* providing extra practice in addition and subtraction.

Resource Card 7 (Notation cards) involves place value to 20.

Resource Cards 8 and *9* (Fancy dress) involve number sequence to 20.

Workbook **2**

Teaching notes

THE 2p AND 5p COINS
Introductory activities

Ma 1/2 2/2b
M/A AS/A
P/2 N/2d M/2b

Money activities involving the 1p coin occur in Heinemann Mathematics 1, Workbooks 4, 5, 6 and 7. The 2p and 5p coins should be introduced by practical activities and discussion involving the teacher and a group of children. Some suggestions are given below.

1 Shopping with 1p and 2p coins

Discussion should establish that

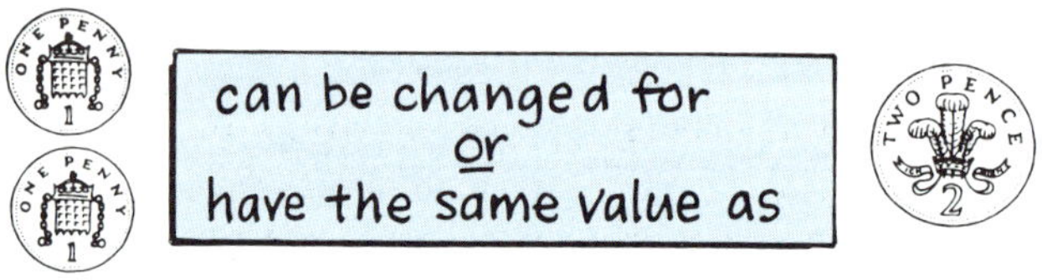

Give each child in the group some 1p and 2p coins. Provide a range of articles priced from 2p to 5p which the children can buy. It is important to discuss the various ways of paying for the articles. For example,

four 1p coins.
or two 2p coins
or one 2p coin and two 1p coins.

2 Collection boxes (1p and 2p coins)

Put 1p and 2p coins in boxes, up to a value of 9p.
The children then put a label beside each box to show the amount it contains.

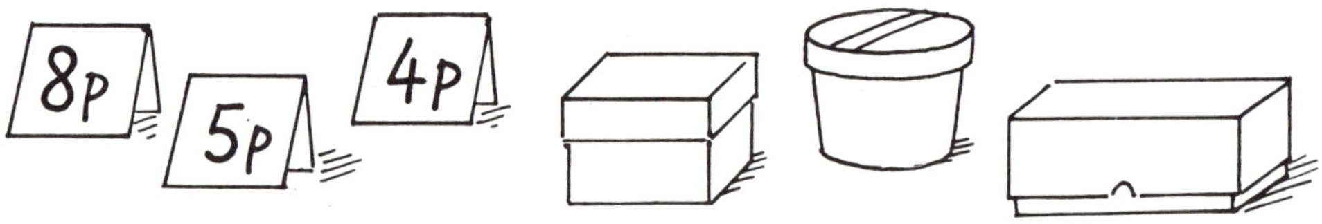

3 Shopping with 1p, 2p and 5p coins

It should be emphasised that

Discuss with the children *other* ways of putting out 5p, using 1p and 2p coins. For example, two 2p coins and one 1p coin.

Price the articles in the class shop from 5p to 9p. Encourage the children to pay for them using a 5p coin first.

4 Collection boxes (1p, 2p and 5p coins)

Extend Activity 2 to include the 5p coin. Limit the totals to not more than 9p.

5 Individual activities

Shopping cards

The child puts out coins to buy the article.

Envelopes and stamps

The child puts money for the stamp inside the envelope.

Slot machines

The child puts money through a slot in the top of a margarine tub according to the amount on the label on the front.

Sweet tubes

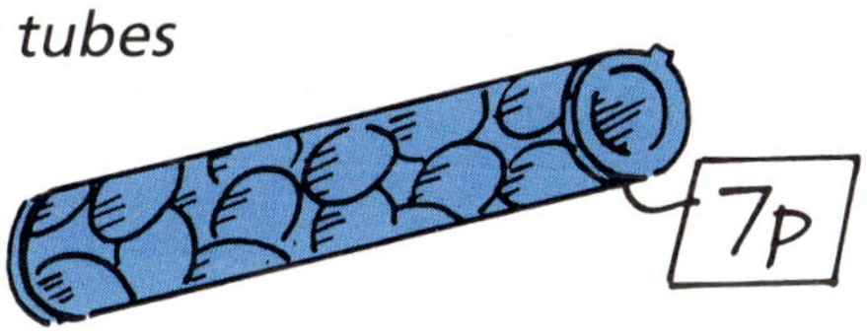

Put a mixture of 1p, 2p, 5p coins (up to 9p) in a tube. The child finds the total and attaches a label to show this amount.

Purses

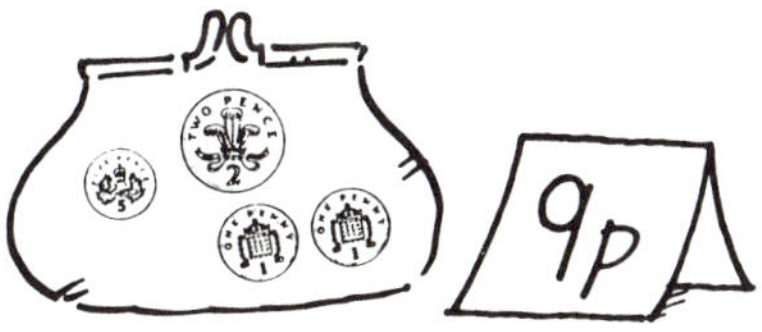

Gummed coins are stuck on to different coloured cardboard purses. The child then places the correct money card on top and says how much is in the purse.

Posting boxes

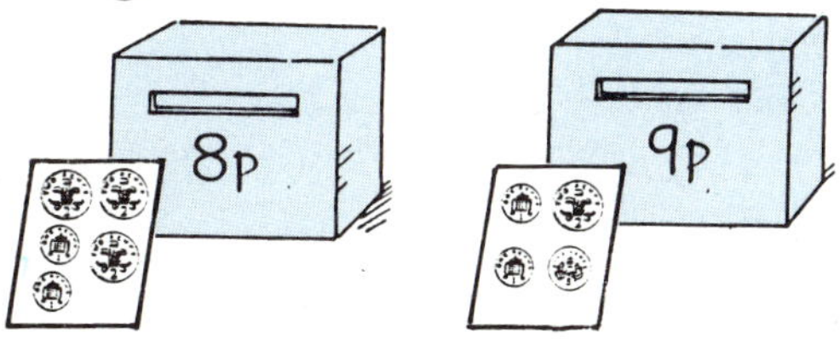

Prepare boxes with a total on them and a slot for posting cards. The cards consist of gummed coins or stamps of coins with varying totals. The child has to post the cards in the correct boxes.

Workbook Pages 1 to 3 *1p, 2p and 5p coins* *Money to 9p*

Ma 1/2 2/2b		
M/A	AS/A	PSE
P/2	N/2d	M/2b

Teaching, discussion and practical work using coins are necessary before the children try these workbook pages.

On Page 1, the children have to write the value of the missing coin inside the appropriate circle. Some children may wish to lay out the coins on top of the page as an aid.

Problem solving

On Page 3, the children should put out coins before drawing them. Their drawings need not show the actual size of the coins.

Problem solving

There are unique answers involving three coins for the problem solving activities at the foot of Page 2 (5p, 1p, 1p) and Page 3 (5p, 2p, 2p).

THE 10p COIN
Introductory activities

Ma 1/2 2/2b
M/A AS/A
P/2 N/2d M/2b

It should be emphasised that

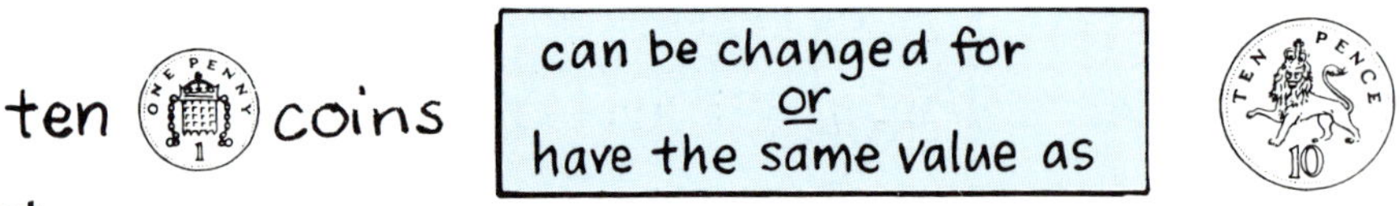

1 Bus ticket

Give each child in the group 1p, 2p and 5p coins. The children have to put out 10p for a ticket in various ways, which are then discussed.

Emphasise the  and  combinations of making up 10p.

2 Parking machine

To buy a parking ticket each child has to put appropriate coins into the slots in a large cardboard box. The amount put in should be checked either by the teacher or the group each time a ticket is bought.

3 Phone calls

A box similar to the one used in Activity 2 can be made for making a phone call costing 10p.

4 Purses, collection boxes, etc.

Have available purses and/or collection boxes which contain coins totalling mostly 10p. Include some with totals of 7p, 8p, 9p. The children have to find how much is in each purse or box.

Ma 1/2 2/2b
M/A AS/A PSE
P/2 M/2b

Problem solving

Workbook Pages 4 and 5 *10 pence*

Page 4 should be tackled after some of the practical work outlined above. This page will have to be carefully explained to children to ensure that they put out the coins, count what they have put out, and then find the coin to make the total 10p.

The problem solving example at the foot of Page 4 has two answers which should be discussed:

 and 

This is also true for the last example on Page 5 where Lili can spend 3p and 7p *or* 4p and 6p.

MONEY: 1p, 2p, 5p AND 10p COINS
Additional activities

Workbook 2

Ma 1/2 2/2b
M/A AS/A
P/2 M/2b

1 Coin rubbings

The children can use real coins to make coin rubbings for both sides of each denomination. Discuss and display the rubbings.

2 Bingo (*for 2 to 4 players*)

Provide the children with coin cards (with various totals, including different collections of coins with the same total) and various playing cards (each with four different values on them, to match the coin cards).

coin card

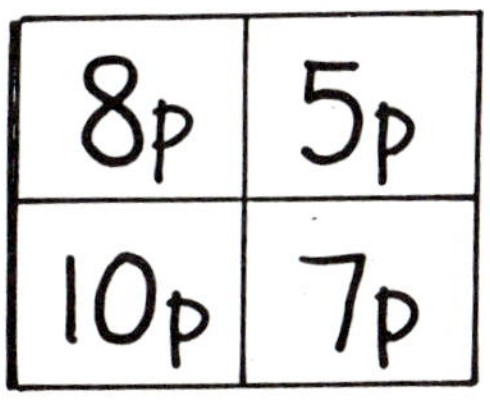

playing card

Each player takes a playing card. Coin cards are placed face down. Each child in turn picks a coin card. If it matches a total on his or her playing card, it is placed on top. If not, it is returned to the bottom of the pile. The winner is the first child to have his or her playing card covered.

3 Resource cards

Assessment and Resources Pack

Resource Cards 3, 4, 5 and 6 (Fair game) provide a track game involving adding collections of coins on coin cards.

CHANGE FROM 5p AND 10p
Introductory activities

Ma 1/2 2/2b
M/A AS/A
P/2 N/2d M/2b

Shop assistants sometimes give back change by 'counting on'. Some children may however find it easier to 'take away' what is spent from the amount tendered and then put out the coins for the change. The following activities emphasise the 'counting on' method.

1 Shopping: change from 5p

- Each child in the group has a 5p coin.
  One child acts as the shopkeeper.
  Ask a child to buy a specific item, for example, the pencil.
  'What will your change be?'
  '4p and *what* makes 5p?'
  The shopkeeper puts out a 1p coin as change.
- 'Buy the ball.' (3p)
  'What will your change be?'
  '3p and *what* makes 5p?'
  The shopkeeper puts out a 2p coin as change.

Some children may initially put out the change as 1p and 1p as they count on from 3p. (3p and 1p is 4p; 4p and 1p is 5p.) Other prices can then be considered.

2 Shopping cards

Using shopping cards, an individual child puts out coins to show the change from 5p when the article shown on the card is bought.

3 Shopping: change from 10p

Price the articles in the class shop from 1p to 9p. Children find it easier to find change from 10p by counting on for articles priced 5p to 9p than for articles priced 1p to 4p. Practical work and discussion should be graded accordingly.

4 Individual activities

Shopping cards

Provide shopping cards with prices in the range from 1p to 9p.
The child has to put out coins to show change from 10p.

Birthday cards

Make a collection of old birthday cards and price them from 1p to 9p.
The child has to put out change from 10p as before.

Buy a pencil

Ask a child to buy a pencil, rubber or crayon each day with a 10p coin.
The child has to put out the change.

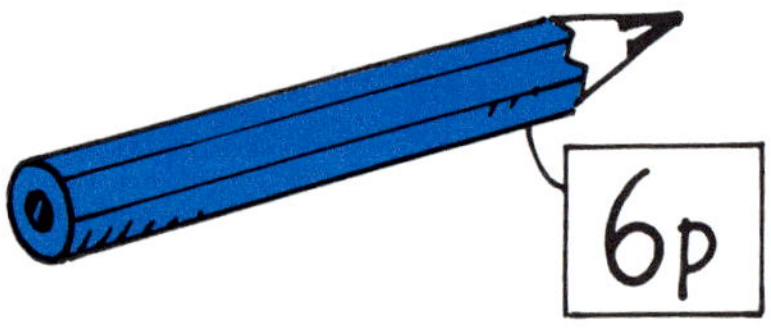

Ma 1/2 2/2b
M/A AS/A
P/2 M/2b

Workbook Page 6 *Change from 5p and 10p*

Much teaching, practical work and discussion should occur before the children try this workbook page. The children should put out the change and draw the coins, which need not be actual size, in the boxes provided.

The activity can be extended by getting the children to make their own stickers to sell. Prices can range from 1p to 9p. A 10p coin is tendered each time and the change found.

NUMBER SEQUENCE TO 20
Introductory activities

Ma 2/2a
M/A
N/2a

The suggestions which follow include ideas for teaching 'number after' and 'number before'.

1 The number strip and number line

Number strip

Number line

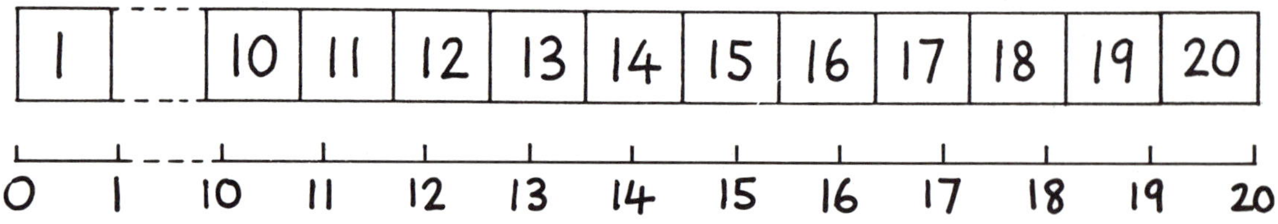

Using a number strip from 1 to 20 or a number line from 0 to 20 enables children to see these numbers in sequence.

- Point to each number in turn and ask the children to recite the number names.
- Point to a number and say, 'What number is this?', and so on.
- Ask a child to point to fourteen, and so on.
- Cover one of the numbers with your hand and say, 'What number is hidden?'.
- 'What is the number after thirteen?' and so on.
- 'What is the number before seventeen?' and so on.

Workbook 2

2 Houses

Ask each child to draw a house. Give each child a different number from 10 to 20 for his/her house. Then ask the children to make a display of the houses in order. Ask for house numbers before/after certain numbers. (Keep the display of houses for use with the activity on page 38.)

3 Birthday cards

Provide each child with a card folded to represent a birthday card. Give each child a number from 10 to 20 to write on his or her card. Display the cards in order on a 'clothes line' attached with clothes pegs or paper clips. Use the cards for discussion as outlined in Activity 1 above.

4 Skaters

Give each child a number from 10 to 20, which they can fix to their jumper like a skating competitor.

- 'Here is the order for the competition: 11, 12, 13, 14, and so on.'
  Children come forward as their number is called.
- 'Stand up – the number after twelve, etc.
  the number before nineteen, etc.'

This activity links up with the skating scene presented in Workbook 2, Pages 7 and 8.

5 Flashcards

- Read out a number from a flashcard and ask the children to write it down. Show the children the flashcard as a check.
- Show the children a flashcard. For example,

  'Write the number after this one.'
  'Write the number before this one.'

6 Resource cards

Resource Cards 8 and 9 (Fancy dress) provide ordering activities for the numbers 1 to 20.

Assessment and Resources Pack

THE CALCULATOR
Introductory activities

Ma 2/2a
RTN/A
N/2a

Many children have access to a calculator at home and may already have played with one. The calculator can, however, be a very useful teaching aid.

- Make sure the children know how to switch the calculator on and off. (This will not be necessary for solar powered calculators.)
- Let them play with it to see what they can find out.
- Show them how to 'enter' and 'clear' numbers from 1 to 20.
- For the numbers 10 to 20, ask them to
  'Enter twelve in the calculator.' Check. 'Clear the calculator.'
  'Enter fourteen', and so on.
  'Enter the number after fourteen.' Check, and so on.
  'Enter the number before twenty.' Check, and so on.
- The children should work in pairs: one with a set of number cards from 10 to 20 and the other with the calculator. One child reads out a number and the other child enters it in the calculator.
  They then check, for example,  against 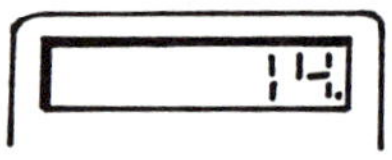

Ma 2/2a
RTN/A
N/2a

Workbook Pages 7 and 8 *Numbers to 20*

Teaching, discussion and practical work using some of the ideas above, or similar ideas, is essential before the children try these workbook pages. The seats at the top and bottom of the pages form continuous rows across Pages 7 and 8.

On Page 7, the outlines of two skaters are completed by correctly joining the dots numbered from 1 to 20 in order.

COUNTING TO 20
Introductory activities

Ma 2/2a
RTN/A
N/2a

In this section, the children count or put out a number of objects from 11 to 20. They also learn that, for example, fifteen is 1 more than fourteen.

1 Beads on a string

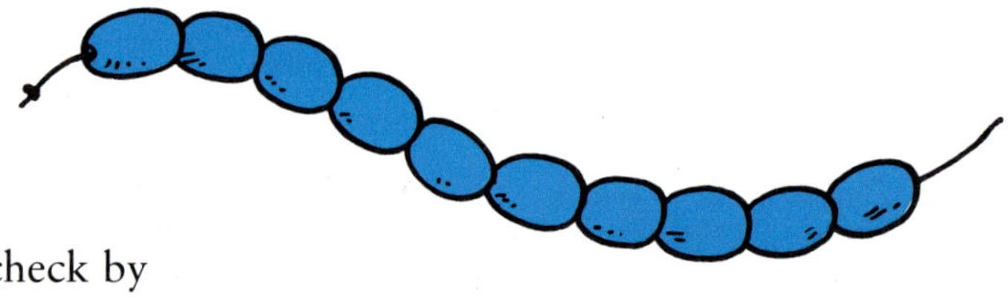

Ask the children to
'Put 10 beads on a string.'
'Now put 1 more on.'
'How many have we now?'
If necessary get the children to check by counting from one again.
Repeat for 12, 13, up to 20 beads.

2 Spots

Make a large outline shape of a monster, clown or dog on card and lay it flat.
Use counters as spots and say
'How many spots on the clown?'
'Put sixteen spots on the monster?'
'How many spots on the dog?'
'Take off 3. How many are left?' and so on.
The child counts to find the answer each time.

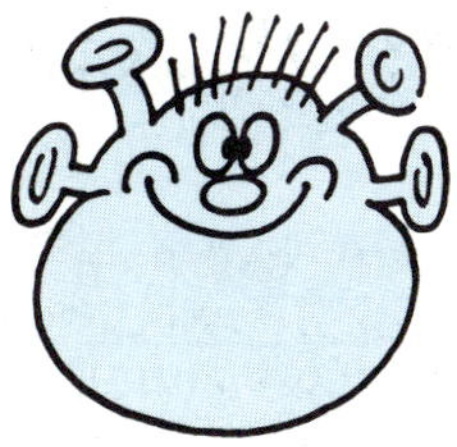

3 Candles on a cake

Prepare a large plasticine cake with eleven candles made from blunted cocktail sticks.
'How many candles on the cake?' (11)
'Put on five more.'
'How many candles now?'
At first, the child will probably count from one to find out. Later he/she may count on from 11.

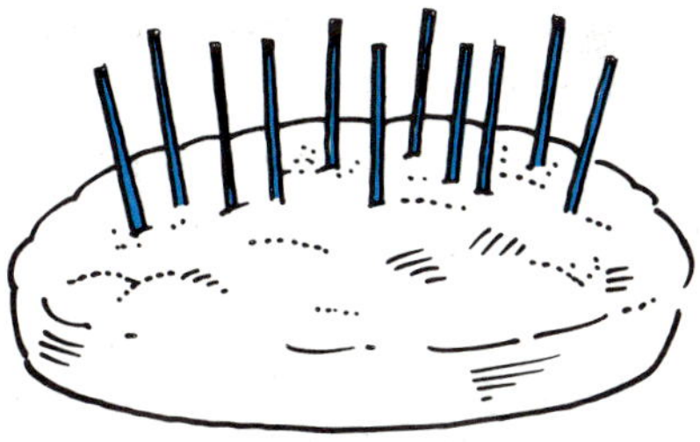

4 Apples on a tree

Provide a large cardboard tree shape on which cardboard apples can be fixed using Blu-tack.
'Put fifteen apples on the tree.'
'Three fall off.'
The child takes three off.
'How many apples are left?'
The child counts.

5 Buttons on a coat

Similar work to the above can be done using buttons and a coat shape cut from cardboard.

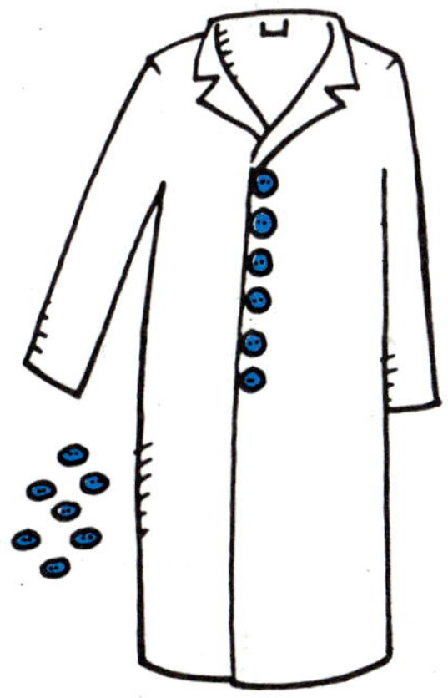

6 Individual activities

Individual children can undertake activities using specially prepared and labelled materials such as beads on strings, counters in envelopes, cubes in boxes, pegs on a pegboard, etc.

For example, using counters and envelopes, the activities could be of the following types:

Workbook Pages 9 and 10 *Counting to 20*

A discussion about a jeweller's shop window would be a good introduction to these workbook pages. Make sure the children can locate the items to be counted. It may be necessary for children to mark or tick each item as they say the appropriate number name so that they do not lose count.

Ma 2/2a
RTN/A
N/2a

COUNTING TO 20
Additional activities

Ma 2/2a
RTN/A
N/2a

Provide counting and drawing cards like the following:

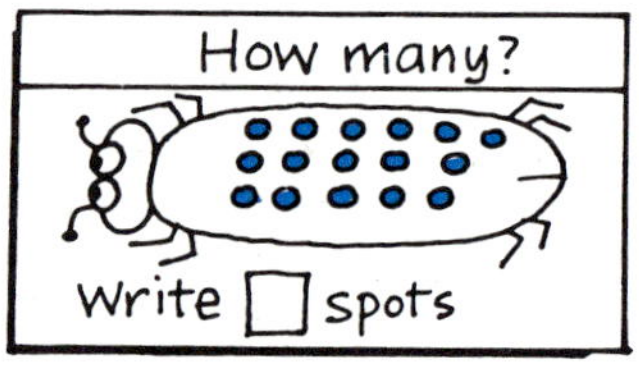

NUMBER NAMES TO TWENTY
Introductory activities

Ma 2/2a
RTN/A
N/2a

The number names one to ten were introduced in Heinemann Mathematics 1, Workbook 4. The following activities concentrate on the number names eleven to twenty.

1 Flashcards

Use cards showing [11] to [20] and the number names [eleven] to [twenty].

Display the number cards in order. The children then match the number names to the number cards, one at a time, in order.

2 Delivering letters

Use the display of houses and house numbers from 11 to 20 prepared for Activity 2, on page 35 of these notes.
Write number names on envelopes and give an envelope to each child. Say to the group:

'The postman calls at number fourteen.'
The child with the 'fourteen' envelope then delivers it to house number 14, and so on.

3 Seat numbers

Number a row of seats in the classroom from 11 to 20. Give each child a ticket with a number name on it and say to the group:

'Ticket number twelve take your seat.'

The child with ticket number twelve then sits down at number 12, and so on.

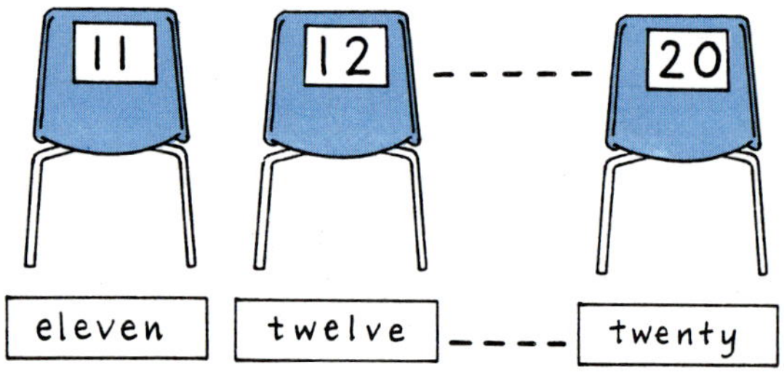

4 Calculators

Provide each child with a calculator. A child then picks a number name card and *shows* it to the group. Each child then enters this number into the calculator. The teacher should check the children's calculator displays. The procedure can then be repeated for each child in the group.

5 Counting activities

The counting activities outlined on pages 36 and 37 could be related to number names rather than numerals. For example,

'Count the number of objects in the box and put the correct number name card beside it.'

Workbook Pages 11 and 12 *Number names to 20*

Ma 2/2a
RTN/A
N/2a

Point out to the children that they should work *across both pages*. The numbers which the children write on the calculators do not need to be digital in style. In the counting activity on Page 12, the children may need to tick or cross out each penguin as it is counted, so that they do not lose count.

TOWARDS PLACE VALUE: NUMBERS TO 20

Introductory activities

Ma 2/2a
RTN/A
N/2a

This section deals with expressing numbers such as 13 as 10 + 3 and conversely with expressing 10 + 3 as 13. Some practical suggestions to cover both types of example are given below for teacher and children working together.

1 Buttons on a coat

Use the coat shape prepared for Activity 5 on page 37. Give the children some buttons and say

'Count out 13 buttons. Put 10 buttons on the coat.
How many buttons are left over?'

The children or teacher should write this out as

$13 = 10$ and 3

or $13 = 10 + 3$

Repeat the activity for other numbers of buttons up to 20.

2 Socks on a line

Put up a string clothes line. Use cardboard or real socks and clothes pegs and say

'Count out 18 socks.
Put 10 on the line.
How many socks are left over?'

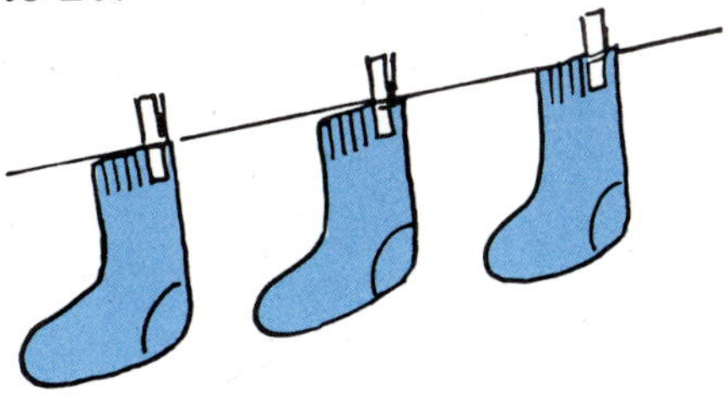

Write $18 = 10 + 8$

3 Cakes on a tray

Use plasticine cakes in cake cases, made previously by the children. Ask them to count out 14 cakes and put 10 on a tray leaving 4 on the table.

Write $14 = 10 + 4$

4 Cars in a car park

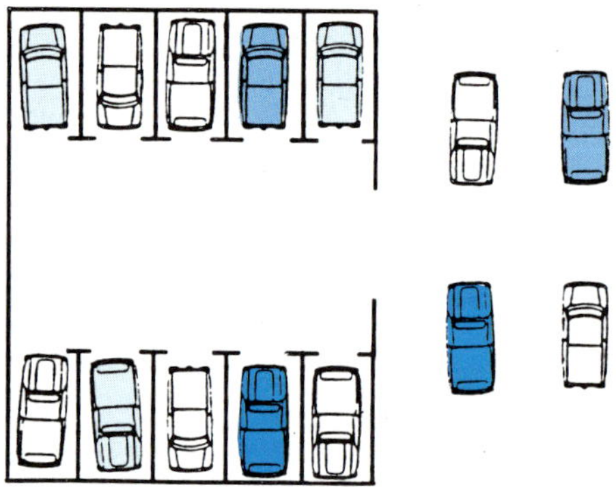

Use a large piece of cardboard to represent a car park with ten parking places.

If toy cars are not available cubes can be used. Park 14 cars as shown.

Write 14 = 10 + 4

5 Discussion

Towards the end of some of the above activities, the children should be encouraged to look at their written results to see if they can see a pattern, i.e. 18 = 10 + 8. Without using material, the teacher can ask

'What could I write for sixteen?'
'Sixteen is ten and what?'

and write 16 = 10 + 6

Material can then be used to check the result.

Ma 2/2a
RTN/A.
N/2a

Workbook Pages 13 and 14 *Towards place value*

Page 13 is a practical page. Children can use counters or cubes to represent bees. The page contains work similar to the practical activities which the children should already have encountered and which are outlined above. At the foot of Page 14, the last three examples are not illustrated. The children may need to use materials to find answers.

Some of the following activities in which, for example, 10 + 3 is written as 13 can now be introduced.

6 Sweets in a jar

Provide a jar containing ten beads with three beads beside it.

'There are 10 sweets (beads) in the jar.'

The children can check by counting.

'How many are not in the jar?' (3)
'How many altogether?' (13)

Some children may be able to count on in ones from 10 – ten, eleven, twelve, thirteen.

Write 10 + 3 = 13.

Other examples, such as 10 + 7 = 17, can then be considered.

7 Christmas cards

Provide a packet of ten Christmas cards and two loose cards.

'There are 10 cards in this packet. How many are not in the packet?' (2)
'How many altogether?'

Write 10 + 2 = 12

8 Cubes in a box

Use a box with the label [10] on it and with ten cubes inside.
Put 3 loose cubes beside the box.
'How many altogether?'

Some children may have to count the cubes inside the box.
Write 10 + 3 = 13

Ma 2/2a
RTN/A
N/2a

Workbook Page 15 *Towards place value*

In all the examples on this workbook page the individual items in the group of ten can be counted if necessary. Children should however be encouraged to 'count on' from 10.

9 Additional activity

Assessment and Resources Pack

Resource card 7 (Notation cards) provides small cards such as [1 0] and [4] [8] [9] etc. By overlapping cards such as, for example, [1 0] and [8] to produce [1 8], it can be shown that 18 is 10 and 8.

PLACE VALUE TO 20
Introductory activities

Ma 2/2a
RTN/A
N/2a

In this section numbers such as 15 are expressed as 1 ten + 5 units and, conversely, 1 ten + 5 units is written as 15. Interlocking cubes, such as Unifix or Multilink, are ideal for practical work to illustrate both types of example, as suggested below.

1 Making a ten

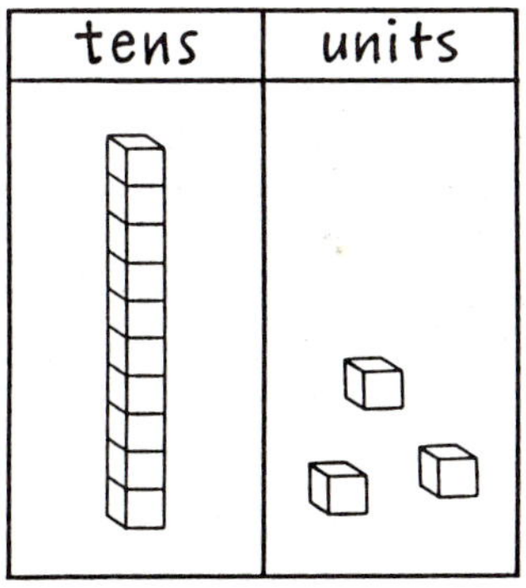

Ask the children to count out, for example, 13 cubes.
'Make a tower of ten.'
The 'ten' can then be placed on a notation card as shown, and the word 'tens' introduced.
'How many cubes are left over?' (3)
Put the 3 cubes on the units part of the notation card and introduce the new word 'units'.

Write 13 = 1 ten and 3 units

Several examples like this can be done with teacher supervision.
In particular, it should be emphasised that 20 = 2 tens + 0 units.

Ma 2/2a
RTN/A
N/2a

Workbook Page 16 *Place value to 20*

This is a practical page where children do similar work to that outlined above. Ten Unifix cubes should fit on top of the ten column on the truck and the 'units' on the rest of the truck. When the page is completed children should be asked to look carefully at each result. For example, [1 | 6] = [1] ten and [6] units.

The last example, involving 20, may cause some difficulty.

2 Tower of ten

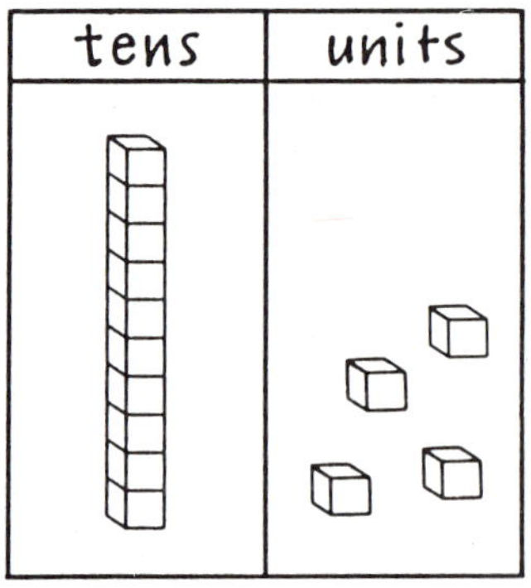

Prepare several towers of ten cubes. Ask the children to put 1 ten in the tens column of the notation card and 4 cubes in the units column.

'How many cubes altogether?'

Some children may say fourteen straight away, while some may count on from 10. Others, who are less sure of the concept of place value, may need to count all the cubes.

Write   1 ten + 4 units = 14

Several examples like this should be done with the teacher.

Ma 2/2a
RTN/A
N/2a

Workbook Page 17 *Place value to 20*

This is a practical page with space provided for laying out materials on top of the page. The work mirrors that outlined in Activity 2 above. However, some children may be able to complete the examples without material and should be encouraged to do so.

PLACE VALUE TO 20
Consolidation activities

Ma 2/2a
RTN/A
N/2a

The following practical activities, together with the work on Workbook Page 18 and Place Value cards 1 to 6, draw together various aspects of place value work. For example, 14, fourteen, 10 + 4 and 1 ten + 4 all represent the same number.

1 Launch the rocket

Prepare a rocket shape on cardboard and sets of cards for all the numbers from 11 to 20, for example,

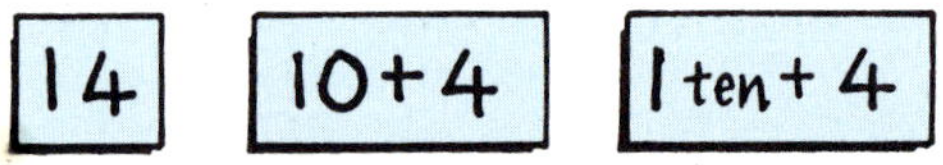

Fix a card to the rocket using Blu-tack, for example the 14 card. To launch the rocket, the children have to place two other cards to match the 14 on the rocket. The starting card, can be any one of the three cards in a set.

2 Cover up

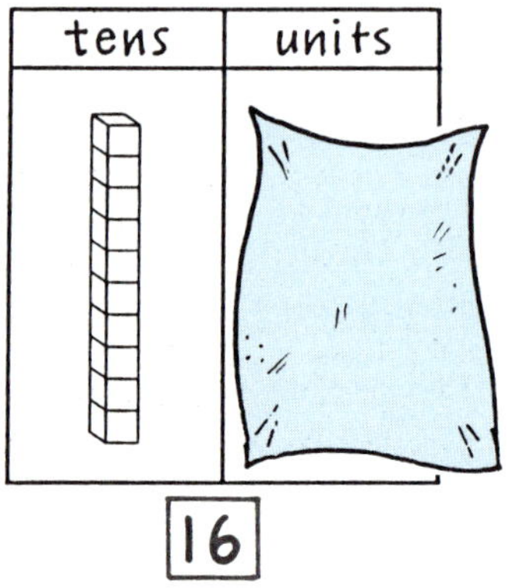

- Cover the units section of a notation card with a cloth. The children then have to say how many units are covered for a specific number, for example, 16.
- Cover the tens section with a cloth leaving 8 units visible in the units column. Ask how many cubes are covered for the number 18. Answers of 'ten' or '1 ten' are both acceptable.

Workbook 2

- Have a box labelled [10 cubes] and some extra cubes. Put out, for example, fourteen cubes as shown together with a number card 14. Cover either the four cubes or the box of ten and ask the children how many cubes are hidden.

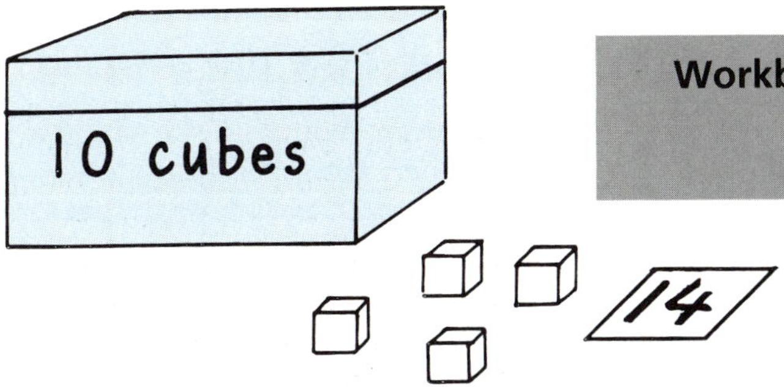

Workbook Page 18 *Place value to 20*
Number/Place Value Cards 1 to 6

Ma 2/2a
RTN/A
N/2a

Some of the consolidation activities outlined above should be done before children try the Workbook page and cards. Workbook Page 18 involves number names as well as place value work. Some children may wish to write, for example, 17 beside seventeen as an initial step.

Cards 1 to 6 are mostly practical and can be done in any order. For Cards 3 and 4 it would be an advantage if the children had done some of the consolidation activities in 2 on page 42. For the example at the foot of Card 5 the children should make a card showing [10 + 5] or [1 ten + 5].

THE NUMBER LINE TO 20: COUNTING ON
Introductory activities

Ma 2/2a
RTN/A
N/2a

In this section children use a number line from 0 to 20 to find answers to examples like 14 + 3 by 'counting on' from 14.

1 Introduction of the number line

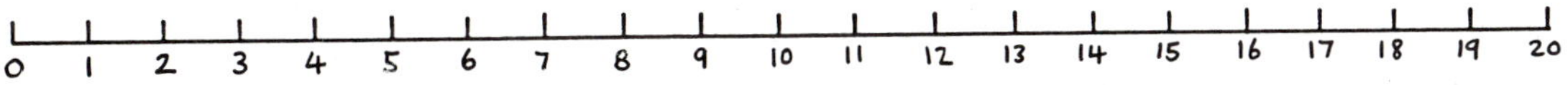

Use a number line drawn on card or on a chalkboard. Point out that it starts at 0 and that the marks on the line are numbered.

Some teachers may already have introduced the number line in connection with the 'Number sequence to 20' section on page 34.

- Repeat some of the number line activities suggested on page 34.
- 'Start at 14.' Child puts a finger on 14.
  'Count on 3.' Child makes 3 jumps of one.
  'What number do you land on?' Child reads off 'seventeen'.
  Write 14 + 3 = 17.

Repeat the sequence for other numbers. The movements along a number line could be contextualised by having a cut-out rabbit or kangaroo hop along the line.

- 'What is 11 + 4?'
  See if the children know what to do.
  Repeat for other examples.

Ma 2/2a
RTN/A
N/2a

Workbook Page 19 *Number line: counting on*

Children should be shown how to put a dot on the number line at the starting number, before counting on. Putting a dot at the finishing number is also a good idea.

COMPLEMENTARY ADDITION
Introductory activities

Ma 2/2a 3/2b
RTN/A FE/B
N/2c A/2e

Suggestions for practical activities to introduce examples of the type 3 + □ = 7 are given below. Teachers should make their own selection.

1 Ducks on a pond

Prepare a pond shape using a large piece of blue paper or card. Divide the pond into two parts using 'greenery' made from tissue paper. Use either counters or cardboard cut-outs to represent ducks.

'Put 3 ducks in this part of the pond.'
'How many more ducks to make 7 altogether?'
'3 and what make 7?'

Place the 3 + □ = 7 card as shown.

Put a duck in the empty part of the pond on the other side of the greenery.

'How many ducks are there now in the pond?' (4)

Put another duck in the pond.

'How many ducks now?' (5)

Repeat until a total of 7 ducks is reached.

'How many more ducks have we put in?' (4)
'3 and what make 7?'

Complete the 3 + □ = 7 card to give 3 + [4] = 7

Do other examples using the above language.

2 Cherries on a cake

The same idea could also be taught using cherries (counters) on a plasticine cake.

3 Birthday cards

Use birthday cards to find the answer to 5 + □ = 10. Put out 5 cards and then more cards, one at a time, until 10 is reached.

4 Apples on a tree

Prepare a cardboard tree shape and card apples which are red on one side and green on the other. To find 3 + □ = 8, put 3 red apples on the tree and then add green apples, one at a time, until 8 is reached. The 5 added green apples will stand out clearly.

Write 3 + [5] = 8

Workbook **2**

5 Crosses on the board

Draw four crosses on the chalkboard using white chalk.
To find '4 + □ = 9'
or '4 and what make 9?'
add coloured crosses one at a time, until 9 is reached.
Write 4 + [5] = 9

Ma 2/2a 3/2b
RTN/A FE/B
N/2c A/2e

Workbook Pages 20 and 21 *Complementary addition*

The essential practical work outlined above should help children to complete Workbook Page 20. The idea of complementary addition is difficult for children. Some children may be able to complete Workbook Page 21 through their secure knowledge of addition facts to 10. Many however may need to use counters or cubes to find the answers. Whichever method is used, it is essential that children can interpret, for example,
6 + □ = 10 as '6 and what make 10' or '6 and how many more to make 10?'

DIFFERENCE IN PRICE
Introductory activities

Ma 2/2b
M/A AS/A
N/1e M/2b

The comparative language 'How much more?' and its association with the '–' sign was introduced in Heinemann Mathematics 2, Workbook 1. Here the 1p coin is used to introduce the language 'difference in price' and its association with the '–' sign.

1 Shopping

Use articles from the class shop or shopping cards.

- Put out 1p coins as shown below.

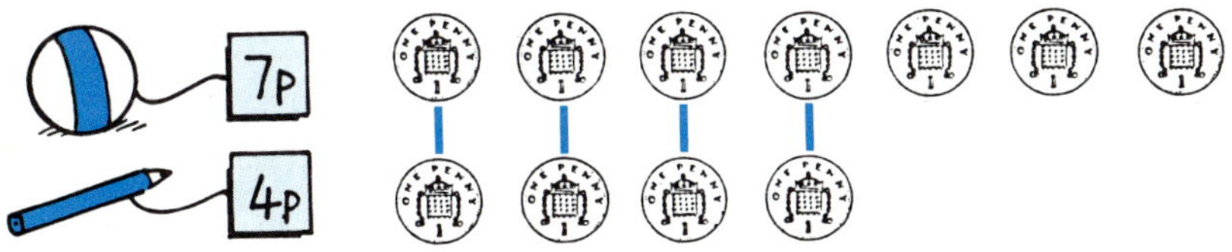

Discuss with the children that the prices are *different* and that the *difference in price* can be found by matching. The *unmatched* 1p coins show the difference in price:
a flashcard showing [difference in price] may be helpful.

- Examples where the smaller amount is laid out first should also be done. For example,

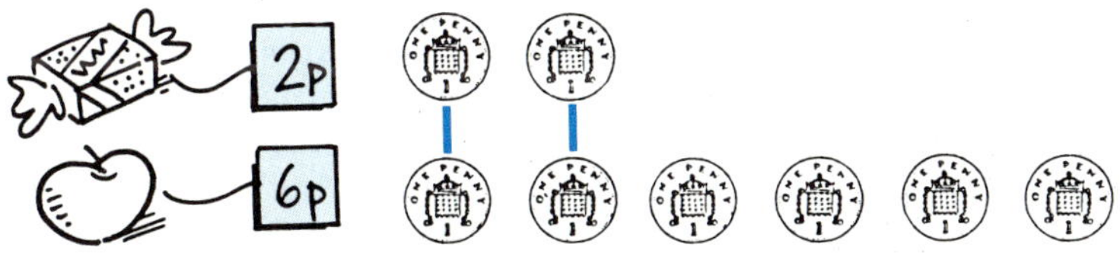

- Ask the children to pay for these articles by putting out 1p coins on top of the shopping cards. Then ask the children what the difference in price is.

Check whether the children match the 1p coins to find the answer.

- After the children have completed several shopping activities, try to establish, through discussion, that the answers can be found *by subtraction*. Some teachers may wish to record answers as

$10 - 8 = 2$ *or* $10p - 8p = 2p$ *or* $\begin{array}{r} 10p \\ -8p \\ \hline 2p \\ \hline \end{array}$

Ma 2/2b
M/A AS/A
N/1e M/2b

Workbook Page 22 *Difference in price*

The practical work, discussion and teaching described above are essential before the children try this workbook page. Most children will need to use 1p coins at least initially. When the page is completed it would be worthwhile reiterating that the difference in price can be found by *subtracting* the two prices involved.

DIFFERENCE BETWEEN
Introductory activities

Ma 2/2ab
AS/A
P/2 N/1e

The comparative language 'How many more?' and its association with the '–' sign was introduced in Heinemann Mathematics 2, Workbook 1. Here 'difference between' and its association with the '–' sign is introduced through matching.

1 Flowers

Prepare a card showing two rows of ten flower stems together with twenty detachable flower heads.

'Put 6 flowers on the top row.
Put 2 flowers on the bottom row.
Are the numbers in both rows the same or different?
The difference between 6 and 2 is 4.
We write this as 6 – 2 = 4'

A flashcard showing **difference between** would be helpful. Do several examples like this, including examples where there are fewer flowers on the top row than on the bottom row. Stress that the recording should be, for example 8 – 3 = 5 and not 3 – 8 = .

2 Crosses

Mark rows of 6 and 2 crosses on a chalkboard to find the difference between 6 and 2.

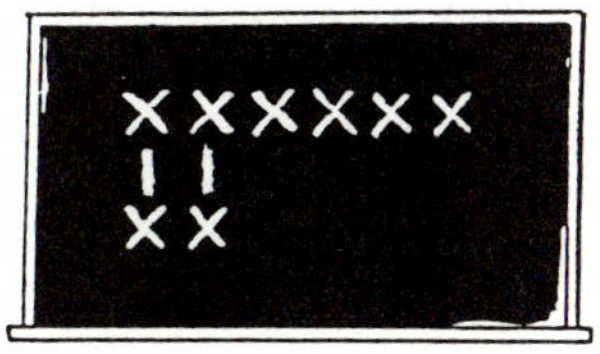

3 Counting materials

Various materials can be used by the children when they attempt practice examples.

Cubes

Beads on a string

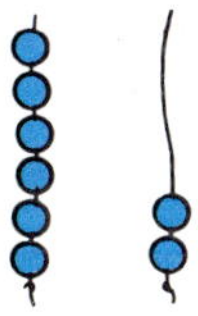

Pegs in a pegboard

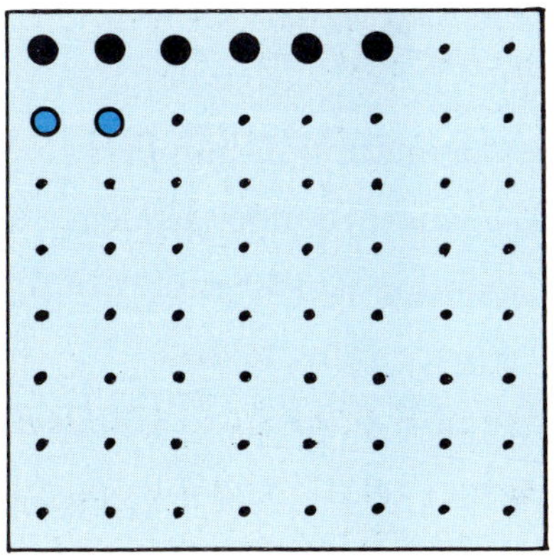

For all the above activities,

- emphasise that 'difference between' can be found by matching and that the unmatched items show the difference, for example,

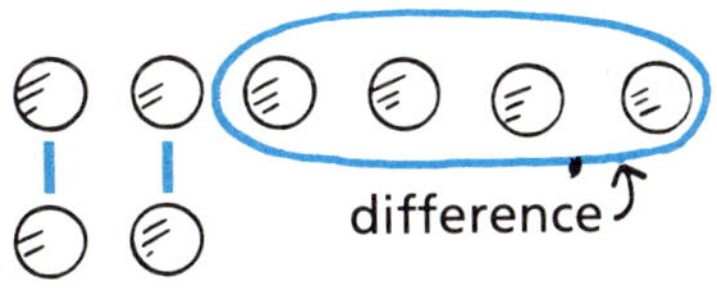

- Stress that the recording for a 'difference between' situation uses the '–' sign.

Workbook Page 23 *Difference between*

Ma 2/2ab
AS/A
N/1e

Practical work, discussion and teaching as outlined above should take place before the children try this page. In the last three examples, some children may need to use counters or cubes to represent the articles, to enable them to find the difference between by matching. Other children may already have a sound understanding that the difference between can be found by subtraction.

Workbook 3

Estimation Place value to 100 Money to 50p

Ma 1/2 2/2ab,3a 3/2ab 3/3a
RTN/A,B M/B AS/B
PS/B FE/B PSE
P/2 N/2abcde,3a A/2de,3a

Overview

This section

- introduces estimation of numbers to 20
- extends the whole number sequence to 100
- includes counting to 100 and 'counting on'
- introduces place value to 100
- explores number patterns to 100 and introduces odd and even numbers
- extends money to 50p and introduces the 20p coin.

	Teacher's Notes	Workbook 3	Workcards
			Number/ Estimation
Estimation to 20	50	1	1 to 5
Number sequence to 100	51	2 to 6	
Counting beyond 20	55	7, 8	
Counting in tens	57	9 to 12	
Place value to 99	61	13 to 15	
Place value to 99: additional activities	65		
Counting on	66	16	
Number patterns to 100	67	17 to 19	Number/ Calculators
Calculator work	69		1 to 9
Odd and even numbers	70	20	
Number to 100: additional activities	70		
Money to 50p	71	21 to 23	
Extension		*3, 5, 6, 7, 13, 14, 18, 19, 20*	
Problem solving		*6, 18*	

Key words and phrases

estimate	nearest	one more than
number before	complete	one less than
number after	greater number	towers of ten
tens, units	smaller number	odd numbers
continue the patterns	answers	even numbers

twenty, thirty, forty, fifty, sixty, seventy, eighty, ninety, one hundred

Resources

Useful materials

- small objects for counting such as beads, buttons, counters, bricks, pegs, sticky shapes, straws
- interlocking cubes
- plastic or real coins: 1p, 2p, 5p, 10p, 20p
- calculators
- wall number strip to 100, bus/house masks to suit (see page 51)
- number cards 20 to 100 [20] [21] [22] .... [100]
- flashcards of key words and phrases (see above)

Assessment and Resources Pack

Assessment

Check-ups

Check-up for Workbook 3

Assessment in Context

'Treasure Island' context: Questions 2, 7, 8, 11, 24, 25, 31, 32

Resources

Contexts

'The street' context contains activities about estimation of number to 20.
The 'Islands' context includes activities about number sequence and place value to 100.

Problem Solving Activities

1 Tens and units (Place value)
4 The race (Number sequence to 100)
6 Number pairs (Numbers to 100)

Resource Cards

Resource Card 7 (Notation cards) can be used to show numbers to 100 in place value form.

Resource Cards 10 and *11* (Three stories) provide sequences of numbers less than 100.

ESTIMATION TO 20
Introductory activities

RTN/A
N/2e

The idea of estimating a number of objects up to 10 is described in the Teaching notes for Workbook 3 of Heinemann Mathematics 1. A child's ability to estimate depends on his/her previous experience of handling and counting actual objects. Some suggested activities for extending this work to 20 are given below.

1 String of beads

Ask the children to count the number of beads on a string of say 12 beads. Produce other strings (up to 20 beads) and ask the children whether, without counting, there are more or less than 12 and 'How many beads do you think there are on this string?' The children should then check the number of beads by counting. Repeat the activity for other strings of beads.

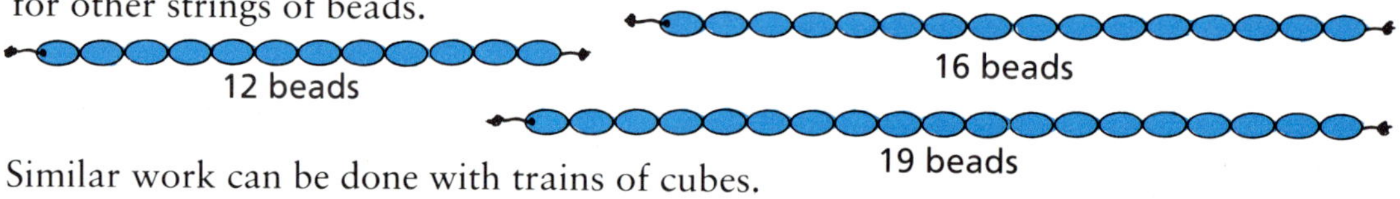

Similar work can be done with trains of cubes.

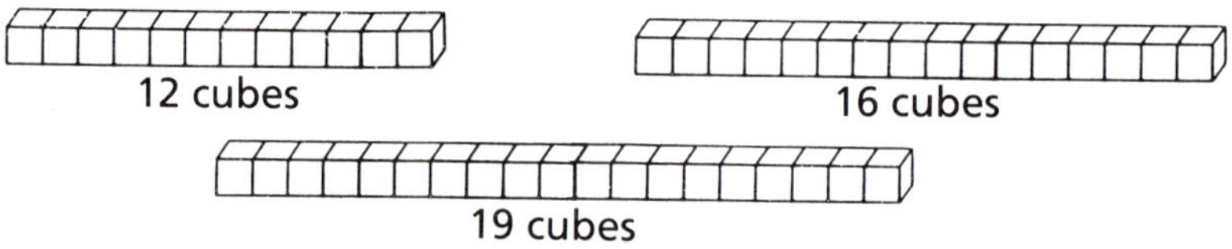

2 Precious stones

Use plastic bags containing different numbers of precious stones, from 10 to 20. The stones can be represented by beads, cubes, pegs or counters. Ask the children to write down an estimate of how many stones there are in one of the bags. They should then count them, without opening the bag, to check. Continue the process of estimating and counting for the other bags. The children's estimates should improve with practice.

3 Spots

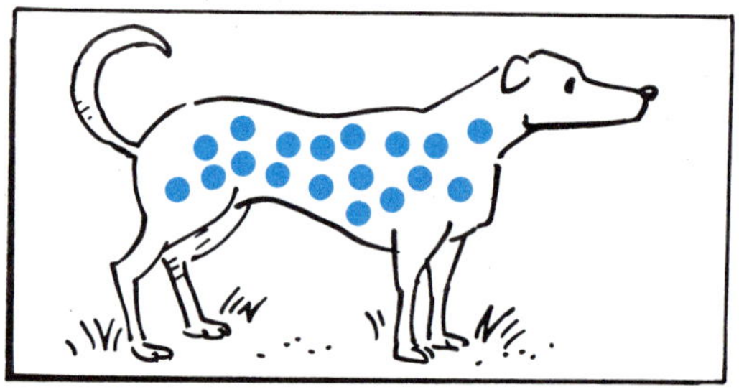

Prepare a large outline-drawing of a dog. Pick up a handful of counters from a set of between 10 and 20. Place them on the dog.

The children can estimate and count as for Activity 2.

4 Shape cards

Prepare cards with up to 20 sticky stars or shapes on them. Show the children a card and ask them to estimate the number of stars. The card should be turned over before the children have time to count the stars.

Number/Estimation Cards 1 to 5 *Estimation to 20*

RTN/A
N/2e

Cards 1 to 4 require children to estimate the number of objects in a picture *before* counting them. Working in pairs, one child could cover the objects after a short time to prevent counting before estimating.

For Card 4, paper cups, cake cases and a tray are required.

Card 5 requires the teacher to provide a suitable plastic tub and cup, each of which holds no more than 20 beads.

Workbook Page 1 *Estimation to 20*

RTN/A
N/2e

This page is best done by the children working in pairs. Each child is allowed a brief look at each set of insects before one of them hides it. The estimates should be recorded *before* the insects are counted. Estimates within 2 or 3 of the actual count are excellent at this level.

NUMBER SEQUENCE TO 100
Introductory activities

Ma 2/2a
RTN/B
N/2a

Counting to 20 is dealt with in Workbook 2. Some children may be able to say the counting sequence beyond twenty, perhaps up to one hundred. This ability can be developed and consolidated using practical activities and discussion. Here are some suggestions.

RECOGNISING THE NUMBERS TO 100

1 Number strip

A wall-mounted number strip to 20 could be extended perhaps one decade at a time. The work is mostly oral until the correct number sequence is established.

18	19	20	21	22	23	24	25	26	27	28	29	30

The children repeat the sequence saying twenty, twenty-one, twenty-two, twenty-three, and so on.

- Highlighting the decade numbers 10, 20, 30, 40, 50, etc. helps children to locate numbers more easily.
- Bus and house masks could be prepared to fit the number strip.

'What number is the bus?'
'Show me bus number 26.'
'What number is the house?'
'Show me house number 24.'

. . . and so on.

- Use the number strip for discussion of number after and number before.

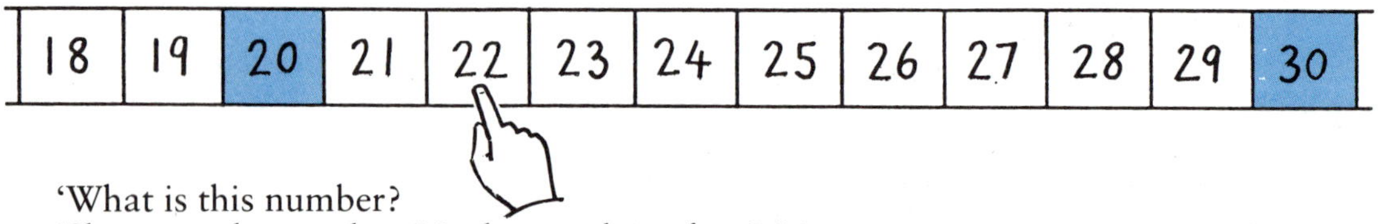

'What is this number?
'Show me the number 25, the number after 25.'
'Show me the number 22, the number before 22.' . . . and so on.

This activity can be made more demanding if either single numbers or groups of numbers on the strip are covered.

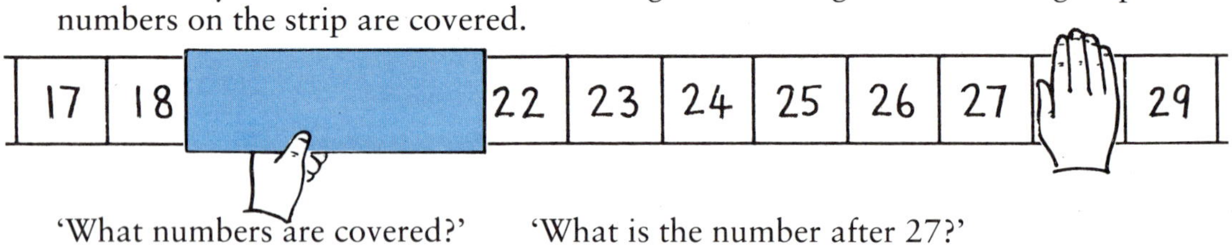

'What numbers are covered?'
'What number is after 18?'
'What number is before 22?'

'What is the number after 27?'
'What is the number before 29?'
. . . and so on.

- The number strip can be extended one decade at a time up to 100. All the above activities can be repeated, initially within the new decade only and afterwards throughout the whole strip.

- The children should know the following important oral sequences:

  10, 20, 30, 40, 50, ... , 100

  and complete decades: 30, 31, 32, 33, ... , 39 and so on.

2 Cloakroom pegs

These can be used for realistic number work.

'What number is the coat on?'
'Hang your coat on peg number 23.'

3 Board for keys

Many schools have boards for keys which could be used for number work.

'Is there a key on 27?'
'Put this key on number 23.'
. . . and so on.

This activity is related to the scenario on Workbook 3, Page 2.

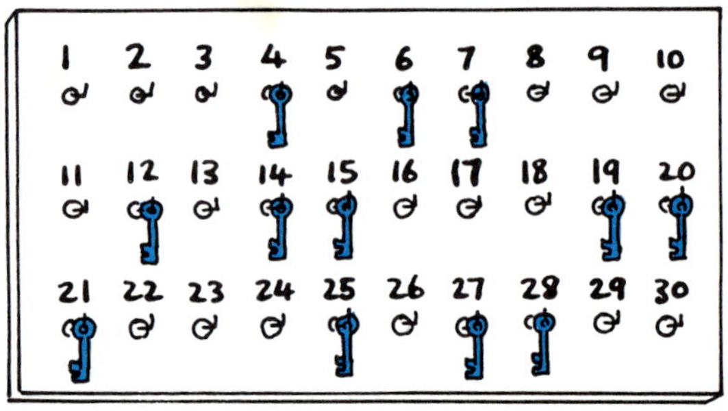

4 Calculator

'Press any number key.
Now press any other number key.
Tell me the number shown.'

'Press keys to show 34.'
. . . and so on.

WRITING THE NUMBERS TO 100

1 Using the number strip

At first children could practise writing sequences of numbers using the wall number strip for reference.

'Write all the numbers from 23 to 27.'
'Write all the numbers in the thirties.'
'Write all the numbers which begin with a 4.'
'Write all the numbers which end with a 4.'
'Write the number 51.'
'Write the number after 51, before 51.'
'Write the number one more than 72, one less than 72.'

Particular care is needed with pairs of numbers like 14 and 41 which some children confuse. Gradually the children should rely less on reference to the number strip as they learn the sequence.

2 Covering parts of the number strip

'Write in order the numbers covered.'
'Write the number after 55, before 51.'
'Write the number one more than 42, one less than 50.'

A row of numbered house shapes can be used instead of a number strip. This would allow children to deliver letters, etc.

3 Calculator

A calculator can be used as a teaching aid to reinforce the ideas of 'one more than' and 'one less than', by 'adding one' and 'subtracting one', respectively. The sequences of keys must be introduced. For example, one more than 72 is found as follows:

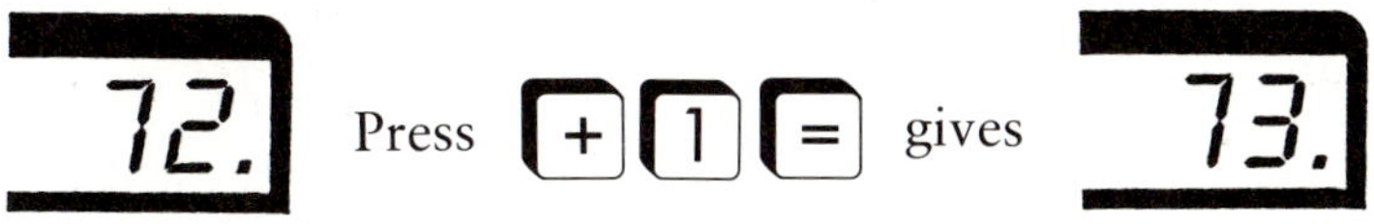

and one less than 58 as:

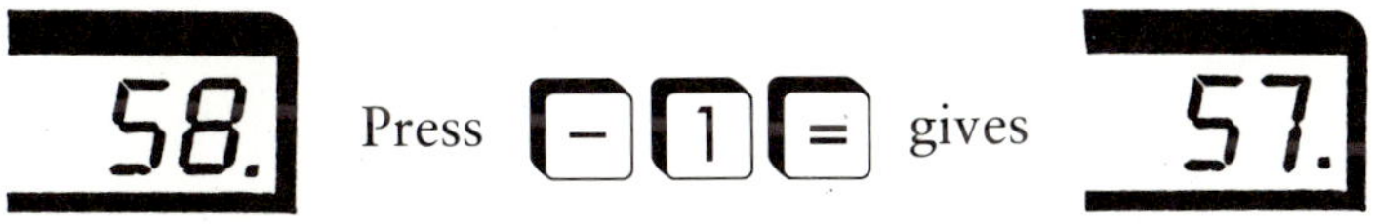

Some children should be encouraged to generate and write down numbers beyond 100. For example, they could start at 97 and add on 1 to give 98, 99, 100, 101, 102, . . . 110, and so on.
The numbers should be read aloud, particularly one hundred and one, one hundred and two, and so on.

ORDERING THE NUMBERS TO 100

The number strip shows the numbers in their correct sequence. All the preceding activities should help to establish this correct order of the numbers. Here are some further ordering activities.

1 Join numbers in order

Prepare worksheets showing numbers or draw them on a chalkboard. Ask a child to join these numbers in order starting at the smallest number.

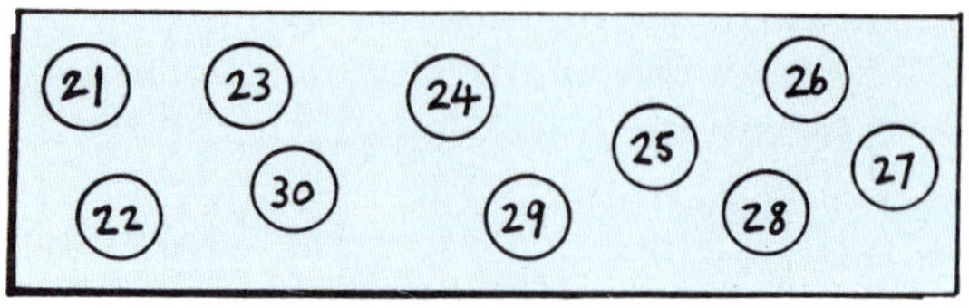

2 Numbered cards

Put out a set of numbered cards (or tablets) spread face up at random. A child or a small group of children could then arrange them in order in a row. When the cards have been arranged correctly one or more could be turned over and the children asked to say the number *before* turning each card back.

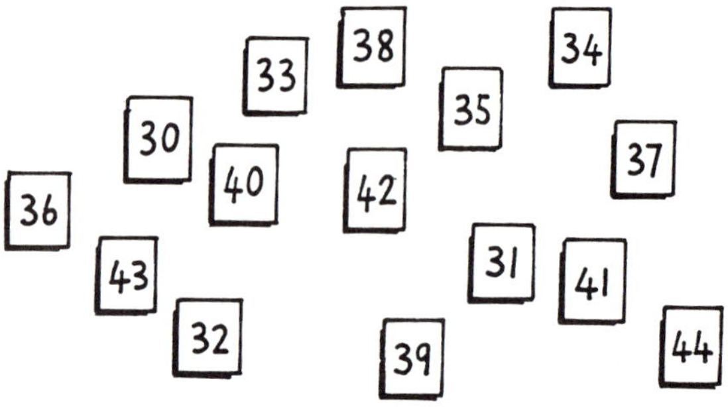

3 Picture cards

Numbered pictures like this can be cut into smaller cards as shown. The children have to arrange the cards in numerical order to recreate the picture.

Assessment and Resources Pack

4 Resource cards

Resource Cards 10 and *11* (Three stories) in the *Assessment and Resources Pack* provide pictures of three fairy tales:

'Goldilocks' – number sequence 59 to 64
'Cinderella' – number sequence 77 to 82
'Sleeping Beauty' – number sequence 95 to 100.

Ma 1/2 2/2a
RTN/B
P/2 N2a

Workbook Pages 2 to 6 *Number sequence to 100*

These pages provide a check on the progress of children who have experienced the preceding introductory activities.

The calculator work on Pages 3 and 4 involves adding or subtracting one.

Extension

The final activity on Page 3 is extension work because children have to write numbers beyond 100. To help teachers check the work on Page 5 each correctly coloured quilt has an obvious pattern.

Extension

The lower part of Page 5 is considered extension work because of the more complicated instructions, where the children are asked to colour squares for numbers before or after the given ones.

Extension/ problem solving

Page 6 is extension and problem solving work. The children should find each correct path and colour it before writing the missing numbers. The gold should be numbered 65 and the jewels 90 if the page is completed correctly.

COUNTING BEYOND 20
Introductory activities

Ma 2/2a
RTN/B
N/2a

Counting to 20 was introduced in Workbook 2. This is now extended beyond 20. Sets to be counted should number in the twenties, thirties or forties at first.

1 Using the children

A class of more than 20 children can be counted each day by individual children. Alternatively the children can 'number off' in sequence '1, 2, 3' and so on, the last number giving the count.

For fewer than 20 children, there could be a count of hands or feet.

2 Objects in containers

Prepare containers of objects for the children to count – pencils, crayons, pens, rulers, cubes, counters, etc. Ask the children to count them as they take them out and check as they put them back. They could record the number on a label on the container.

3 Counting out sets

Instructions for children to count out a specific number can be given either orally or in writing. For example,

'Put 42 pegs in the pegboard.'
'Put out 35 straws.'
'Make a wall with 28 bricks.'

4 Filling containers

'Fill the carton with beads.'
'Count how many it holds.'

Similarly for other containers:

'How many bricks does the box hold?'
'How many cards cover your desk?'
'How many straws can you put in the tin?'

Other opportunities for counting in realistic situations are: cards in a pack, toys in a box, coats in the cloakroom.

5 Worksheets

Here are some sample activities.

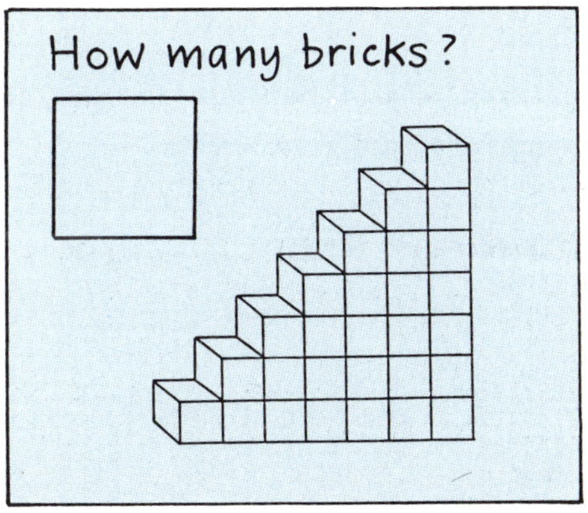

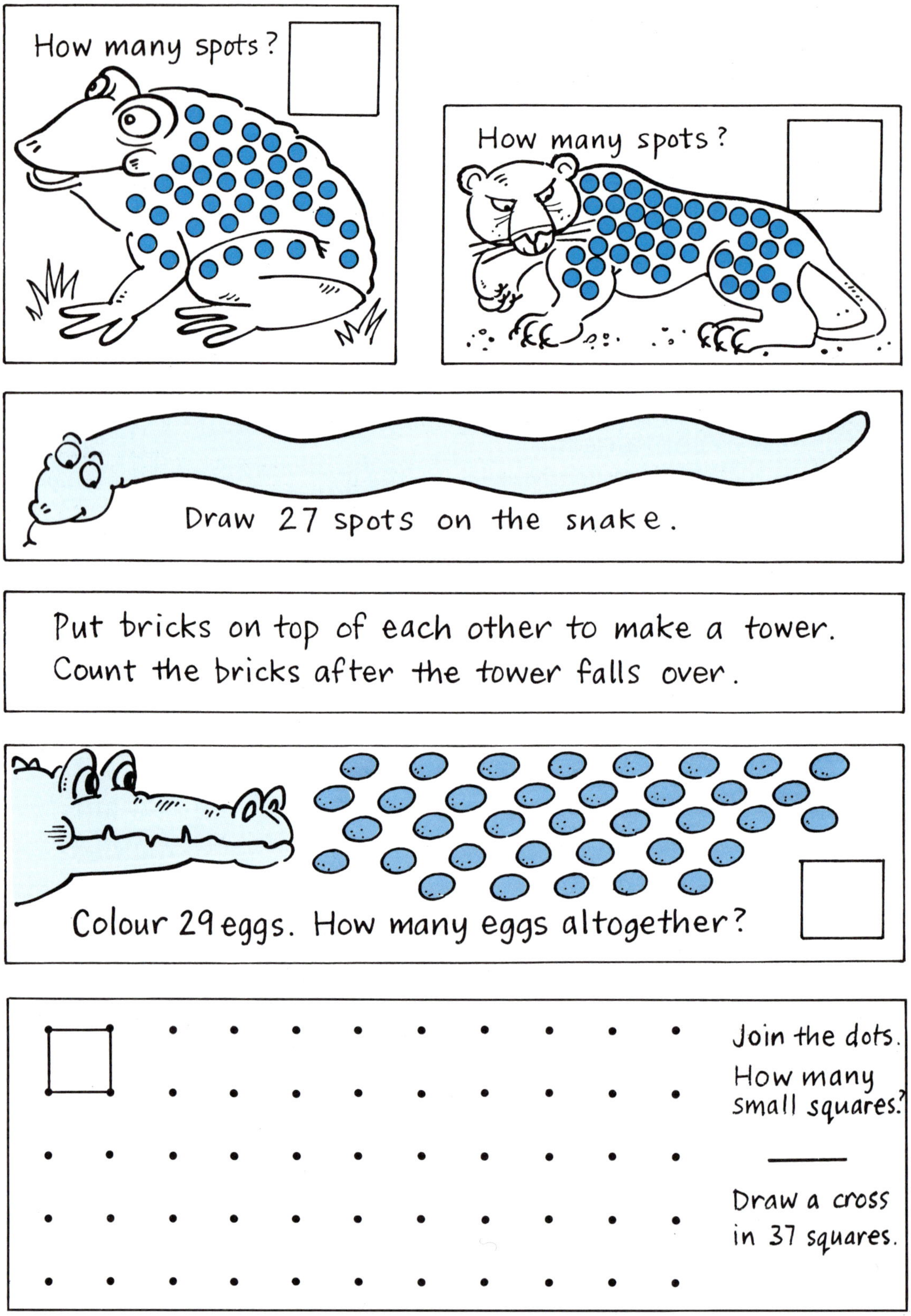

Ma 2/2a
RTN/B
N/2a

Extension

Workbook Pages 7 and 8 *Counting beyond 20*

These pages provide further practice in counting beyond 20. The children could tick the spots on the animals to keep a tally as they count them on Page 7.

The work at the foot of Page 7 is extension work since it requires the knowledge of how 'noughts and crosses' games are played and won.

COUNTING IN TENS
Introductory activities

Workbook 3

Ma 2/2a
RTN/B PS/B
N/2a

Sets of more than twenty objects have so far been counted in ones. As a bridge to proper understanding of place value, the sequence 10, 20, 30, ... , 100 can now be used to count in tens. Activities to establish this sequence and introduce counting in tens are given below.

1 Number strip

Use a number line or strip from 1 to 100 to emphasise once more the sequence 10, 20, 30, ... , 100. These numbers could be highlighted using a different colour.

Count on from 20 in ones – '20 and one, two, three, four, ... , ten more makes 30, and another 10 makes 40, and another 10 makes 50', and so on.

2 Number cards

- Use number cards to make up the sequence from 10 to 100.

Remove a card and ask the children which number is missing. Give practice in saying the sequence.
Use one card at a time to ask questions such as
'What number is ten more than 50?'

- Use number name cards to match. For example,

. . . .

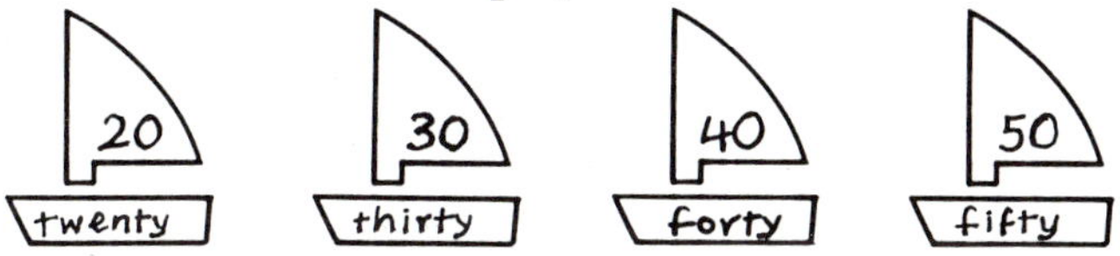

. . . . .

3 Dot-to-dot

Use a simple picture or pattern on the chalkboard or a large sheet of paper to give practice with the sequence.

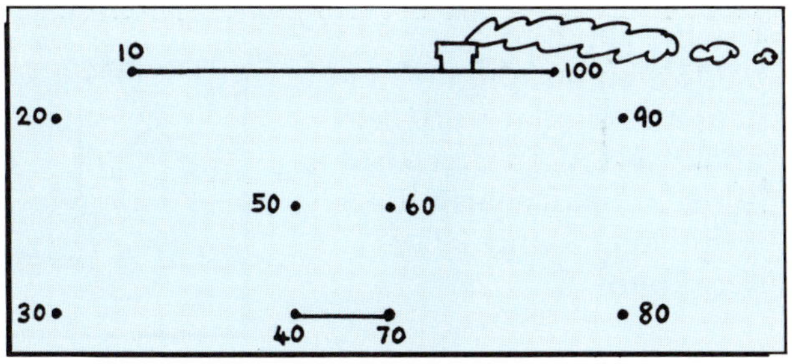

4 A calculator sequence

Discuss what happens when 10 is added to 10, then to 20, 30, and so on up to 100.

Provide each child in the group with a simple calculator on which they can work or demonstrate the sequence to the group by keying in 10 to show

Add 10 by pressing

to give

Without clearing the calculator, add 10 again to give 30 . . . and so on, with the children predicting what the next answer will be.

5 Sets of ten

Use plasticine cakes in cake cases or use cubes to represent cakes. Ask each child in a group to put 10 cakes on a plate. Help them to count how many there are altogether by counting in tens.

ten, ... twenty, ... thirty, ... forty, ... fifty, ... sixty.

Ask a child to lay out plates for, say, 30 cakes by counting in tens. Repeat for other totals from the 10, 20, 30, . . . 100 sequence. It is worthwhile checking one of these totals by counting in ones.

Other ideas can be used for such activities. For example,

- 10 ice cubes (blue cubes) in each tray

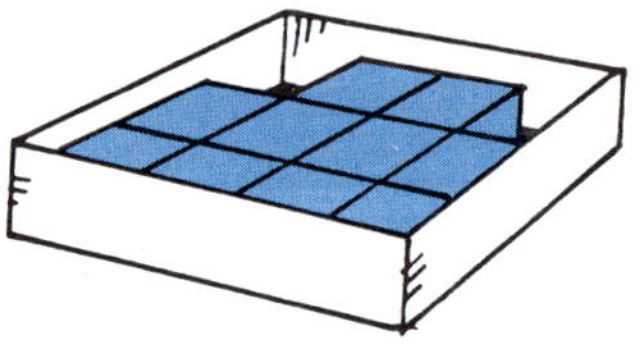

- sets of 10 pencils

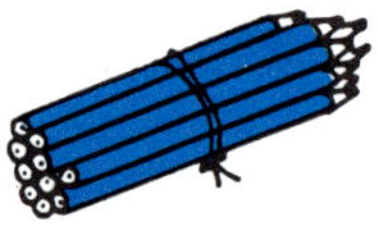

- 10 fish fingers (rods) in each box
- 10 cassettes in each box
- any cheap materials, foods, which come in packs of 10.

Each time the appropriate number card, for example 40, and/or number name card forty can be attached to the set.

6 Buses

Give each child a sheet showing a drawing of a bus with 10 large windows. Each child then draws 10 passengers, one at each window, on his/her bus.

Use the children's completed bus pictures in activities similar to those about sets of 10 described above. This scenario links with Pages 9 and 10 of Workbook 3.

Ma 2/2a
RTN/B PS/B
N/2a

Workbook Pages 9 and 10 *Counting in tens*

The activities of these pages aim to consolidate the sequence 10, 20, 30, . . . , 100 and counting in tens. Careful explanation for each section of the pages is required, particularly with the calculator activity where the format of recording and the continuous nature of adding, without clearing, may cause difficulties. When counting passengers on Page 10, it is important that the children count '10, 20, 30, ...'.

FURTHER COUNTING IN TENS
Introductory activities

Workbook 3

Ma 2/2ab
RTN/B
N/2a

The next section introduces grouping in tens and counting where there are also extra 'ones' to be counted, as well as sets of 10. Possible activities are given below.

1 Sets of 10

Introductory activity 5 opposite can be repeated and extended. For example,
'Count four trays of ten ice cubes (blue cubes).'

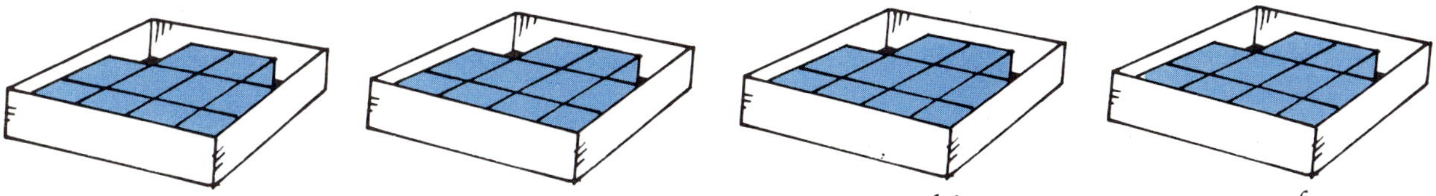

ten, ... twenty, ... thirty, ... forty.

'Add on single cubes one at a time.'

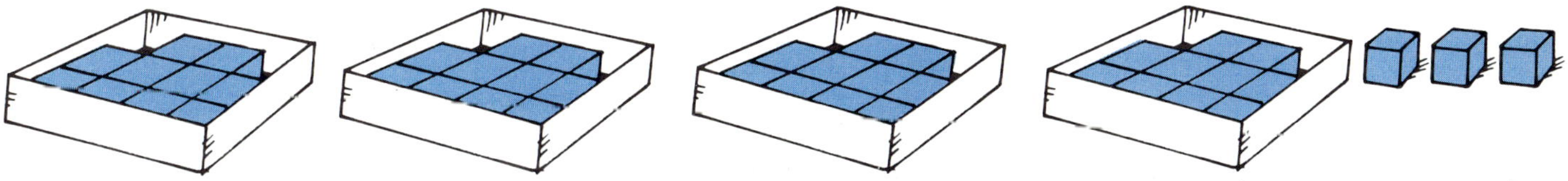

ten, ... twenty, ... thirty, ... forty. . . one, two, three

'Forty and three is 43.'

A number card [43], or notation cards [40] and [3] overlapped to give [4|3], can be placed beside the set. (Notation cards are supplied in the *Assessment and Resources Pack*, Card 7.)

Assessment and Resources Pack

Give the children plenty of practice in counting sets like these and also in laying out sets of numbers like 57 by putting out tens and then ones. Different materials and scenarios could be used.

2 Collecting for charity

The technique of counting in tens is often applied to collections of coins in real-life situations. Prepare a collecting can containing plastic 1p coins and with a favourite charity illustrated on it. Ask the children to help you in counting the 1p coins by putting them into piles of ten.

seventy-six pence

Repeat with other amounts and also ask the children to lay out amounts, such as 35p, using already counted piles of 10. These activities are related to Page 11 of Workbook 3. Counters might be used if sufficient 1p coins are not available.

3 Individual activities

Individual follow-up activities are suggested below.

Chalk sticks

Counting out packs of ten and singles to fulfil orders written on small cards.

Money box

Counting how much is in a money box containing 1p coins only. Buttons in a button box could also be used.

Flowers

Drawing round sets of 10 and counting in tens.

Sheets of paper

Counting collections of objects by arranging them in groups of ten, for example, sheets of paper, postcards, pencils, etc.

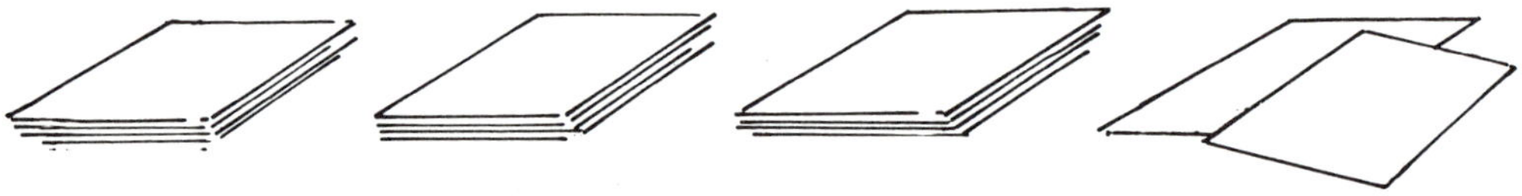

ten, ... twenty, ... thirty, ... two, ... thirty-two.

4 Notation cards

A further step towards place value is to point out the structure of the numbers which the children are counting in tens. For example, using cards,

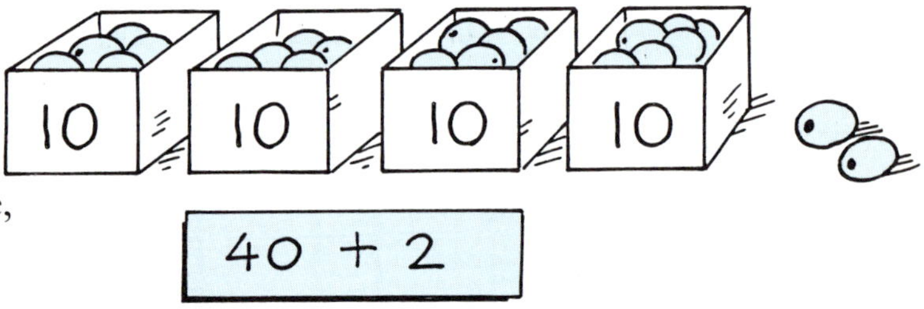

Assessment and Resources Pack

Notation Cards, such as those supplied in the *Assessment and Resources Pack* (Card 7), can also be used to illustrate this structure by overlapping the cards.

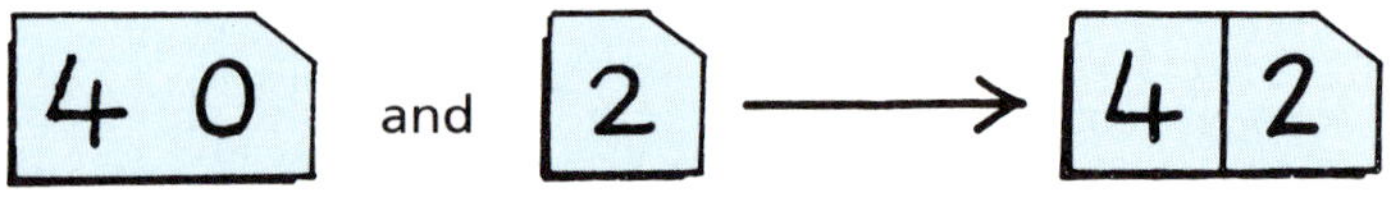

Activities like these are related to the form of recording used on Workbook 3, Page 12.

Workbook Pages 11 and 12 *Counting in tens*

Page 11 depends on previous experience of laying out and counting 1p coins in piles of 10. The children are expected to count these by saying 'ten, twenty, thirty, ...', i.e. counting the tens first and then dealing with the single 1p coins.

The new feature of Page 12 is the use of the 60 + 3 format in recording. The children should count each set and record the total, i.e. 63, in the answer box *or* the diagram. Finally they colour the labels at the foot of the page to match these diagrams.

Workbook 3

Ma 2/2a
RTN/B M/B
N/2a

PLACE VALUE TO 99
Introductory activities

Ma 2/2a
RTN/B
N/2a

Previous sections have considered counting in tens and recording as 63 and as 60 + 3. The next section extends these ideas as it

- uses interlocking cubes and other materials to lay out tens and units
- introduces further forms of recording which make the place value structure of the numbers clear

63   60 +3   6 tens + 3 units   6 tens + 3.

Activities to introduce these ideas are suggested below. Children require extensive practical experience of such activities, or others of the teacher's choice, and also practice with the associated language and recording, to develop ideas of place value. This is a process well worth the time spent on it as such ideas underlie a proper understanding of the number system.

1 Towers of ten

Ask the children to count a set of interlocking cubes by grouping them in tens.

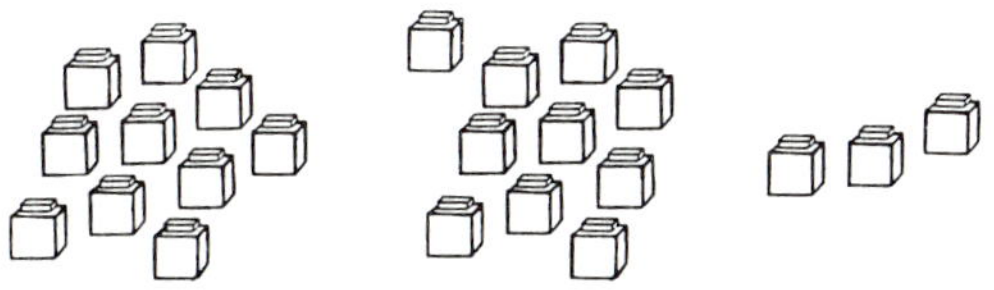

The cubes can be counted,   ten, ... twenty, ... three, ... twenty-three.

Ask the children to make towers of ten by fitting the cubes together. They can then place these on top of a card with column headings. The word 'units', introduced in Workbook 2 and also used on Workbook 3, Pages 13 and 14, will require explanation. Some teachers may prefer to use 'ones' instead.

Refer to this arrangement as '2 tens and 7 units'.

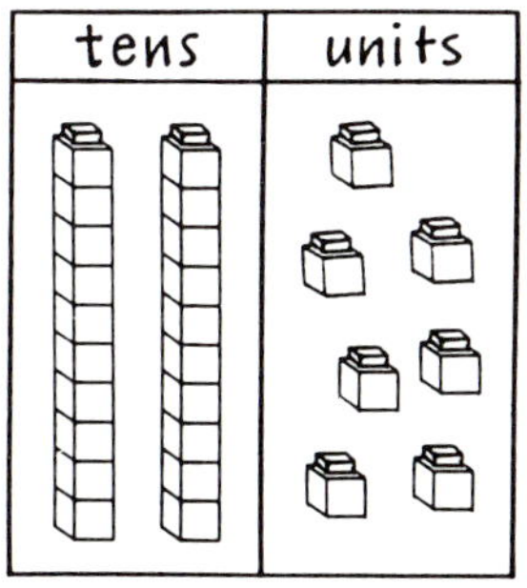

Ways of representing this number can then be discussed:

27   20 + 7   2 tens + 7 units   2 tens + 7

This should by repeated for other numbers less than 100. The activity is related to Page 13 of Workbook 3, which might be introduced at this point.

2 Other materials

Use other materials for practice in grouping into tens and units. For example,

Straws and elastic bands

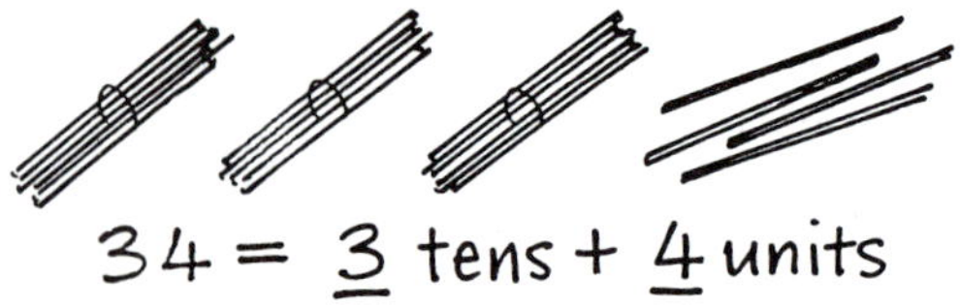

1p coins or counters

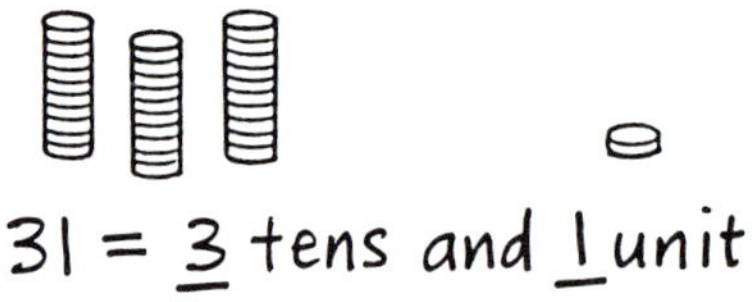

tubs and pencils

The language may still be 'ten, twenty, thirty, forty . . . . one, two, three, four, five, six, seven, eight . . . . forty-eight'. The new aspect will be talking of forty-eight as '4 tens and 8 units'.

3 Individual and group activities

Cube box

Individual children can count how many cubes are in the box by making up towers of 10 and then recording.

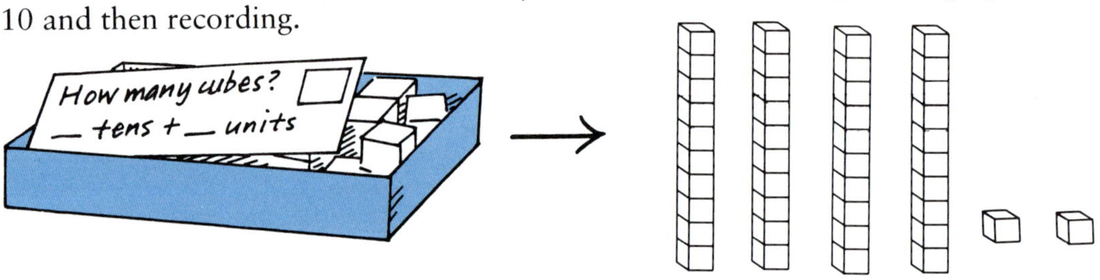

Envelopes

The children can, as a group, find out how many things there are in envelopes or boxes containing simple classroom materials. They would do this by, for example, bundling pencils in tens, bundling straws in tens, placing pegs in strips of ten, and so on.

Recording might use a simple worksheet. For example,

Worksheet

Individual children could colour tens and units for a given total on a worksheet. For example,

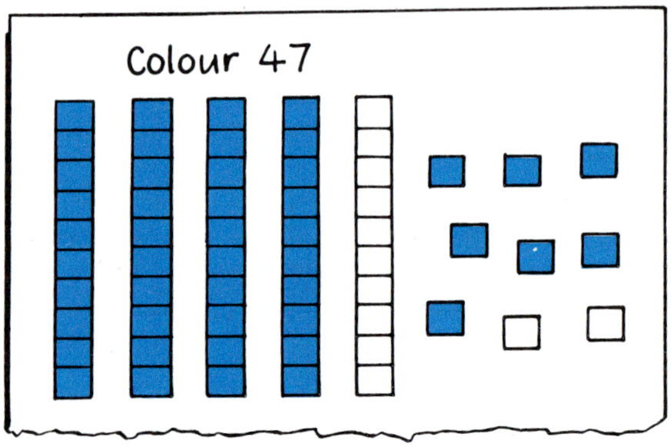

Ma 2/2a
RTN/B
N/2a

Workbook Page 13 *Place value to 99*

This page continues the practical activities using interlocking cubes suggested on Page 61. Some children will begin to express numbers like 59 as 5 tens and 9 units without laying out materials.

Extension

The last section of the page is more difficult extension work where pupils are expected to think of 24 as 2 towers of ten and 4 units when colouring.

The completed page should be discussed to emphasize the pattern:

$$\boxed{5}\boxed{9} = \boxed{5}\text{ tens} + \boxed{9}\text{ units}$$

Oral examples such as 'What will 75 be?' can then be attempted *without* material: 75 = 7 tens + 5 units

4 More towers of ten

Give the children practice in the reverse process of laying out tens and units and then deciding how many cubes there are altogether. Put some cards like this one

4 tens + 3 units

in a bag. A child takes out a card and then lays out corresponding material using already constructed towers of ten.

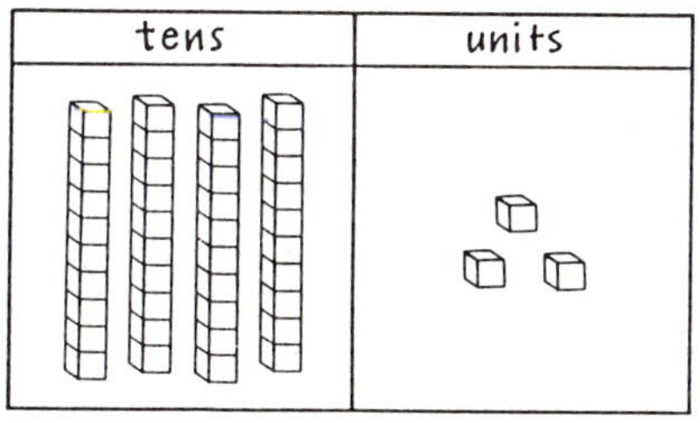

All the children in the group can then be asked how many cubes there are altogether. They are likely to think of the 4 tens as 40 and 3 more makes 43.

Some children may wish to count in ones, showing that their concept of place value is still insecure.

Page 14 of Workbook 3 includes activities like this about 'towers of ten'.

5 Individual activities

Beads

A child can lay out materials, already in tens, and count how many there are altogether. For example, using strings of 10 beads:

Put out 3 tens and 2 units.
How many beads altogether? ☐

Such activities can also be associated with simple scenarios. For example,

Packets of sweets

Bags of pirate gold

Worksheet

A worksheet format will enable individual children to colour tens and units and then find a total. For example,

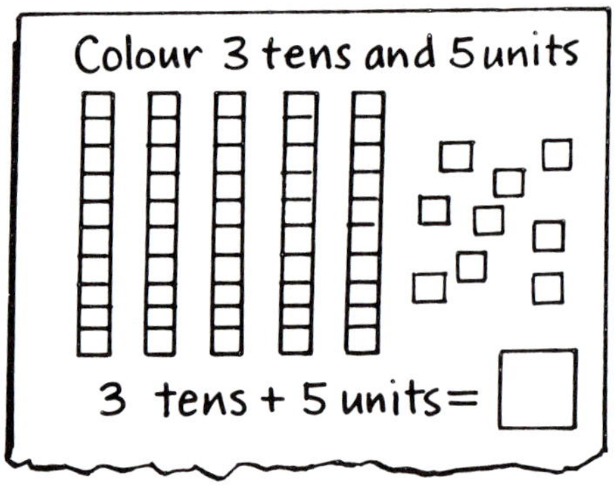

6 Matching activities

Use simple matching activities to relate the three forms of recording which the children have already met.

| 53 | 50+3 | 5 tens + 3 units |

The shorter form 5 tens + 3 can also be introduced as it appears on Workbook 3, Page 15.

Lay out Unifix or similar materials and ask the children to choose cards to match the materials. Simple cards can be made to provide scenarios for matching different forms of recording. For example,

Caterpillars

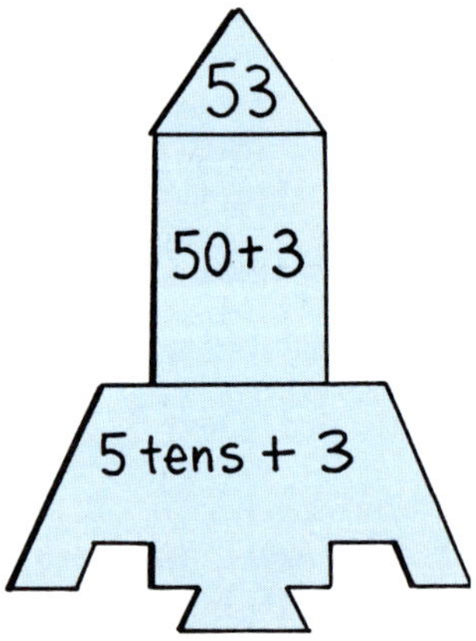

Rockets

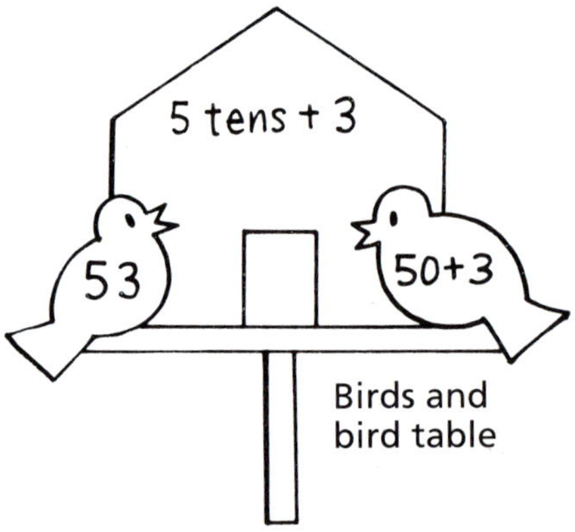

Birds and bird table

Ma 2/2a
RTN/B
N/2a
Extension

Workbook Pages 14 and 15 *Place value to 99*

Page 14 continues the practical activities suggested in Activity 4 on page 63. The extension section at the foot of the page is intended to be done by counting the number of tens . . 1, 2, 3 . . , and then the units.

The scenario on Page 15 involving three sizes of luggage and an airport conveyor belt will require discussion as not all children will be familiar with such a scene.

PLACE VALUE TO 99
Additional activities

Workbook **3**

Ma 2/2a 1/2
RTN/B PSE
N/2a P/2

1 100 grid

Children can colour squares on a 100 grid by counting in tens and units. For example,

82

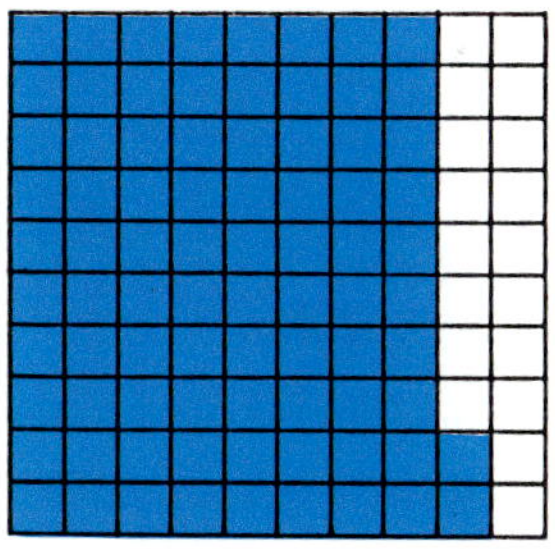

2 Dice game *(for 2 players)*

Each player has a notation card. Towers of ten and single cubes are also available. Each player throws a die and takes the appropriate number of tens *or* units.

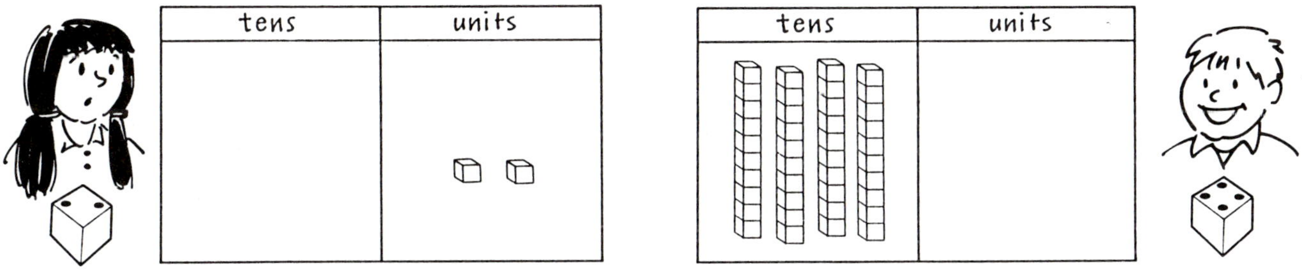

On each player's next throw the number is used to complete the empty column.

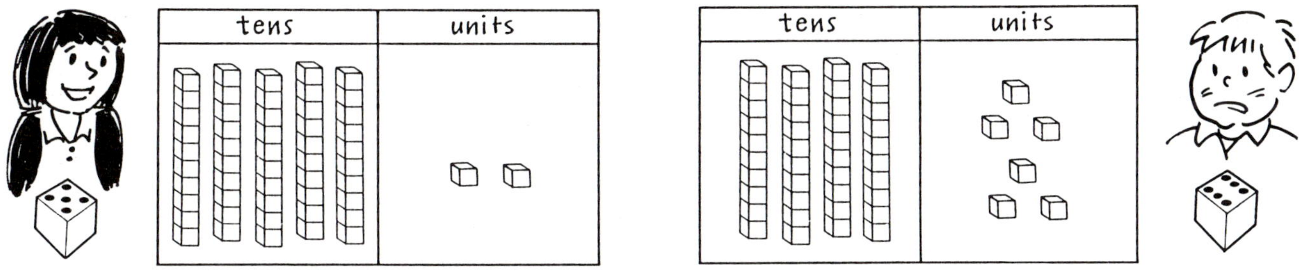

The larger number wins. The game can also be played so that the smaller number wins.

3 Card game *(for 2 players)*

Prepare a set of target cards as shown.

22 64 55 82 33 73 44 91

Have a set of towers of ten and some units available. Each player starts with 5 tens and takes one of the cards from a face-down pile. For example, 73

On each turn a player can either add on 1 ten *or* 1 unit or take away 1 ten *or* 1 unit. The player's aim is to be the first to make the number on his/her target card. The player who starts should always win but only if he/she follows the best strategy.

COUNTING ON
Introductory activities

Ma 2/2a 3/3a
AS/B
N/2a A/3a

The activities below can be used to introduce counting on 1, 2, 3 or 4 from numbers between 10 and 100.

1 Stepping stones

Use a diagram showing numbered stepping stones similar to the ones at the top of Workbook 3, Page 16. For example,

Choose a starting number, say 70, and ask the children to jump on 2.
'Which number will you land on?'
Repeat this process to build up a written pattern like the one below.

70 + 2 = 72
72 + 2 = 74
74 + 2 = 76
76 + 2 = 78
78 + 2 = 80

Repeat for other starting numbers and other sizes of jumps, for example 3 or 4.

Other patterns can be created by jumping on 1, 2, 3 or 4 from the same number each time. For example,

69 + 1 = 70	77 + 1 = 78
69 + 2 = 71	77 + 2 = 79
69 + 3 = 72	77 + 3 = 80
69 + 4 = 73	77 + 4 = 81

2 Number lines

Another type of pattern involves using a number strip or number line from 1 to 100. The starting numbers for each pattern have the same number of units and all the jumps are the same size. For example,

42 + 4 = 46
52 + 4 = 56
62 + 4 = 66
72 + 4 = 76 . . . and so on.

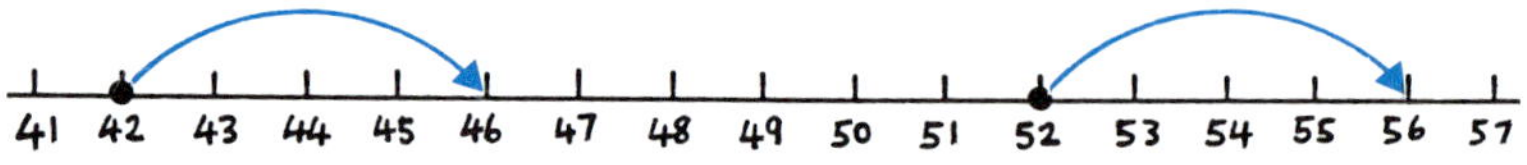

Use a number line to discuss such patterns with the children. Some may be able to appreciate that, for an example like the one above, each answer ends in a 6 because 2 and 4 are 6.

3 Mental work

Some children might be encouraged to count on in their heads. For example, 63 + 2 could be done by saying '64, 65' to count on two.

Workbook Page 16 *Counting on*

Experience of using a number strip or number line to explore patterns, as described in the introductory activities above, will be necessary before the children attempt this page. They should draw 'jumps' on the page, if necessary, to help them with the examples.
The last two examples at the foot of the page are not covered by the section of number line on the page. The children might do these by looking at a number line in the classroom or by using the pattern of earlier examples or by counting on mentally. There should also be discussion of the patterns on the completed page.

Ma 2/2a
AS/B
N/2a

NUMBER PATTERNS TO 100
Introductory activities

Ma 2/2a 3/3a
PS/B RTN/B
N/2a A/3a

This section aims to encourage children to explore the numbers 1 to 100 through patterns and puzzles. The follow-up Pages 17 to 20 of Workbook 3 deal with the following:

Page 17 Patterns on a 100 square
Page 18 Puzzles involving place value and the numbers 1 to 100
Page 19 Patterns created by adding on 10 using a calculator.
For example,

4 + 10 = 14
14 + 10 = 24
24 + 10 = 34 . . . and so on

Page 20 Odd and even numbers

Calculator Cards 1 to 9 are referenced from the foot of Page 19. They contain a variety of activities involving numbers less than 30.

A selection of introductory activities related to Pages 17 and 18 are suggested below.

1 1 to 100 board

Use the type of 1 to 100 number board where the numbers are put on by the children. Some versions have number tags which fit on hooks, others have number tablets which fit on a grid. Start with a few of the numbers missing which the children have to put in the correct places.

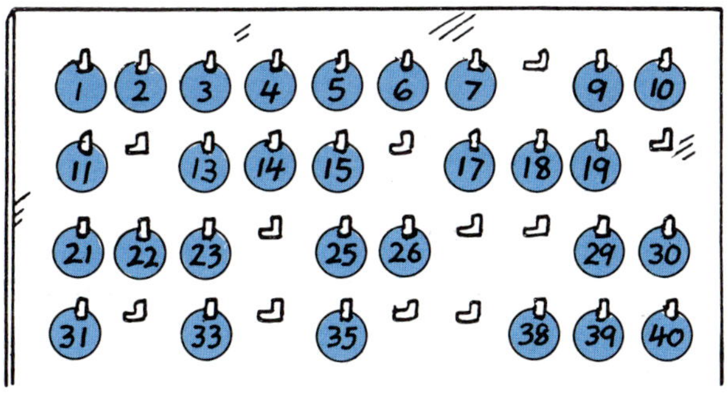

2 100 square

The activity above can be done in another way by using a large paper grid for the numbers 1 to 100 with some of the numbers covered.

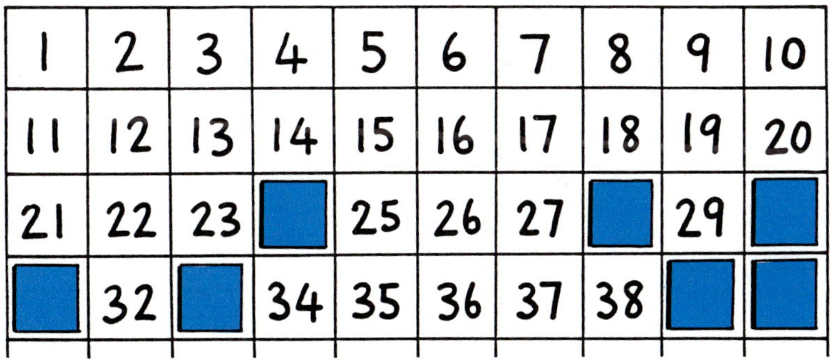

Ask a child to uncover a specific number, such as 39. Alternatively, the child could suggest what one of the covered numbers is and then check by removing the cover.

3 Patterns on a 100 square

Point out patterns involving counting on 2 or 3 or 4 and ask the children to predict the 'next number'. For example,

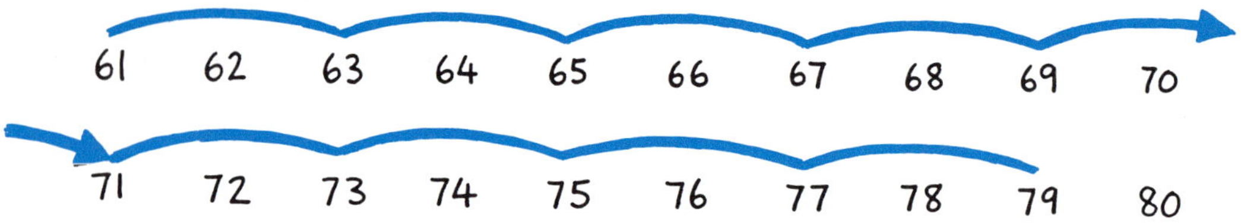

A pattern of counting on 10 produces

8
18
28
38

. . . . and so on.

Page 17 provides follow-up practice for activities of this type.

4 Puzzles

Ask the children questions such as

'Find the number 2 more than 89.'
'Which number has 6 tens and 4 units?'
'Which number is one less than 4 tens and 3 units?'
'Find the number 10 more than 85.' . . . and so on.

A child can point to the answer or stick a counter on top of the appropriate square using Blu-tack.

Ma 2/2a	1/2	3/3a
PS/B	RTN/B	PSE
N/2a	P/2	A/3a

Workbook Pages 17 and 18 *Number patterns to 100*

Page 17 involves missing numbers and sequences on a 1 to 100 grid, as a follow-up to the introductory activities described above. Further oral questions can be asked about the completed grid, for example, 'What number is on the knights' shield?'

Extension

Problem solving

Page 18 contains puzzles involving the numbers 1 to 100. This is extension work which will not be suited to all children as a lot of reading is required. The first three puzzles require the children to draw on the castle picture of Page 17. The remaining questions do not involve the 100 square. This should be explained to the children.

5 Patterns involving adding on 10

Introduce patterns of this type by using a calculator. For example,

Start with [9.] Press [+] [1] [0] [=] to add ten, giving [19.]

Continue the pattern:

$9 + 10 = 19$
$19 + 10 = 29$
$29 + 10 = 39$ . . . and so on.

Colouring these answers on a 1 to 100 square shows up the pattern as a vertical column. Repeat for other starting numbers less than 10.

Ma 2/2a,3a
AS/B
N/2a A/3a

Workbook Page 19 *Pattern: adding on 10*

Extension

This page is extension work which continues the discovery of patterns like those in Activity 5 above. Some children may start to generalise from these patterns and realise that any whole number, such as 49, when 10 is added gives a number with 1 more ten and the same number of units, i.e. 59. This work is not suitable for all children.

Ma 2/2ab 3/2b
AS/B FE/B
N/3a,2b A/2e

Number/Calculators Cards 1 to 9

These cards deal mainly with addition and subtraction of numbers within 20. The cards are referenced from Workbook 3, Page 19 which also involves calculator work, but they can be used earlier or later to suit individual preference.

Card 1 involves 'adding on' to reach a target number. Discuss the worked example at the top of the card with the children.

'Key in 3.'
'You have to make 3 become 8.'
'Is 8 larger or smaller than 3?'
'Will you add or subtract?'
'What will you add?'
The process becomes

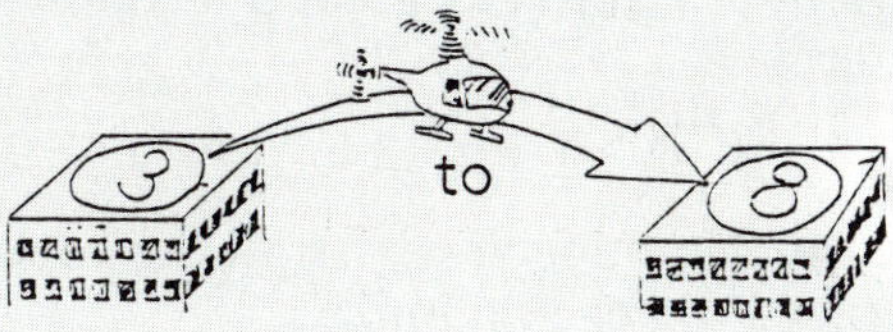

press [+] [5] [=] to give 8.

This is then recorded as $3 + 5 = 8$

Card 2 deals with subtraction and should be explained in a similar way to Card 1.

Cards 3 and 4 involve a series of target numbers. The children might be encouraged *not* to clear the answer in the calculator display each time so that they can start the next step without re-entering. On Card 3, the children should discover that they add on 3 each time giving

$3 + 3 = 6$
$6 + 3 = 9$
$9 + 3 = 12$ . . . and so on.

Extension

Card 4 is extension work which involves addition *or* subtraction of a series of different numbers to move from one boat to the next.

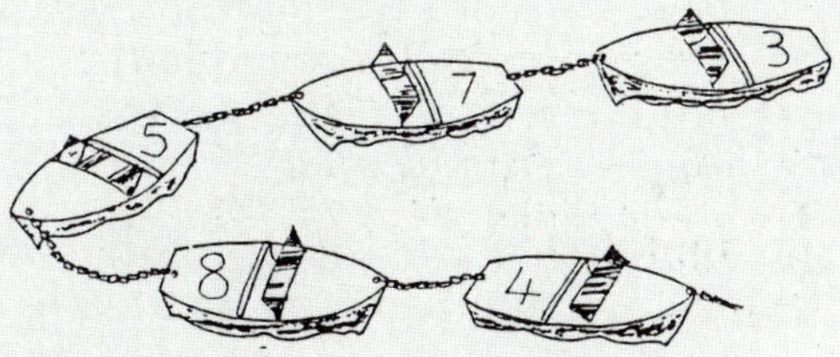

$3 + 4 = 7$
$7 - 2 = 5$ . . . and so on.

Card 5 is similar in style to Cards 1 and 2 but involves 10 in each example. For example,

$7 + 10 = 17$ $15 - 10 = 5$ $16 - 6 = 10$

Cards 6 and 7 contain similar games where children choose two numbers to subtract (Card 6) or add (Card 7). The games depend on a knowledge of basic number facts and the use of a calculator to check.

Card 8 invites children to choose pairs of numbers which add to 20.

Card 9 involves more difficult complementary additions. For example,

$18 + \square = 20$ $26 - \square = 20$

The children are not expected to know the addition and subtraction facts used on Card 9. Some may count on or back to discover the answers and check them with a calculator. Others may simply guess and check repeatedly to find the answers.

ODD AND EVEN NUMBERS
Introductory activities

Ma 3/2a
PS/B
A/2d

1 Counters

Show the children how to arrange sets of counters in pairs.

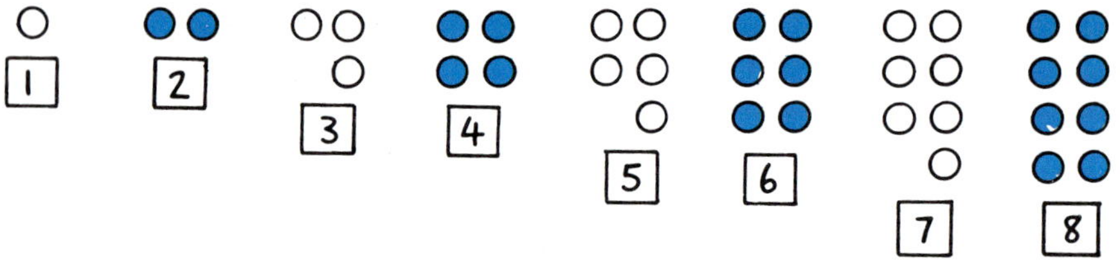

Discuss the patterns so that the children see that some of them have one counter without a partner. Explain that these are **odd** numbers. Ask them to continue the pattern.

1 3 5 7 9 11 13 15 . . . and so on.

The other numbers, where all the counters have partners, are **even** numbers.

2 4 6 8 10 12 14 16 . . . and so on.

Plastic squares can be used instead of counters.

2 Colouring odd and even numbers

Use a number strip or 100 square to show the pattern of odd and even numbers.

23	24	25	26	27	28	29	30	31	32	33

1	2	3	4	5	6	7	8	9	10
11	12	13	14	15	16	17	18	19	20
21	22	23	24	25	26	27	28	29	30
31	32	33	34	35	36	37	38	39	40
41	42	43	44	45	46	47	48	49	50
51	52	53	54	55	56	57	58	59	60
61	62	63	64	65	66	67	68	69	70
71	72	73	74	75	76	77	78	79	80
81	82	83	84	85	86	87	88	89	90
91	92	93	94	95	96	97	98	99	100

Ma 3/2a
PS/B
A/2d

Workbook Page 20 *Odd and even numbers*

This page gives practice in listing odd and even numbers. The extension section of the page is more difficult and may not be suitable for some children. The children may need to refer to a 100 square, shaded as indicated above, to determine that 65 is odd and 100 is even.

Extension

Some children may even realise that odd numbers have units digits of 1, 3, 5, 7 or 9 while even numbers 'end' in 2, 4, 6, 8 or 0.

NUMBERS TO 100
Additional activities

Ma 1/2 2/2a
RTN/B PSE
P/2 N/2a

1 What is my number?

Think of a number on the 1 to 100 number square and ask the children to guess which number it is. Reply to guesses with

'Much more than that.'
'Less than that.' . . . and so on.

until they get close. Final clues can be of the type

'It has 7 tens.' 'It has 5 units.' '2 more than that.' '1 less than that.'

Workbook 3

2 Three numbers

This activity does not involve a pattern but does depend on a knowledge of the size of numbers to 100. Give each child a cardboard strip with three number boxes on it.

Ask each child to pick a number card or tablet from a bag. Each puts the number on any one of his/her squares, where it must stay.

Each draws another number and puts it on the card, if possible. This continues until one child has three numbers in *ascending* order, for example

MONEY TO 50p
Introductory activities

Ma 2/2ab
M/B AS/B
N/2cd

Money to 10p, involving 2p, 5p and 10p coins, was introduced in Workbook 2. This is now extended to 50p with emphasis on counting collections of coins and laying out coins to match a given value. The 20p coin is also introduced. A selection of practical activities is given below.

1 Purses

- Use plastic or real coins laid on card purses to revise counting of totals to 10p or less.

- Revise different ways of making up 10p:

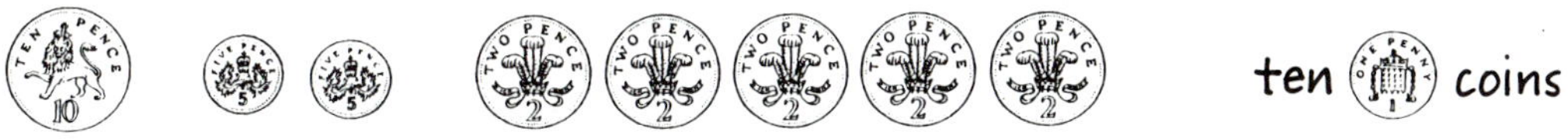

- Introduce amounts greater than 10p by counting in tens. Rearrange the coins from the purse and help the children to count them in tens.

ten, . . . twenty, . . . thirty, . . . thirty-five . . . thirty-six

Repeat for other amounts up to 50p.

- Provide the children with purses made from two pieces of card or paper, with coins inside, to give them practice in counting.

2 Collecting for charity

Collecting for charity was used previously as a context for Workbook 3, Page 11. The idea can be used again to count collections involving 10p coins.

Tell the children they are going to count how much has been collected in each can.

ten, twenty, thirty, forty, two, four, six, seven . . . . forty-seven pence.

At first the amounts can be made up of a few 10p coins and some others. The other coins should total less than 10p.

3 Phone calls

The idea of paying for a phone call from a phone box can be used to introduce putting out coins to match a given total. Explain that

'It costs 34p to phone Gran.'
Each child should put out

first and then deal with the other 4p.
The reward for this can be putting the coins in the slot and, perhaps, saying 'hello' to Gran.

4 Individual activities

The following activity gives practice in counting sets of coins.

Pocket money

The child counts the amount of money in each pocket of an old jacket.

The activities below provide practice in laying out sets of coins for a given total.

Slot machine

The child pays for crisps, drinks, etc. priced from 10p to 50p.

Envelopes and stamps

The child puts money in the envelope, or on top of it, to pay for the stamp.

Class shop

The child buys items from the class shop.

Shopping cards

The child puts out money to pay for the article on the shopping card.

Workbook Page 21 *Using the 10p coin*

Ma 2/2ab
M/B AS/B
N/2a

This page gives practice in counting collections of coins and laying out coins to match totals to 50p. Children will need practical experiences of the types described in the introductory activities before they do this page. They should count or lay out the 10p coins first.

5 Menu: Introducing the 20p coin

Use large pictures of food cut from magazines to form a simple menu.

. . . and so on.

Ask the children to choose a dish and lay out money to pay for it.

Show them how to use a 20p coin instead of two 10p coins. Help the children to count the total starting with the 20p coins.

twenty, . . . forty, . . . five and two is seven and one is eight . . . . forty-eight pence

Repeat for other dishes and other amounts.

6 Other activities

Activities 1 to 4 can be repeated using 20p coins as well as 10p, 5p, 2p and 1p coins. Other activities include

- Bus tickets – role play of driver issuing tickets which the children pay for using coins.
- Meals – cards showing a meal for which the children lay out coins.

Workbook Pages 22 and 23 *The 20p coin* *Money: counting in tens*

Ma 2/2ab
M/B AS/B
N/2ad

These pages give practice in counting collections and laying out coins for totals up to 50p and involving the 20p coin.

When paying for the items on Page 23 some children will use 20p coins while others may use 10p coins instead. Discussion should highlight that collections like these have the same value of 24p.

The final example on Page 23 may lead to some children suggesting the use of a 50p coin.

Workbook 4

Addition and subtraction to 13
Halves and quarters

Ma 1/2 2/2bc,3a 3/2a
RTN/A M/A PM/A
AS/B PS/B PSE
P/2 N/2bcd,3d A/2a

Overview

This section

- extends addition and subtraction to 20 using materials
- systematically introduces and consolidates addition and subtraction facts for 11, 12 and 13
- includes money and calculator work
- introduces practical activities about halves and quarters.

	Teacher's Notes	Workbook 4
Addition and subtraction to 20 using materials: introductory activities, consolidation	77	1, 2
Stories of 11	79	3 to 6
Addition and subtraction stories of 11: consolidation	83	
Stories of 12	83	7 to 9
Addition and subtraction facts to 12: further activities, consolidation	87	10 to 12
Stories of 13	88	13, 14
Addition and subtraction facts to 13: further activities, money	90	15 to 19
Addition and subtraction to 20: Calculator work	92	20
Halves and quarters	93	21 to 23
Extension		*2, 12, 15, 16, 19*
Investigation		*4, 7, 8, 13*
Problem solving		*6, 11, 12, 16, 17, 18, 19*

Key words and phrases

2 more than	odd	half	quarters
3 less than	even	halves	subtract . . . from . . .
answer	greater than	halving	

Resources

Useful materials

- small objects for counting such as beads, bricks, buttons, counters
- interlocking cubes
- 1p coins
- cardboard number line 0 to 20
- wallpaper number strip 1 to 20 (see page 78)
- flashcards of key words and phrases (see above)
- a large coloured picture of 'Islands' (see *Assessment and Resources Pack* below)
- sets of picture cards of creatures and plants found on the islands
- coloured pencils
- shapes for folding
- calculators

Assessment and Resources Pack

Assessment

Check-ups

Check-up for Workbook 4

Assessment in Context

'Treasure Island' context: Questions 3, 9, 10, 12, 15, 16, 17, 21, 22

Resources

Contexts

The 'Islands' context is related to the theme running through the first 18 pages of Workbook 4. A large coloured picture of these islands is provided with the Pack.

Problem Solving Activities

8 Papers (Addition and subtraction to 13)
5 Fish (Halving)

Resource Cards

Resource Cards 12 and *13* (Islands picture): addition facts to 13

Resource Cards 14 to *17* (Islands game): subtraction facts to 13. Further practice is provided by *Resource Cards 37–40*.

Teaching notes

THE 'ISLANDS' CONTEXT

Most of the work in this workbook is related to an 'Islands' context. While the context is used specifically to introduce and develop addition and subtraction facts related to 11, 12 and 13, it can also be used to develop many other aspects of the mathematics curriculum.

Further ideas and suggestions on how to develop the context more fully are contained in the *Contexts* booklet in the *Assessment and Resources Pack.*

SETTING THE SCENE

It is important when using a context to develop new mathematical ideas that the 'scene is set' before the mathematics is introduced. This helps to give the children a clearer understanding of what is happening and a purpose to the activities.

In the 'Islands' context the children are setting off on an expedition to find the lost treasure in the Golden Sea. On their journey they will meet many interesting creatures, like the Nim-nams, and have to solve a variety of problems before they finally locate the treasure.

One way of introducing the context is to display the large picture of the islands which is included in the *Assessment and Resources Pack.* This can be used as a large map and shows the five islands in the Golden Sea.

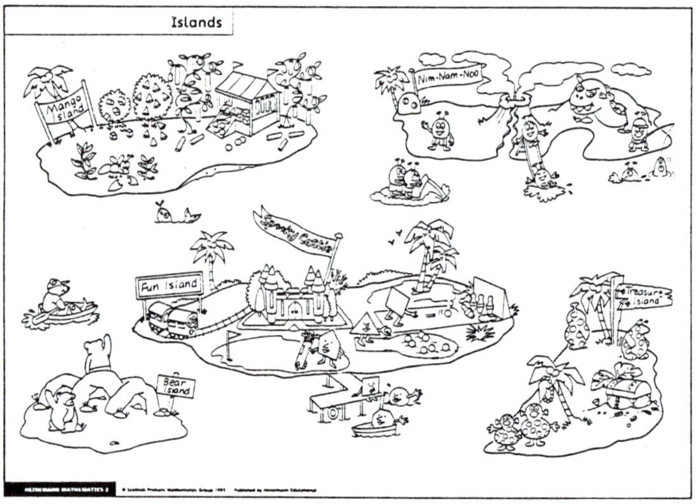

An invitation can be issued to the children, for example:

It would be helpful if the wall display showed only the basic information about the islands, thus allowing it to be used in an interactive way with the children. For example,

- Twelve Nim-nams placed on Nim-Nam-Noo can help to introduce addition and subtraction stories of 12. Pictures of plants or animals or materials (cubes, counters) can be placed on top of the map to investigate other number stories.
- The characters and items which the children meet on the islands and when using Pages 1 to 18 of Workbook 4 can provide a stimulus for other worksheets and cards produced by the teacher.

Two children, Amy and Jack, appear on some pages of Workbook 4 in connection with the 'Islands' theme. These characters should be introduced to the children before they use the workbook pages.

ADDITION/SUBTRACTION TO 20 USING MATERIALS
Introductory activities

Workbook 4

Ma 2/2b 1/2
AS/B M/A
N/2d P/2

This section introduces practical activities in adding and subtracting within 20. The intention is to extend the children's appreciation of the concepts of adding and subtracting to larger totals before concentrating on the systematic exploration of number stories for 11, 12 and 13 in later sections. Possible introductory activities related to the 'Islands' theme are given below.

1 Catch the boat

- Provide **two** boats made of card and either cut-outs of people, toy people or cubes.

  Some people are put into each boat and the total found by counting. For example,

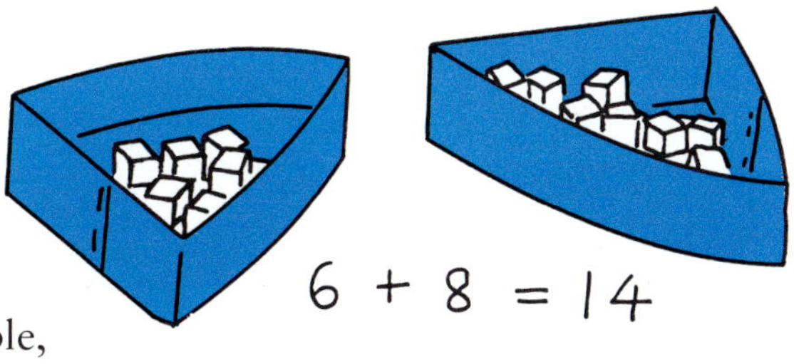

- Use **one** boat. Put a number of people in the boat. The children can practice subtracting by either 'landing' some of the people on an island or allowing them to go swimming. For example,

  Alternatively the children could role-play being the passengers in the boats.

2 Feed the sea-snakes

- Prepare a set of cut-out sea-snakes, each of which should be long enough to hold up to 20 cubes or counters.

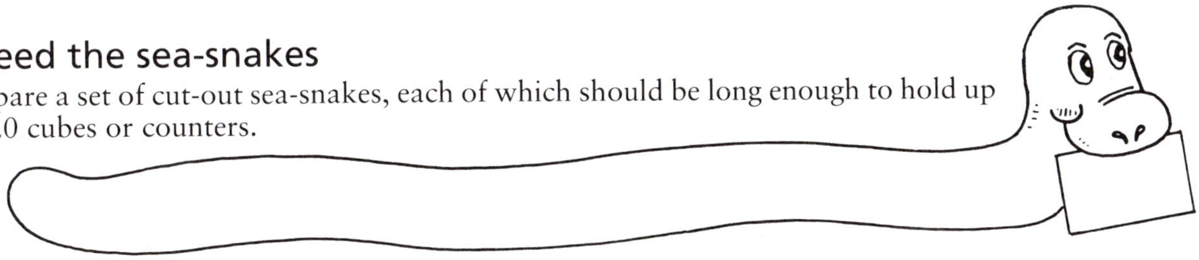

  Use two colours of counters or cubes, a set of cards with additions, for example,

  8 + 10   9 + 4 ... and a set of answer cards 18   13 ...

  The children select a card, put out the coloured counters for each number in the addition to show how many fish the sea-snake has eaten and then place the answer card to show the total.

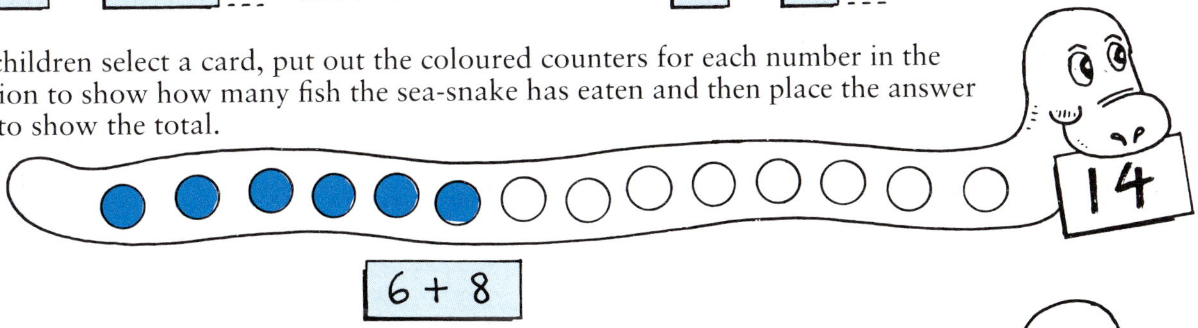

- For subtraction, the children put the total number of counters on the sea-snake and then remove the number indicated by a subtraction card.

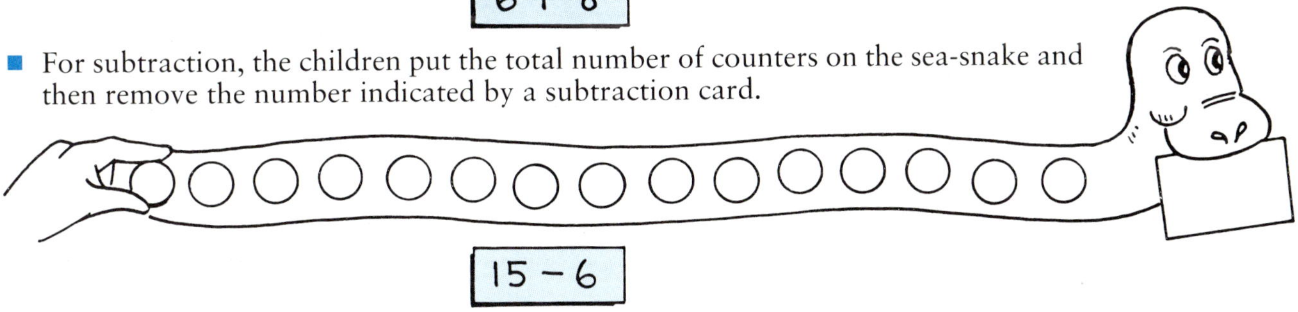

3 Fishing trips

Prepare a sign which shows prices for trips to the islands. There is a similar sign on Page 1 of Workbook 4. 1p coins or other practical materials can be used to help the children to find answers.

Oral work might involve questions such as,

'How much will it cost to go to Fun Island *and* Treasure Island?'
'I have 13p. I go to Nim-Nam-Noo. How much will I have left?'
'I have 15p. Which two islands can I visit?'

Ma 2/2b 1/2
AS/B M/A
N/2d P/2

Workbook Pages 1 and 2 *Addition and subtraction to 20*

On Page 1, the children are asked to use materials, such as cubes or pennies, to help them to find the total on each flag.

On Page 2, the children are asked to match boats to each island by completing a subtraction story. Cubes or pennies should again be used to find or check answers.

Extension

The extension money activity at the foot of Page 2 requires careful use of the available information on the notice on Page 1, and the amounts of money associated with Amy and Jack. This will require discussion with the children.

CONSOLIDATION
Addition and subtraction to 20

Ma 2/2b 1/2
AS/B
N/2d P/2

Two further activities which will help to consolidate the idea of finding totals and subtracting within 20 are given below.

1 Amy and Jack

Use a large number strip made from wallpaper with the numbers from 1 to 20 on it. Pairs of children can take turns to stand on the strip and play the roles of Amy and Jack.

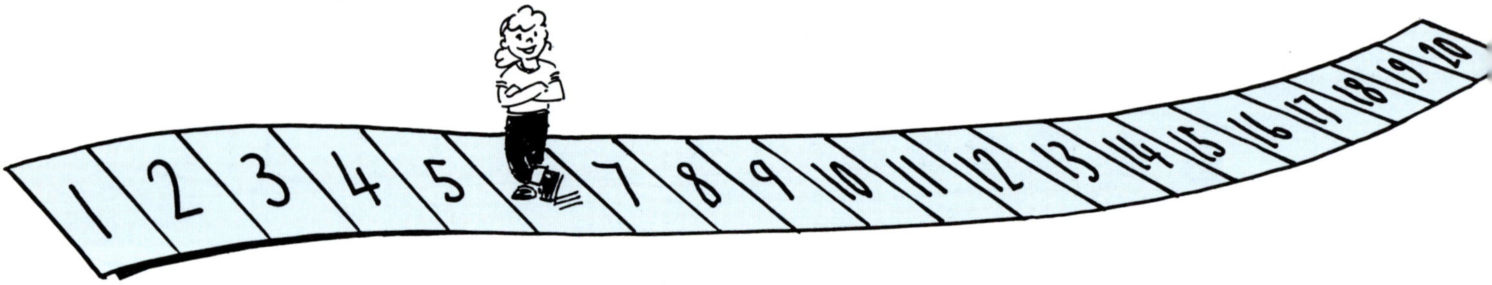

- Amy chooses two cards from a set with the numbers 5 to 10 on them, for example [6] and [8]. She walks along 6 squares and then another 8 squares to land at 14.

  $6 + 8 = 14$

  The children can take it in turns to choose cards and find the landing square.

- Give Jack a card with a number such as [17]. Jack stands on 17. He chooses another card from the pack, say [9], and moves back that number of squares. Where does he land? $17 - 9 = 8$

2 Lucky bags

Each child in a group chooses an addition flashcard, for example [7 + 9], from a bag (or box) and uses counters or cubes to find an answer. The teacher then picks a number from a bag containing the numbers 11 to 20. Any child whose total correctly matches the teacher's number scores 1 point. Repeat for other numbers.

A similar game can be played for subtraction examples within 20.

Workbook 4

ADDITION AND SUBTRACTION STORIES FOR 11, 12 AND 13

This section of work takes each of the numbers 11, 12 and 13 and examines the addition and subtraction facts for each number in turn.

In particular, the related addition and subtraction facts should be highlighted, for example,

$7 + 4 = 11 \qquad 11 - 4 = 7$
$4 + 7 = 11 \qquad 11 - 7 = 4$

It is important that practical work and discussion between teacher and children and among the children themselves takes place before the children start written work. A number of practical tasks are suggested at the beginning of each section on the stories of 11, 12 and 13. While these activities are described for a specific number, they can be adapted and used for the other numbers.

STORIES OF 11
Introductory activities

1 Mango Island

Ma 2/2b,3a 1/2
AS/B PSE
N/2d,3d P/2

This is an island covered in jungle which contains exotic trees, bushes, fruit and flowers. The creatures who live there include ants, flies and other strange insects. Visitors to the island look for many kinds of delicious fruit and berries which grow there. There is a food stall on the island.

Prepare either a wall display or a table-top picture and sets of pictures and objects to represent the creatures and plants the children can find on Mango Island. For example,

Pockets might be used to hold types of trees, children, and so on.
A number of oral activities could be developed using the picture cards in the pockets or other materials to allow the children to investigate the stories of 11.

■ Put 11 trees on the island, some on either side of the hill.

This activity can be repeated for other stories of 11 by moving the trees.

■ Put 11 ants on the island.
'There are 11 ants on the island.'
'Five fly away.'
'How many are left?'

Write 11 take away 5 is 6
$11 - 5 = 6$

Repeat for other numbers of ants flying away and gradually build up subtraction stories for 11.

$11 - 1$
$11 - 2$
$11 - 3$
. . . and so on up to . . .
$11 - 10$

■ It is also important to establish relationships between some of the addition and subtraction facts for 11. For example,

Put 11 children on the island.

Considering the numbers on each side of the hill can lead to the two related addition facts:

$7 + 4 = 11$
$4 + 7 = 11$

Now cover up 4 of the children. 'How many are left?'

$11 - 4 = 7$

Cover the group of 7 children.

$11 - 7 = 4$

Discuss the four facts which are related.

$7 + 4 = 11$
$4 + 7 = 11$
$11 - 4 = 7$
$11 - 7 = 4$

Repeat for other sets of four related facts.

2 Sinking sands

Mark an outline of Mango Island on the classroom floor using chalk. Explain to the children that on the shores of Mango Island there are dangerous sands and that there are only two safe landing areas – represented by mats or hoops placed on the island shape.

Eleven children can land but to do this safely they must stand on the mats.
'How many can land on each part?'

The children can work out the various combinations which can stand on the two mats and record these as, for example,

5 + 6 = 11
6 + 5 = 11

'One group return to the boat. How many are left?'

11 − 5 = 6

'If the other group returns to the boat first, how many are left?'

11 − 6 = 5

Again, the related facts can be displayed together. The activity can be repeated for other combinations which total 11.

5 + 6 = 11
6 + 5 = 11
11 − 5 = 6
11 − 6 = 5

An extension to this activity would be to use three mats as landing places and to investigate different ways of making totals of 11 using three numbers.

3 Mango sale

The children can create pictures or use plasticine to make some typical Mango Island food. This can be set up for sale with price tickets ranging from 1p to 10p.

The children can use 1p coins to help them find out

- which items they can buy which cost a total of 11p. They should be encouraged to look initially for two items and then combinations of three items.
- how much change they receive if, given 11p to spend, they buy one item from the stall.

4 Individual activities

Beads

Beads can be used to find related stories of 11.
Some of the beads can be *covered up* to subtract.

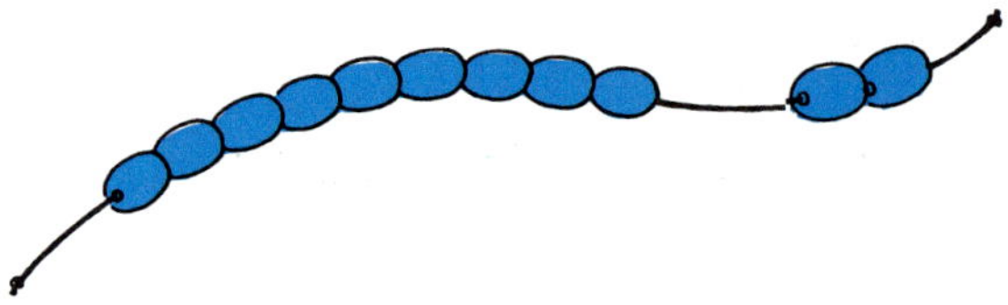

$9 + 2 = 11$ $11 - 2 = 9$

$2 + 9 = 11$ $11 - 9 = 2$

Cubes

Cubes of two colours can be used in a similar way.

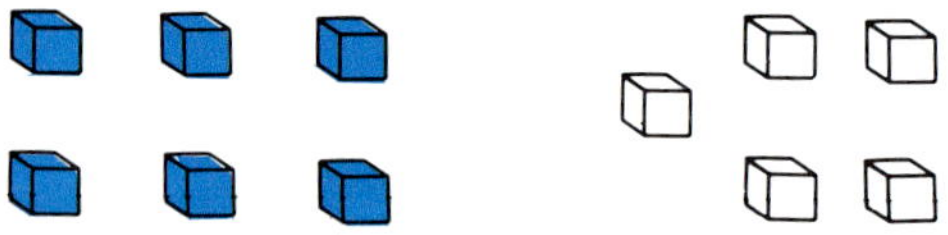

$6 + 5 = 11$ $11 - 6 = 5$

$5 + 6 = 11$ $11 - 5 = 6$

Pegboards and pegs

Pegboards and different colours of pegs can also be used.

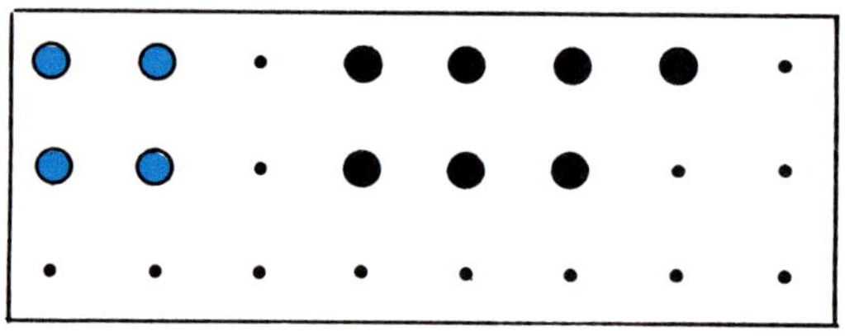

$4 + 7 = 11$ $11 - 7 = 4$

$7 + 4 = 11$ $11 - 4 = 7$

Three colours of pegs can be employed for addition stories.

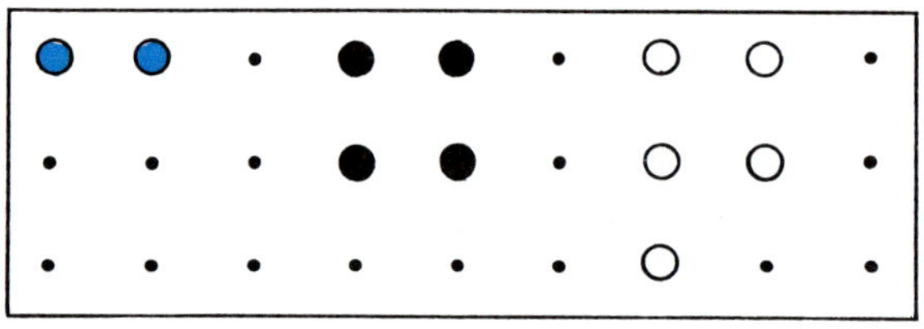

$2 + 4 + 5 = 11$

Ma 2/2b,3a 1/2
AS/B PSE
N/2d,3d P/2

Workbook Pages 3 to 6 *Addition and subtraction facts for 11*

The activities on Page 3 encourage the children to use materials to find, and then record, addition facts for 11. Pictures of objects which can be counted are provided to help them complete subtraction facts for 11.

Investigation

Related addition and subtraction facts are grouped together on Page 4. The children are also given the opportunity to find sets of three numbers which add to 11. Some children will need counters or cubes for this investigation.

Pages 5 and 6 provide further examples to reinforce and consolidate addition and subtraction facts for 11. Horizontal and vertical settings are included on Page 5 while Page 6 applies these facts in a money context where the children buy from the food stall on Mango Island.

Problem solving

The last question involves solving the problem of buying three things for 11p. Some children may need to use 1p coins for this.

CONSOLIDATION
Addition and subtraction stories of 11

Workbook **4**

Ma 2/2b,3a
AS/B
N/2d,3d

Further activities which give practice with these facts are described below.

1 Fruit pies

Two cardboard pies, with 'plums', can be used to reinforce specific facts.

'If we eat the first pie, how many plums are left?'

$11 - 5 = 6$

'If we eat the second pie, how many plums are left?'

$11 - 6 = 5$

2 Crossing Mango River

Use a large paper number strip to bridge a river marked by chalk either in the classroom or playground. Oral work can be done with the children predicting answers where possible and then moving to check them.

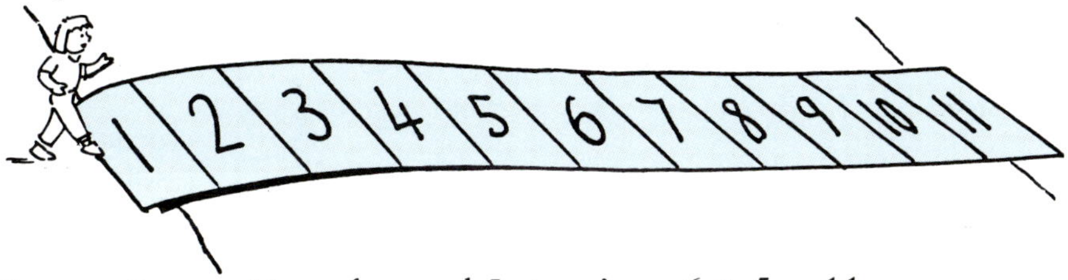

'Start at 6.	Move forward 5 steps.'	$6 + 5 = 11$
'Start at 5.	Move forward 6 steps.'	$5 + 6 = 11$
'Start at 11.	Move back 6 steps.'	$11 - 6 = 5$
'Start at 11.	Move back 5 steps.'	$11 - 5 = 6$

Repeat for other number stories of 11.

STORIES OF 12
Introductory activities

Ma 2/2ab,3a 1/2
AS/B
N/2dc,3d P/2

This section deals with stories of 12 in a similar way to that used for 11. The practical activities below relate to the new island of Nim-Nam-Noo. The individual activities detailed opposite are also appropriate for the new total of 12.

One part of the island of Nim-Nam-Noo is red and the other part green. It is inhabited by little creatures called Nim-nams who wear red or green clothes and like to fish and water-ski. The monster Noo lives in a cave on the red part of the island. She likes to eat jelly and Nim-nams.

1 Noo's lunch

Explain to the children that Noo is always hungry and as a special lunchtime treat she likes to eat pots of jelly. Every lunchtime she eats 12 pots of jelly.

- Today she ate 7 red pots and 5 blue pots.

'How many other ways can she eat 12 pots?'
The children can investigate the addition stories and record their findings.
The children can use cubes or tubs to help them.

- 'Noo eats 12 pots of jelly.
  She eats the 7 red pots first.
  How many blue pots will she eat?'

  $12 - 7 = 5$

  'Noo eats 12 pots of jelly.
  She eats the 5 blue pots first.
  How many red pots are left?'

  $12 - 5 = 7$

Repeat for other numbers which total 12.

2 Nim-nam submarines

- Prepare a red and a green submarine shape and use cubes to represent Nim-nams.
  '12 Nim-nams go on a trip on a red or green submarine. How many go in each submarine?'

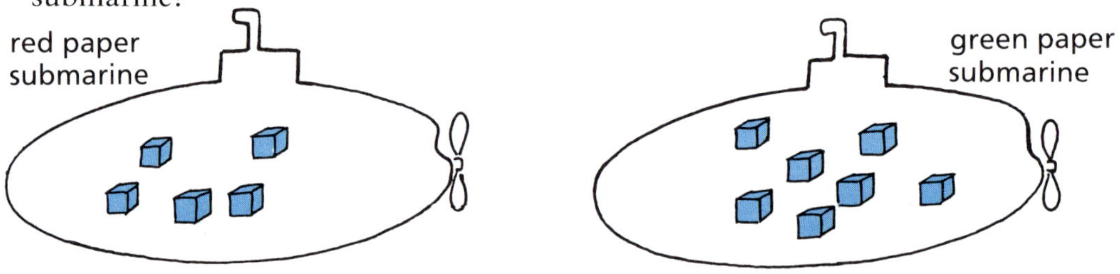

The children can explore the number of Nim-nams that can be placed in each submarine to give totals of 12, using cubes. Addition stories such as $5 + 7 = 12$ can be recorded and, later, systematised as

$2 + 10 = 12$
$3 + 9 = 12$
$4 + 8 = 12$
. . . and so on up to
$10 + 2 = 12$

- Related subtraction facts can also be explored. For example, for the situation illustrated above, $5 + 7 = 12$ and $7 + 5 = 12$, can be linked to $12 - 5 = 7$ and $12 - 7 = 5$ as follows:
  The red submarine goes back to the island. This gives $12 - 5 = 7$.
  The green submarine goes back, giving $12 - 7 = 5$.

An extension to this activity would be to use three submarines – red, green and yellow, and to investigate different ways of making totals of 12 using three numbers.

3 Nim-nam partners game *(for 2 players)*

Prepare two sets of cards with a picture of a Nim-nam on one side and the numbers 2 to 10 on the reverse (a total of eighteen cards).

Spread the cards out on a table so that all the Nim-nams are showing. Each child takes it in turn to turn over two cards. If the sum of the two cards is 12 he/she keeps the cards. If not he/she turns them back again. The winner is the child with the most Nim-nams at the end of the game.

4 Noo's necklace

Use 12 beads to make a necklace for Noo. Ask the children to divide the beads into two sets, for example,

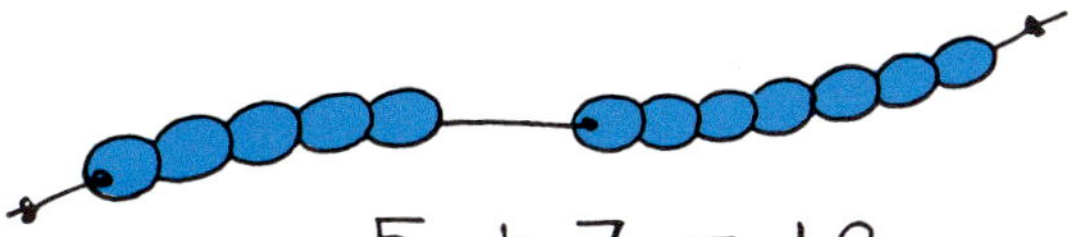

5 + 7 = 12

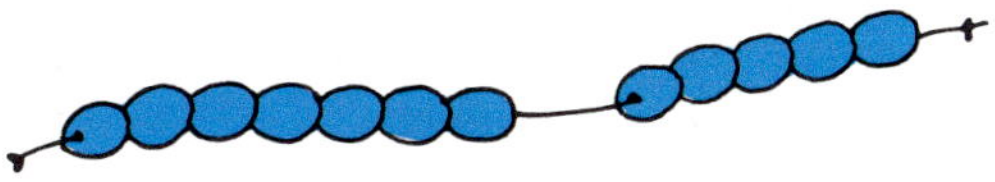

7 + 5 = 12

Repeat for other partitions.
Each time the related subtraction facts can be found by 'hiding'.

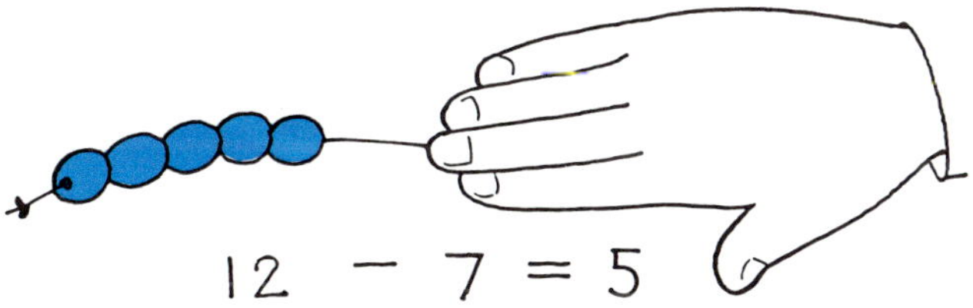

12 − 7 = 5

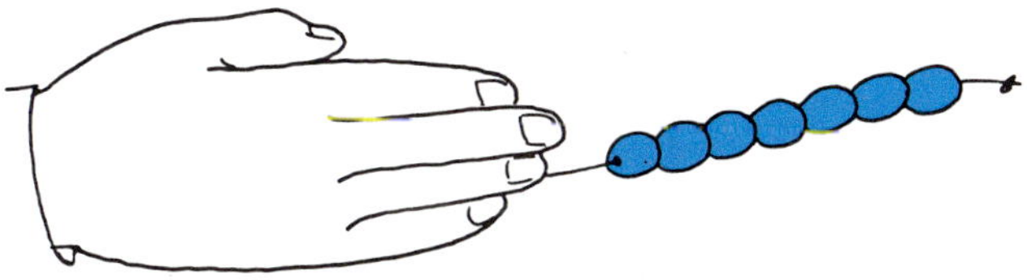

12 − 5 = 7

5 Individual activities

The individual activities suggested on page 82 for stories of 11 can be adapted for stories of 12. Other ideas are given below.

Interlocking cubes

The children could be asked to investigate the stories of 12 using interlocking cubes. For example,

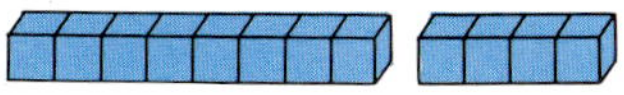

8 + 4 = 12

Take away the 4 cubes : 12 − 4 = 8

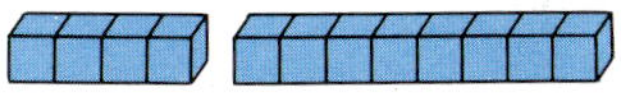

4 + 8 = 12

Take away the 8 cubes : 12 − 8 = 4

Money

Use a set of shopping cards with priced items. The children find items which total 12p using 1p coins, if necessary.

9p + 3p = 12p

Subtraction can use the idea:
'I have 12p.
I buy a balloon.
I have 3p left.'   12p − 9p = 3p

Ma 2/2b,3a
AS/B PSE
N/2d,3d

Investigation

Workbook Pages 7 to 9 *Addition and subtraction stories of 12*

On Pages 7 and 8 the children are encouraged to use materials to help them find or confirm the stories of 12. They can place cubes on top of the island, which stretches across both pages, to represent the Nim-nams.

On Page 8, the children also investigate different ways in which they can add three numbers together to make a total of 12.

Page 9 deals with related addition and subtraction facts for 12 and should only be tackled by the children after extensive practical work and discussion.

ADDITION AND SUBTRACTION FACTS TO 12
Further activities

Ma 2/2b,3a 1/2
AS/B PSE
N/2d,3d P/2

Workbook Pages 10 to 12 provide further activities about addition and subtraction facts for totals to 12. They give further practice, include vertical setting and contain problem-solving activities. Possible introductory activities are given below.

1 Nim-nam house

Prepare a set of flashcards with an addition or subtraction fact on one side, for example 6 + 5, and the answer (11) and an item from a Nim-nam house on the other side, 

. (See Workbook 4, Page 10 for suitable items.)

Show the children the number fact. If the answer is correct, turn it over to reveal an item from the house and discuss what it is.

2 Nim-nam beds

Use two boxes as a Nim-nam bunk bed and cubes to represent the Nim-nams. This model can be used to re-introduce vertical setting for addition and subtraction examples.

Workbook 4, Page 10 can be used at this point.

$$\begin{array}{r} 7 \\ +5 \\ \hline 12 \\ \hline \end{array}$$

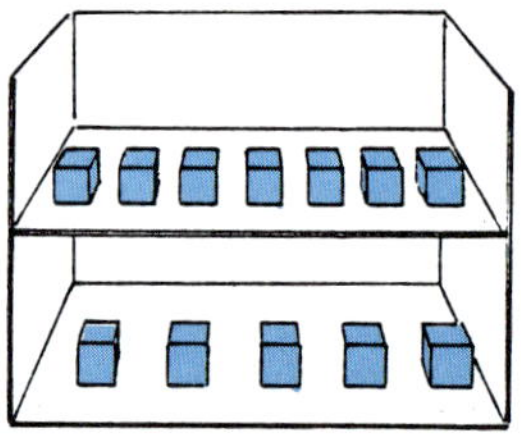

3 Bear Island

This island has caves where friendly bears live. They are very good at adding, subtracting and solving puzzles. Workbook Pages 11 and 12 contain problem solving work and relate to Bear Island. The bears could be introduced by using four numbered drawings, for example,

'Can the bears make a total of 9?' (6 + 3 or 5 + 4)
'Can they make 10?' (6 + 4)
'Can they make 11?' (5 + 6)
'Can they make 12?' (3 + 5 + 4)

Pictures can be placed side by side to make each total. Children should use facts which they have memorized, wherever possible. This activity would make a suitable introduction to Workbook Page 11.

Workbook 4

Workbook Pages 10 to 12 *Addition and subtraction facts to 12*

Ma 2/3a	1/2	3/2a
AS/B	PS/B	PSE
N/3d	P/2	A/2a

Page 10 allows the children to practise addition and subtraction facts to 12 within a scenario related to a Nim-nam house. Some children will require to use materials while others may be able to recall some of the facts. The vertical addition of two or three numbers at the foot of the page is related to the Nim-nam beds activity given in Activity 2 on page 86.

Problem solving

Pages 11 and 12 are problem solving pages which provide activities which allow the children to explore further addition and subtraction facts to 12.

On Page 11, the children have to colour three bears which add together to make 12. Some children may have to write down three numbers in the form of a sum in order to see that the total is 12. Others may be able to use recall of known facts. The activity may be too difficult for some children.
On Page 12, they should answer the three questions at the top before trying to decide which cave is the school cave.

$$\begin{array}{r} 2 \\ 3 \\ +7 \\ \hline \\ \hline \end{array}$$

gives an answer of 12, which is even and greater than 10.

Extension

The extension activity at the foot of Page 12 is likely to be too difficult for some of the children. It may help the children if they have a set of cards, as shown, to help them experiment.

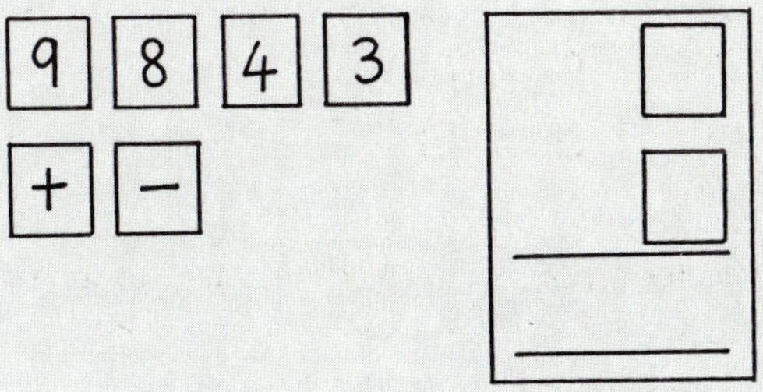

ADDITION AND SUBTRACTION FACTS TO 12
Consolidation

Ma 2/3a
AS/B
N/3d

Further activities to encourage memorisation and recall of number facts to 12 are suggested below.

1 Noo's number bingo *(for 3 to 6 players)*

Prepare a set of bingo cards each containing six numbers from this set: 3, 4, 5, 6, 7, 8, 9, 10, 11, 12. For example,

8	12	5
6	4	3

7	4	12
6	9	8

Each child in the group requires a bingo card. Other materials required are

- a set of coloured counters to place over the answers on the bingo cards
- cubes to help children to work out answers, where required
- flashcards containing addition and subtraction facts to 12.

The teacher shows the children one of the flashcards. The children work out the answer and if they have the number on their bingo card they cover it with a counter. The winner is the first person to cover all the numbers with counters.

2 Noo-minoes *(for 2 players)*

Prepare a set of domino cards showing addition and subtraction facts for 12 on one half of the card and answers on the other, for example,

Use a 'Noo head' to start off the chain of dominoes.

The children take it in turns to place a domino to complete the Noo.

3 Oral work

Nim-nams can be used as a focus for discussion.

- '12 Nim-nams go for a swim.
  6 come out of the water.
  How many stay in?'
- 'There are 12 Nim-nams in two boats.
  How many can be in each boat?'

STORIES OF 13
Introductory activities

Ma 2/2b 1/2
AS/B PM/A
N/2d P/2

FUN ISLAND

Fun Island offers games to play, puzzles and sports of all kinds. Spooky Castle on Fun Island has a friendly ghost.
A context of games and puzzles can be used with the children to explore addition and subtraction stories of 13. Some suggestions are given below from which introductory activities might be chosen.

1 Swimming

Use materials to represent children swimming or lying on the beach on Fun Island.
Various number pairs which add to 13 can be explored to build up addition stories of 13.

$3 + 10 = 13$
$4 + 9 = 13$ . . . and so on.

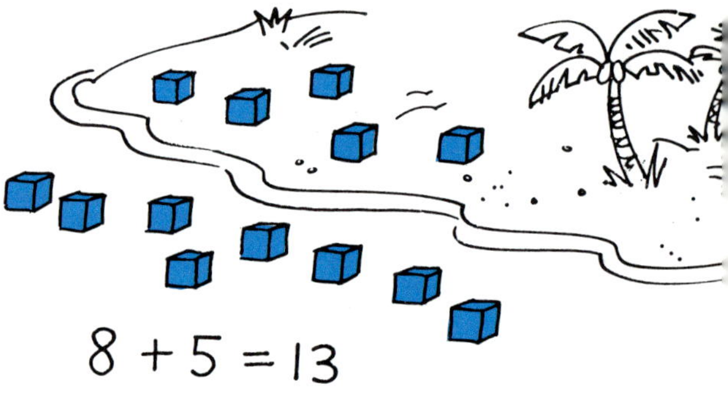

Related subtraction facts can be discovered when some of the children go home from the island.

2 Pegboard puzzles

These puzzles are common on Fun Island and use two or three colours of pegs to investigate different combinations involving 13.

'Use a pegboard and two colours of pegs. Find the different combinations which total 13.
Record your results.'

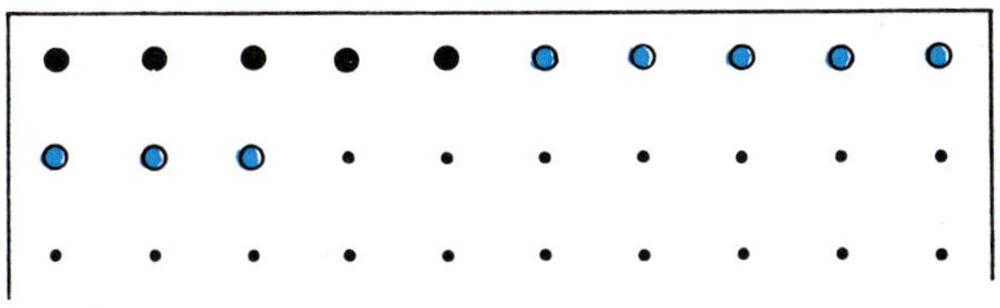

5 + 8 = 13
8 + 5 = 13

'Cover up 5 pegs to give 13 − 5 = 8'
'Cover up 8 pegs to give 13 − 8 = 5'
This activity could be repeated for other combinations.

3 Spooky Castle

The Castle could be

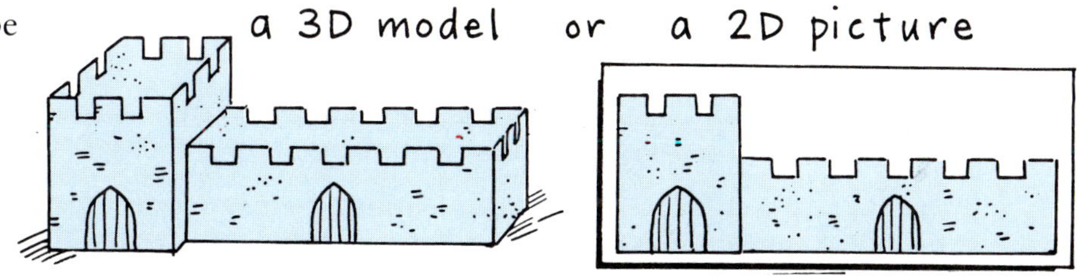

There are two doors into the castle.

- '13 children go into the castle.
  How many can go in through each door?'
  Materials can be placed on the castle to build up stories, for example,

  7 + 6 = 13
  6 + 7 = 13 . . . and so on.

- Related subtraction facts can be introduced in the usual way.

  '13 children go in. 7 come out. How many are left?' 13 − 7 = 6

  '6 come out. How many are left?' 13 − 6 = 7

- Another method would involve a chalk plan of the castle, on the floor or in the playground. The children could go in through the two entrances.

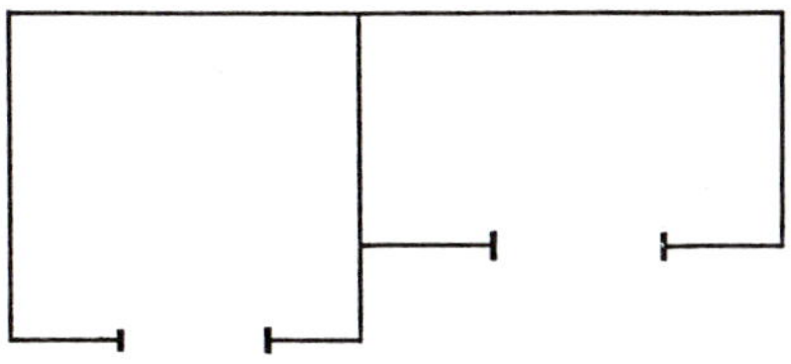

4 Escape from Spooky Castle

Tell the children how many are to go into the castle, using the plan above. Then say how many are allowed to escape. This activity can be built up as follows:

13 children go into the castle?	The children go in.
8 escape	8 children come out of the castle.
How many are left?	Record as 13 − 8 = 5

This activity could also be done with cubes and the 2D picture of the castle.

5 Wobbly bridge

Use a large strip of wallpaper numbered from 1 to 13 to represent the wobbly wooden bridge near the castle. The children walk along this bridge.

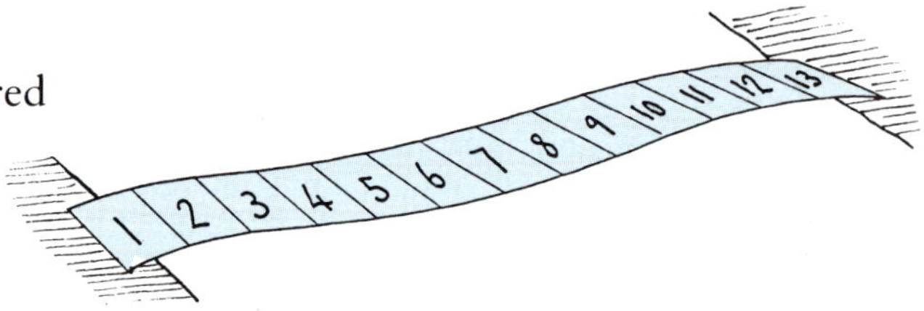

Alternatively, a paper number strip and cubes might be used.

'Start at 9. Move forward 4 steps.'	$9 + 4 = 13$
'Start at 4. Move forward 9 steps.'	$4 + 9 = 13$
'Start at 13. Move back 4 steps.'	$13 - 4 = 9$
'Start at 13. Move back 9 steps.'	$13 - 9 = 4$

Similar instructions could be used to explore other combinations of numbers.

6 Individual activities

The activities given on page 82 for stories of 11 and on page 85 for stories of 12 can be adapted to suit 13.

Ma 2/3a 1/2
AS/B PSE
N/3d P/2

Investigation

Workbook Pages 13 and 14 *Addition and subtraction facts for 13*

On Page 13, the children should place counters on the surfboard and the scooter to help them to find as many of the stories of 13 as they can. The children should use a vertical setting for each story as indicated on the page.

After the children have had the opportunity to discover the stories for themselves it is important that they discuss their findings with other children and with the teacher. At this stage the stories can be organised into a more formal structure.

At the bottom of this page the children have the opportunity to find sets of three numbers which add together to give 13.

Page 14 deals with related addition and subtraction facts for 13 and should only be tackled after the children have experienced practical work and discussion of the kind described in the introductory section.

ADDITION AND SUBTRACTION FACTS TO 13
Further activities

Ma 2/2b,3a 1/2
AS/B
N/2d,3d P/2

Workbook 4, Pages 15 to 18 provide further practice with number stories of 11, 12 and 13. There is extension or problem solving work on each of these pages.

> Page 15 concentrates on language such as
> 'subtract 5 from 13' '6 less than 13' '2 more than 10'
>
> Page 16 contains four problems and it is unlikely that all children would attempt these.
>
> Pages 17 and 18 provide practice examples for addition and subtraction involving 11, 12 and 13 as well as problem-solving examples.

These pages also conclude the 'Islands' theme. The children can be told that they are going to visit Spooky Castle and then find the treasure. The full story involves a train to Spooky Castle (Page 15), Amy and Jack finding a key to go into the castle, going through a door and then finding the key for a trap door (Page 16). They then escape from the castle, take a boat to Treasure Island, go past the spotty monsters and find the treasure (Pages 17 and 18).

Further activities to introduce these pages are suggested below.

Workbook 4

1 Treasure chest game *(for 2 or more players)*

Introduce the language '3 more than' as associated with addition and '2 less than' as signifying subtraction. Also 'subtract 4 *from* 12' should be discussed and related to 12 – 4. Practice with this language can take the form of a game. Each child takes a card with an example such as those shown below.

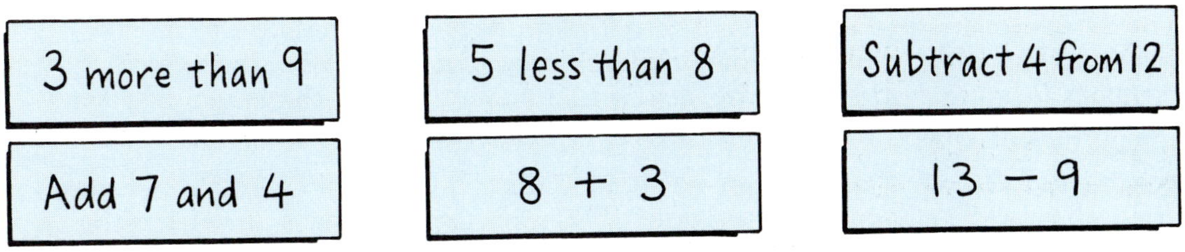

The child reads the card and finds an answer using materials if necessary. The card is then turned over to confirm the answer (written on the back). A correct answer is rewarded by taking a gold coin (counters or coins covered in gold paper) from a treasure chest. The winner is the one to have most coins when the game ends.

The language involved here is directly related to Workbook 4, Page 15.

2 Resource cards

Assessment and Resources Pack

Resource Cards 12 and *13* (Islands picture) provide an activity for a small group which reinforces addition facts for 11, 12 and 13. The picture is a smaller version of the large 'Islands' picture supplied with the *Assessment and Resources Pack.*

Resource Cards 14 to *17* (Islands game) are also for use with a small group. The game provides practice with subtraction facts for 11, 12 and 13.

3 Monster cards

Provide monster cards showing spotty monsters similar to those guarding the treasure on Treasure Island, as depicted on Workbook 4, Page 18.

Each monster has some green spots and some black spots. Ask the children
'How many black spots . . . green spots?'
'How many spots altogether?'
'How can we write this?'
This can lead to the following addition stories for the monsters above:

8 + 5 = 13	5 + 6 = 11	3 + 8 = 11	10 + 2 = 12

Then ask questions like
'How many spots are left if the green ones fade away?'

13 – 5 = 8	11 – 6 = 5	11 – 8 = 3	12 – 2 = 10

Finally, as extension and problem solving work related to Workbook Page 18:
'Has this monster got more black spots or more green spots?'
'How many more?' This could lead to

3 more black spots (8 – 5)	1 more green spot (6 – 5)	5 more green spots (8 – 3)	8 more black spots (10 – 2)

Ma 2/2b,3a 1/2
AS/B PSE
N/2d,3d P/2

Workbook Pages 15 to 18 *Addition and subtraction facts to 13*

Extension

Page 15 is extension work dealing with the language '2 more than', '3 less than', 'subtract . . . . from . . . .'. The language will require oral discussion to associate it with adding and subtracting. Such work may be too difficult for some children.

Extension/ Problem solving

The extension and problem solving activities on Page 16 are unlikely to be attempted by all the children. Some children may see the sequence in the first problem as 'adding on 2' or as the 'next odd number'. The jar showing 6 and 5 at the foot of the page is the odd one out as 6 + 5 is 11 while the other jars total 13.

Problem solving

When children colour the even answers red at the top of Page 17 they should lead down the middle ladder to the red door. There are two possible solutions to the problem at the foot of Page 17: 2 + 4 + 6 or 3 + 4 + 5.

Problem solving

On Page 18, the treasure is in the box marked 9 + 3.

Teachers may wish to use the Islands' scenario which runs through these pages. The story which lies behind these pages is given on page 91 of these notes.

Ma 2/2b
AS/B
N/2d

Workbook Page 19 *Money to 13p*

Extension/ Problem solving

The work on this page is an application of earlier money work together with a knowledge of addition and subtraction facts introduced in Pages 1 to 18. The children may use coins for this work. The last question is more difficult. The children should realise that they do not need to spend all of the remaining 5p. This page is not related to the 'Islands' theme.

ADDITION AND SUBTRACTION TO 20
Calculator work

Page 20 of Workbook 4 provides practice examples involving the use of a calculator for addition and subtraction within 20. The intention is to extend the children's scope in dealing with problems involving addition and subtraction beyond 13. The children should be reminded of the technique for adding and subtracting, the need to press the [=] key to show an answer and how to clear the calculator. It is also worthwhile discussing examples like 5 + 3 + 7 + 4 where the additions can be continuous with [=] being pressed only at the last step.

Ma 2/2b,3a
AS/B
N/2d,3d

Workbook Page 20 *Calculator work*

The teacher should discuss this page to ensure the children understand what they are expected to do. They have to use a calculator as shown at the top of the page to find answers. The examples deal with additions and subtractions beyond 13.

The lower part of the page shows that an answer of 19 on the calculator 'wins a prize'. The first and last children both win.

HALVES AND QUARTERS
Introductory activities

Ma 2/2c
RTN/A
N/2b

This section introduces practical work and appropriate language for halves and quarters. It aims to improve children's understanding that something has been halved when it is cut into *two equal* parts and quartered when there are *four equal* parts. No formal notation for fractions is expected at this level.

1 Folding in half

Show the children how they can fold shapes to halve them. Emphasise that there are two halves which are the same. Each shape can be opened out, labelled, coloured, and used to create a wall display.

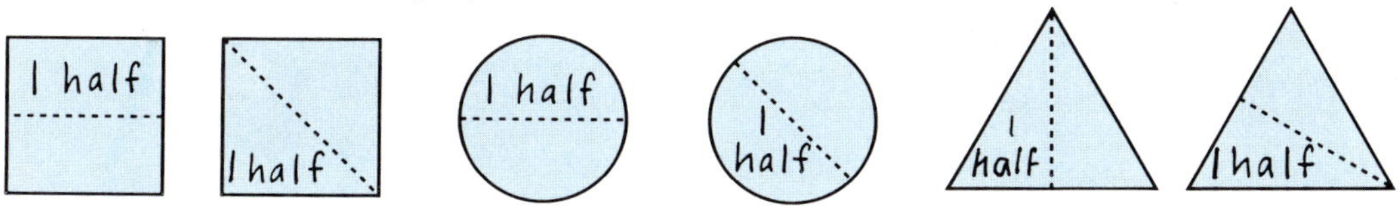

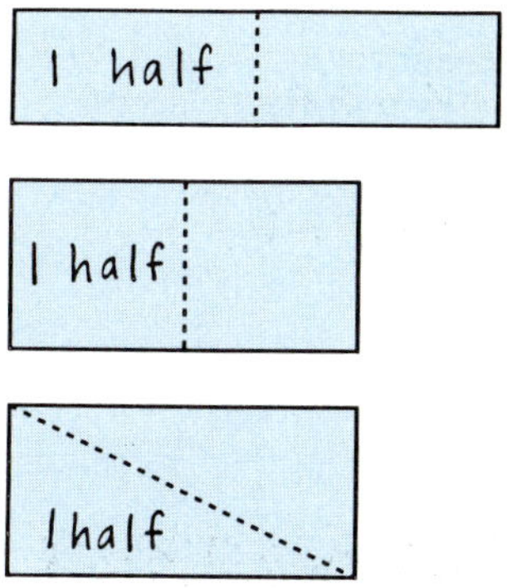

The children could rotate shapes to see how their appearance is affected, for example,

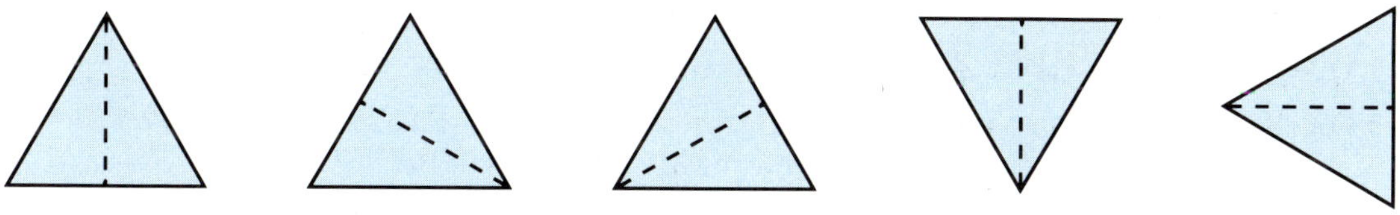

Discuss with the children shapes which are *not* folded in half, for example,

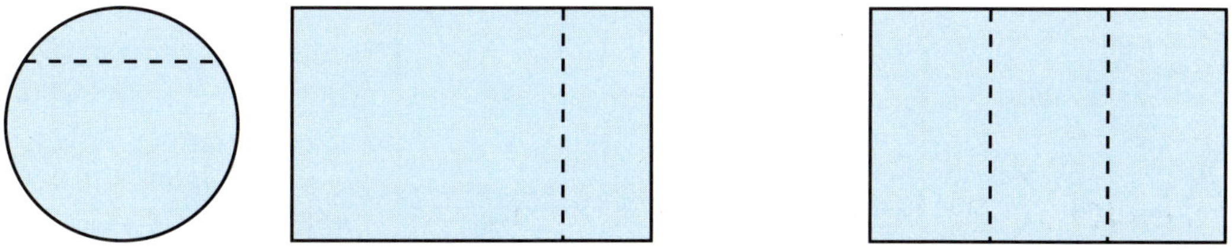

two parts not equal

more than 2 equal parts

These activities are related to Page 21 of Workbook 4.

2 Cutting in half

Objects such as apples, oranges, pies, cakes, pieces of string or ribbon can be cut in half and the two parts discussed.

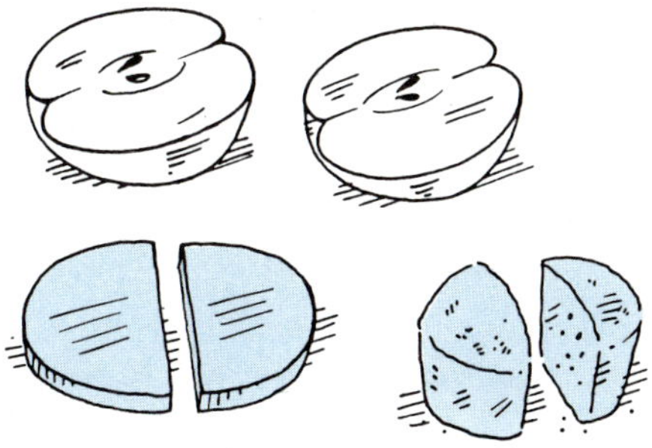

Establish that children who speak about the bigger half do know that for proper halving the two parts must be equal.

3 Half of

Children can use chocolate, biscuits or strips of paper to find a half of, for example, 8 squares.

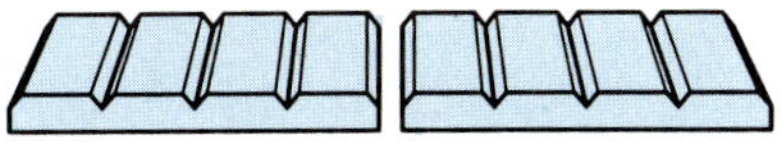

'one half of 8 is 4'

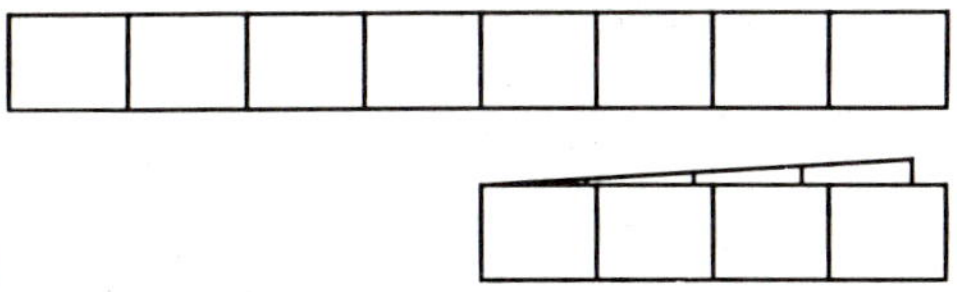

'one half of 8 is 4'

Some children might fold a rectangle in half like this

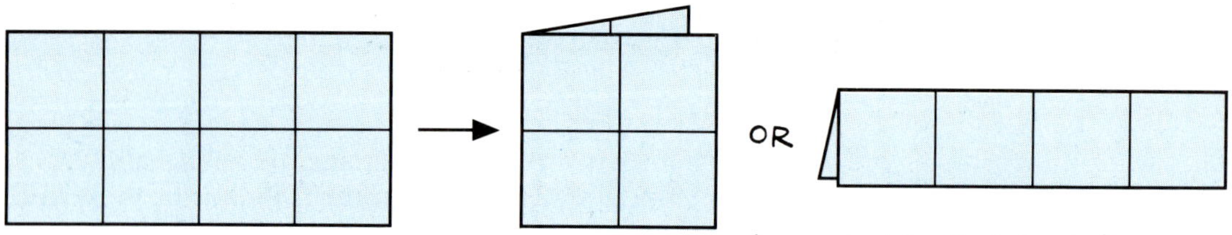

'one half of 8 is 4'

Further activities of this kind are given on Page 22 of Workbook 4.

4 Halving towers

The children can make towers with, for example, six cubes and break them in half. They should check that the halves are the same size.

Repeat for larger towers, say 18 cubes.

Further activities of this kind are contained in Workbook 4, Page 22.

'one half of 6 is 3'

Ma 2/2c
RTN/A
N/2b

Workbook Pages 21 and 22 *Halving*

The activities on these pages are similar to those above. The children need paper shapes to fold for Page 21. They should fold each shape in half. Different folds are possible and these should be discussed.

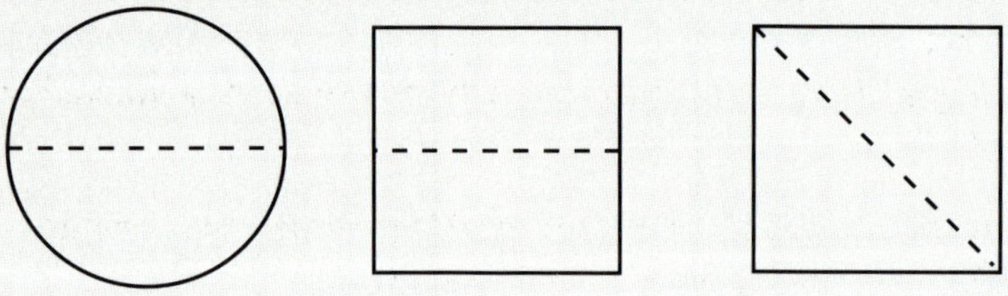

and possibly for the ablest

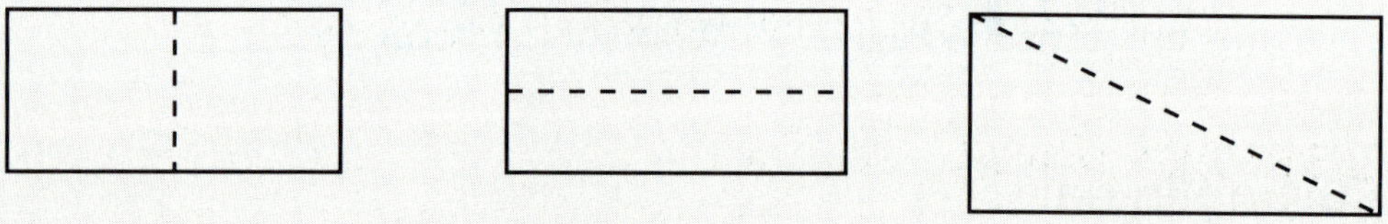

Extension

5 Additional activity: extension

Able children could investigate towers which can be halved and towers which can not. They could record what they discover as follows:

Cubes in towers which can be halved	2, 4, 6, 8, . . . even numbers
Cubes in towers which cannot be halved	1, 3, 5, 7, . . . odd numbers

6 Folding in quarters

Show the children how they can fold shapes to quarter them.
They can fold in half and then fold in half again.

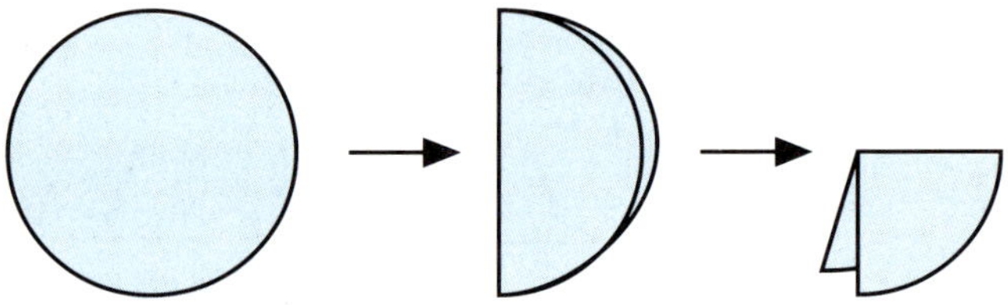

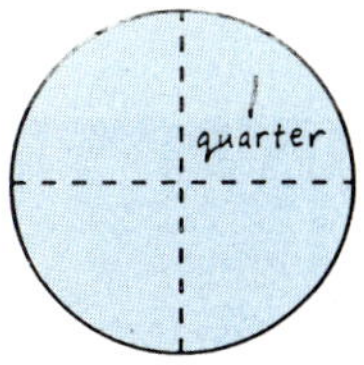

Emphasise that the four quarters are all the same. Each shape can be opened out, labelled, coloured and used to make a wall display.

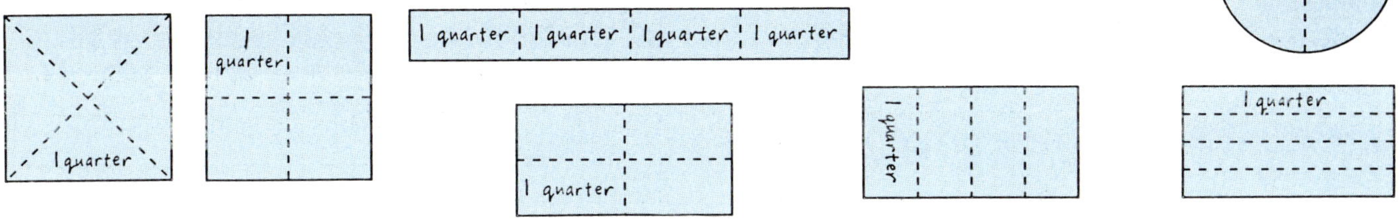

Oral work should emphasise the fact that each whole shape has been folded into four equal parts which are called quarters. Able children may notice that two quarters make one half of any whole.

Shapes can be folded in half twice and *not* show quarters, for example,

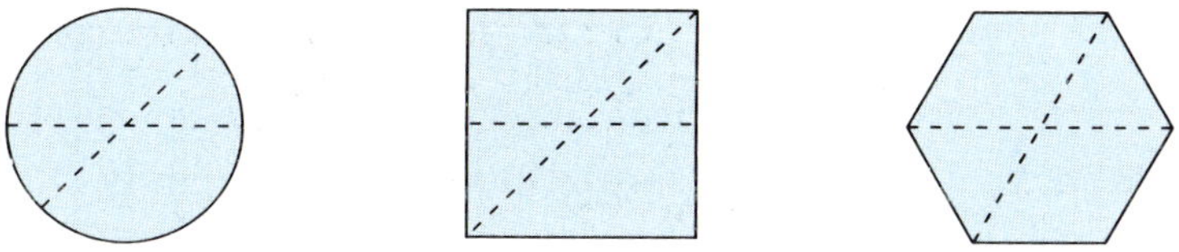

These do *not* show quarters. The 4 parts are not the same.

Children should also realise that a shape shows quarters only when it has exactly *four* equal parts.

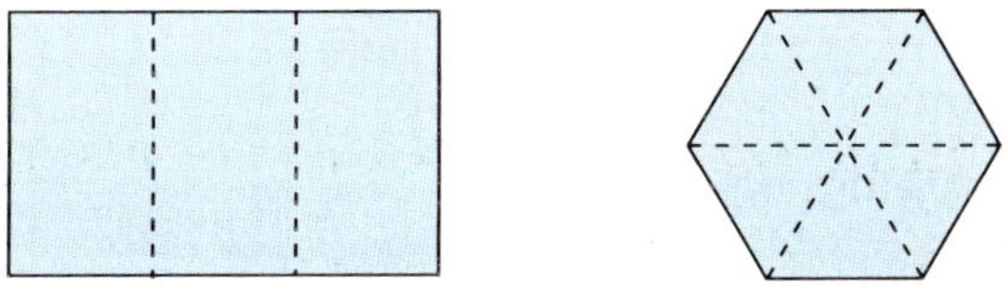

The shapes above do *not* show quarters. There are not exactly four equal parts.

7 Cutting in quarters

Objects such as apples, oranges, pies, cakes, pieces of ribbon, etc. can be halved and then halved again to produce quarters.

Children should realise that the four parts must be equal for proper quartering.

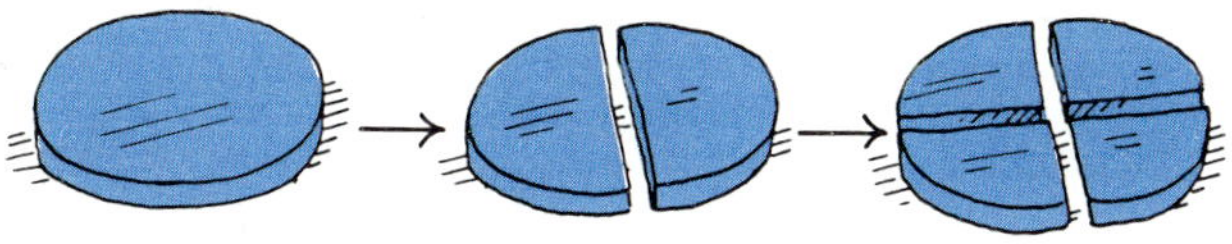

Ma 1/2 2/2c
RTN/B
P/2 N/2b

Workbook Page 23 *Quarters*

The children need paper shapes to fold to show quarters. There are different ways of folding to produce quarters. These should be discovered and discussed and included in the wall display.

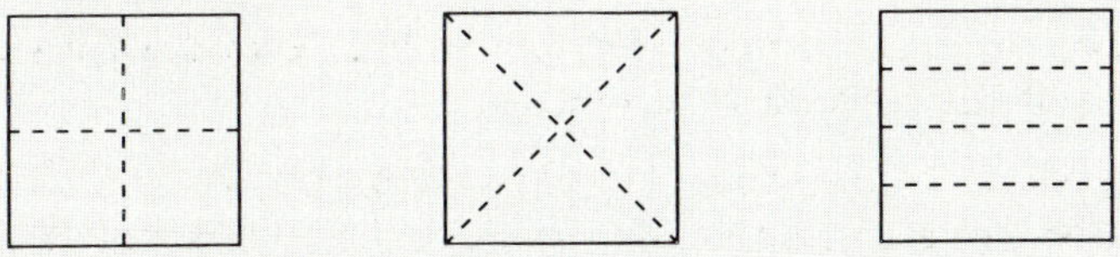

Although the rectangle can be folded along each diagonal and this quarters the *area*, this should not be shown at this level since the four parts are not identical.

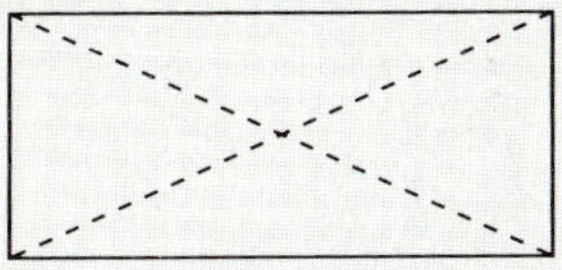

Measure Workbook

Ma 1/2 2/2d,3e
ME/A,B T/A,B PSE
P/2 M/2ac,3b

Overview

This workbook contains seven separate sections dealing with various aspects of measure.
Details of the content, resources and language for each section are given at the start of the notes for that section.

Length 1

Ma 1/2 2/2d
ME/A PSE
P/2 M/2a

Overview

This section

- develops the language of length introduced in Heinemann Mathematics 1 and discusses related practical activities
- introduces practical activities in measuring lengths in non-standard units.

	Teacher's Notes	Measure Workbook	Workcards
Measuring lengths in non-standard units	98	1 to 4	
Measuring lengths in a 'Street' context	100		Measure/ Length 1 to 5
Investigation			*2*

Key words and phrases

taller	wide	further	about	paper clips
tallest	width	furthest	rods	spans
smallest	widest	paces	sticks	measure

Resources

Useful materials

- rods, sticks, straws, paper clips, cubes, strips of card
- flashcards of key words and phrases, see above
- coloured pencils, paper, glue, scissors

Assessment and Resources Pack

Assessment

Check-ups

Measure check-up Page 1

Assessment in Context

'At the fair' context: Questions 25, 26

Resources

Contexts

Length activities are included in both contexts, 'The street' and 'Islands.'

Problem Solving Activities

5 Fish deals with halving a length.

Teaching notes

LENGTH 1: NON-STANDARD UNITS
Introductory activities

Ma 1/2 2/2d
ME/A PSE
P/2 M/2a

This section suggests practical activities to revise length words and introduce the idea of using non-standard units. For most activities it may be better for children to work in pairs or in groups. Their results should then be discussed by the teacher and the class. Some activities are investigations which might involve results from all the children in the class.

1 Exercises

Use activities of the type suggested below to revise and develop length vocabulary:

'Make yourself tall. Make yourself small.'
'Stand nearer to your partner. Stand further from your partner.'
'Jump high. Jump higher.'
'Take five long steps. Take five short steps.'
'Stretch your arms as wide as possible.'
'Stand with your feet wide apart.'
'Point to a high shelf. Point to a low shelf.'
'Hold up your longest finger. Hold up your shortest finger.'

2 Rods, sticks, straws, paper clips and cubes

Show the children how to measure smaller lengths using rods, sticks of equal length, straws or cubes. It is important to stress that the measurement is likely to be 'about' so many units long.

'The car is **about 2 rods** long.'

'Jill's scarf is **about 5 straws** long.

'The box is **about 5 cubes** high.'

'My watch and strap are **about 8 clips** long.'

3 Making a garden

Children can draw objects, associated with a garden, from given measurements. For example, trees, flowers, bird table, wheel barrow, etc. measured using rods.

'Draw a tree 6 rods high.'

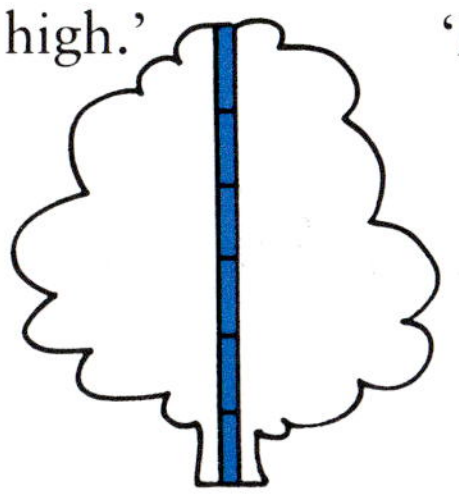

'Make a bird table 3 rods high.'

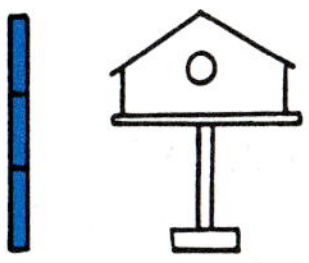

'Draw a barrow 2 rods long, a cat 1 rod tall, a dog 2 rods long.'
'Draw a tub of flowers 2 rods high.' and so on.
These and other objects can be used to make a wall display of a garden scene.

At this point some children might attempt Measure Workbook Pages 1 and 2.

Ma 1/2 2/2d
ME/A PSE
P/2 M/2a

Workbook Pages 1 and 2 *Length: non-standard units*

On Page 1, the child is expected to use paper clips to measure the lengths of objects drawn on the page.

At the end of Page 2 there is an investigation which deals with the widths of plastic bags from shops. These bags should be provided by the teacher and be labelled 1, 2, 3, 4.

Investigation

4 Hands and spans

Using their hands, children can measure the lengths of various objects in the classroom.

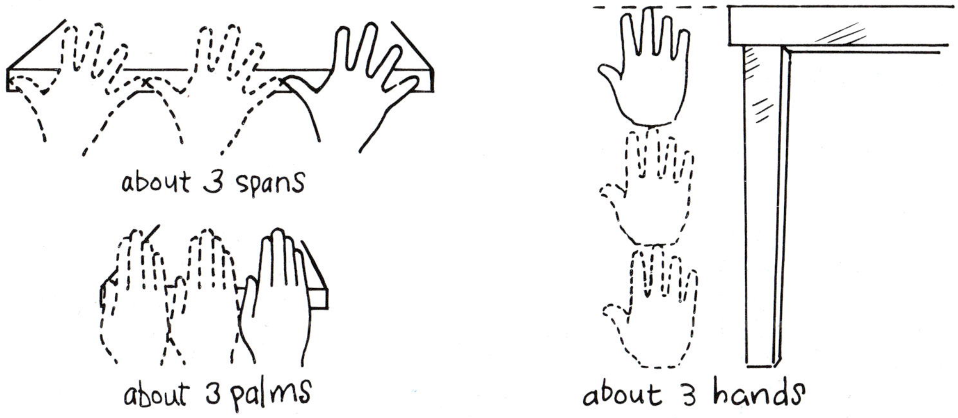

'How long is the window pole?'
'How wide is the desk?'
'How tall is the plant?'

'How high is the door?'
'How high is the window?'
'How tall is the teacher?'

5 Steps and paces

- Encourage the children to solve problems like those below by counting paces or 'feet' (heel to toe steps).

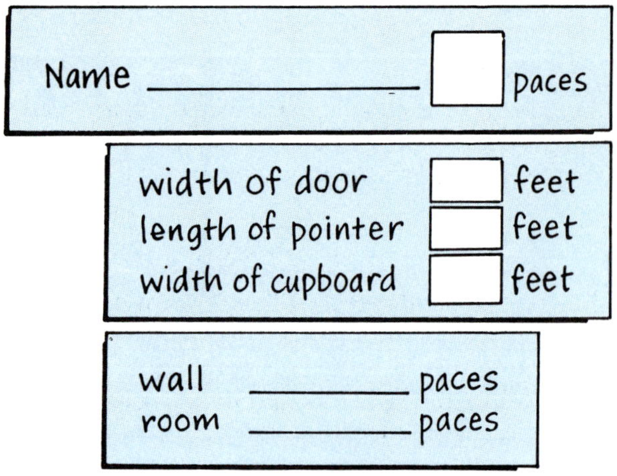

'Who sits furthest from the chalkboard?'
'Who sits nearest to the teacher's chair?'

'How wide is the door?'
'How long is the pointer?'
'How wide is the cupboard door?'

'How long is the classroom wall?'
'How far is it round the classroom?'

- Ask the children to pace out a given distance.

'Put the chair 10 paces from the door.'

'Stand against the wall. Take 6 steps forward.'

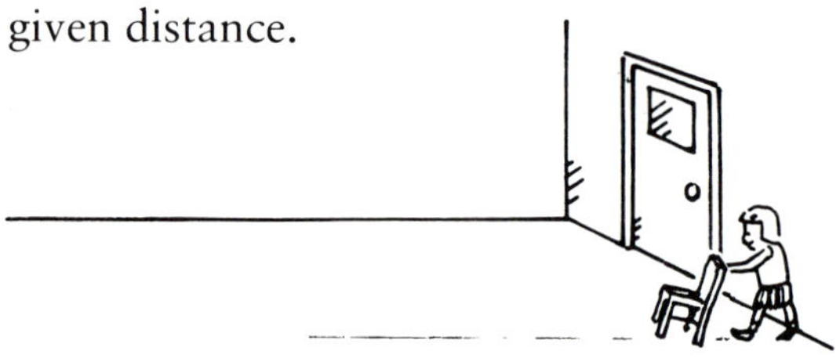

The children will probably finish at different places when following these instructions. This should be discussed to bring out the point that different sizes of unit, such as length of pace, result in different answers.

Ma 1/2 2/2d
ME/A PSE
P/2 M/2a

Workbook Pages 3 and 4 *Length: non-standard units*

On Page 3, the last measurement in each group of activities has to be chosen by the children. On Page 4, the final task requires the use of a long stick as a non-standard unit of measure. An unmarked metre stick would be ideal for this since such a unit will be introduced to the children in the next major section of length work in Heinemann Mathematics 3.

Ma 1/2 2/2d
ME/A PSE
P/2 M/2a

Measure/Length Cards 1 to 5 *Street scene: non-standard units*

These are practical cards which involve the children in making several objects to specified lengths. It is not intended that one child should do all the cards but rather that a group of children should carry out the activities suggested.

The teacher could set up a wall, desk, or floor display of a street scene in which the completed items can be placed. Other groups of children who use the cards could contribute more items to the display.

The street scene could be expanded by children measuring and making items which are not suggested on the cards.

'Draw and make a longer car.'
'Make a fire-engine 3 rods long.'
'Make a church 4 rods high.'
'Draw and make a shorter lorry.'
'Make a bicycle shorter than the car.'
'Make a pram.'

Assessment and Resources Pack

The *Contexts* booklet in the *Assessment and Resources Pack* for Heinemann Mathematics 2 contains a context entitled 'The street'. It provides ideas for a wide range of mathematical activities for an extended project based on this theme. The Length Cards could be used within this project or, perhaps, to introduce the theme.

LENGTH 1: NON-STANDARD UNITS
Additional activities

Ma 1/2	2/2d
ME/A	PSE
P/2	M/2a

The investigations suggested below can be undertaken by either groups of children or by the whole class. The methods used can vary and may depend on the strategies adopted by the children, **including that of choosing their own measuring unit.**

1 Who is the tallest?

The strategies adopted to find out 'Who is the tallest person in the class?' might include:

- Standing all the children closely together and then picking out the tallest.

- Measuring each child using spans or hands.

- Cutting a strip of newsprint to the height of each child and comparing the strips to find the tallest child.

Related activities can be done using similar methods. For example,
'Who is the shortest person?'
'Does the tallest person wear the biggest shoes?'

2 Other investigations

Other investigations might consider:
'Who wears the longest scarf?'
'Who wears the shortest tie?'
'Who has the deepest pockets?', and so on.

Weight

Overview

This section

- develops the language of weighing introduced in Heinemann Mathematics 1
- introduces the use of non-standard units.

	Teacher's Notes	Measure Workbook
Weighing in non-standard units	103	5, 6

Key words and phrases

balance	heaviest	weighs more	weighs about
balancing	lightest	weighs less	

Resources

Useful materials

- two-pan balance
- sets of non-standard units such as cubes, bricks, clothes pegs, washers, coins
- selection of objects for weighing such as ruler, pen, cup, saucer, tin, prepared package, vegetables – carrot, potato, onion (perhaps made of plasticine)

Assessment and Resources Pack

Assessment

Check-ups

Measure Check-up Page 2

Assessment in Context

'At the fair' context: Question 15

Resources

Contexts

'The street' context contains activities about weight.

Problem Solving Activities

13 Fruit
9 Sausage and egg

WEIGHT: NON-STANDARD UNITS
Introductory activities

Ma 1/2 2/2d
ME/A
P/2 M/2a

The idea of using a two-pan balance to compare the weights of objects was introduced in Heinemann Mathematics 1. The language used was 'heavier', 'lighter' and 'about the same weight as'. This work is now extended to using non-standard units such as cubes or pegs to compare and order objects by weight.

1 Using cubes

Place an object, such as a pencil, on the pan of a two-pan balance. Ask the children to find how many cubes balance the pencil. They should add cubes one at a time until the pans are as level as possible.

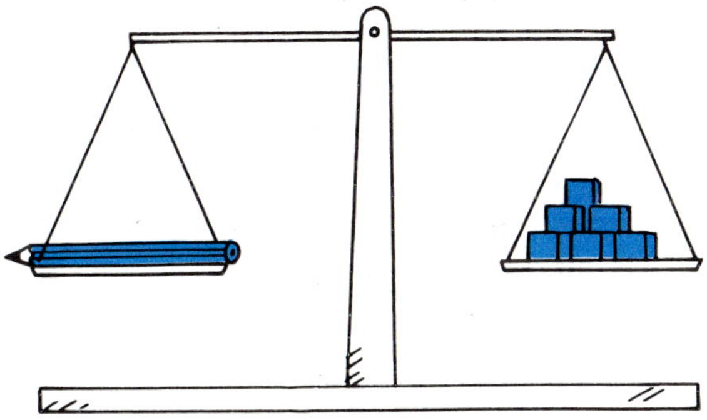

The children may have to add one cube too many and take it off again to achieve the best balance.

This can be recorded as
'The pencil weighs about 6 cubes.'
Repeat for another object and then compare weights.
'The marker weighs about 8 cubes.'
'The marker weighs more than the pencil.'

2 Heaviest, lightest

Extend Activity 1 above to weighing three objects which can then be ordered by weight to find the heaviest and lightest. Other non-standard unit such as clothes pegs, cotton reels, marbles, washers, can be used.

3 Weight table

The children can work in pairs or small groups to compare and record the weights of objects on a weight table.

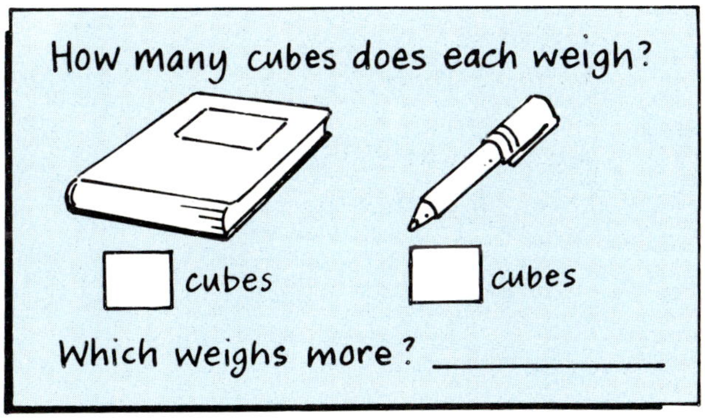

This work is linked to Workbook Page 5 where the language 'weighs more' and 'weighs less' is used.

4 Using a variety of non-standard units

The children should also weigh the same object using different non-standard units.

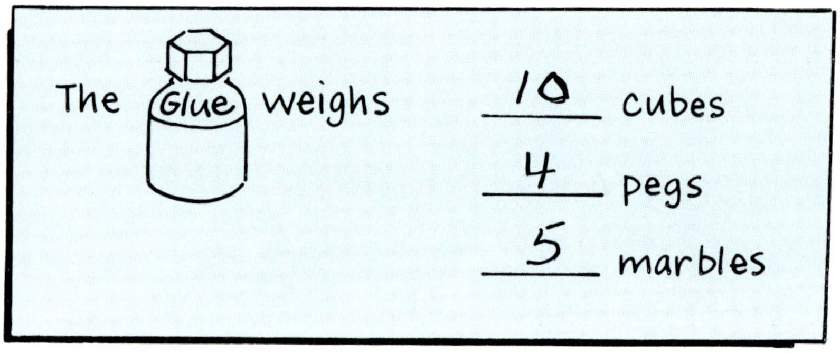

Some children may be able to say why more cubes than marbles are needed to balance the glue jar.

Ma 1/2 2/2d
ME/A
P/2 M/2a

Workbook Pages 5 and 6 *Weight: non-standard units*

The top of Page 5 shows an orange and a pear balanced by cubes which can be counted. The remaining activities on these pages are practical and are similar to those suggested above.

The vegetables on Page 6 could be real or made of plasticine.

Flashcards of the names of the objects at the foot of the page may be needed for some children.

5 Additional activities

Extension activities for some children might include challenges such as
'Find out which weighs more 10 pegs or 8 cotton reels.'
'Find the heaviest/lightest thing on the weight table.'

Capacity and volume

Ma 1/2 2/2d
ME/A
P/2 M/2a

Overview

This section

- develops the language of capacity and volume
- introduces the use of non-standard units of capacity and volume.

	Teacher's Notes	Measure Workbook
Non-standard units of capacity	106	7, 8
Non-standard units of volume	107	9
Extension		*7, 8*

Key words and phrases

cupful	holds most	pack
spoonful	holds least	find out
ladle	holds about	

Resources

Useful materials

- sink or water bucket or basin or baby bath
- dry sand
- plastic containers, beach bucket, ice-cream carton, bowl, bottles of different size and shape, jug, eggcup, doll's cup, pan, cake case, paper cup, yoghurt carton, ladle, spoon
- building blocks or bricks, sets of books
- boxes or cartons marked with a red, blue, green and yellow circle (for Workbook Page 9)

Assessment and Resources Pack

Assessment

Check-up

Measure Check-up Page 2

Assessment in Context

'Treasure Island' context: Question 6

Resources

Contexts

'The street' and 'Islands' contexts both contain activities about capacity.

Teaching notes

CAPACITY: NON-STANDARD UNITS
Introductory activities

Ma 1/2 2/2d
ME/A
P/2 M/2a

Heinemann Mathematics 1 introduced comparison of capacity by pouring and the language 'holds more' and 'holds less'. This work is now extended to comparing and ordering containers by filling, using a variety of non-standard units.

1 Which holds more?

Use two plastic containers and a cup. Show the group of children how to fill the cup and pour into one of the containers, while keeping count. Labels can be used by the children to record about how many cupfuls each container holds.

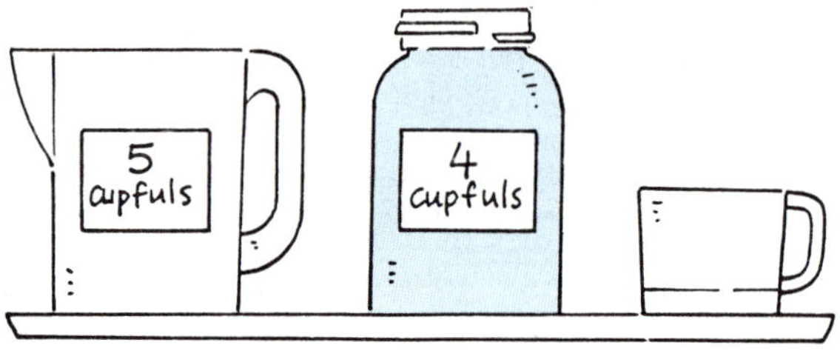

Discussion should also lead to language such as 'about', 'a little more than', 'almost 7 cupfuls'. Discuss which container holds more/less.

This activity is similar to those on Measure Workbook Page 7.

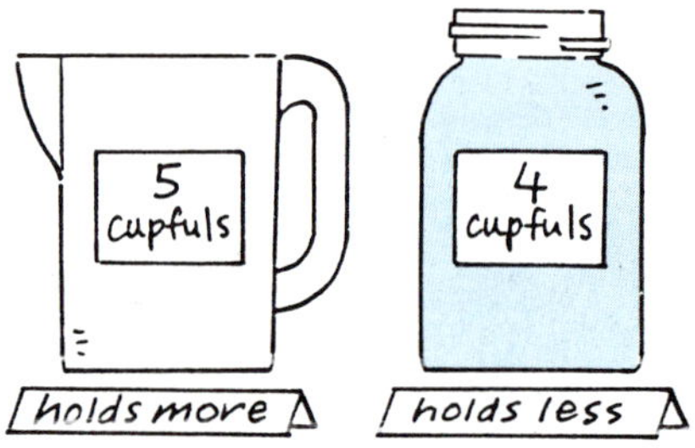

2 Individual and group activities

A small group of two or three children can be challenged to find out which teapot holds more cupfuls.

Two small cups and a large spoon can be used for a similar activity to find which holds more spoonfuls.

Measure Workbook Page 7 has similar activities.

3 Which holds most/least?

Extend activities like those above to ordering three or more containers using non-standard units such as ladlefuls, spoonfuls, cupfuls.
For example,
'Which plate holds most cereal?'

A large spoon and cereal (or sand) can be used. Discussion should introduce the language 'holds most' and 'holds least' and flashcards for these phrases would be useful.

Measure Workbook Page 8 has activities of this kind.

4 Using different non-standard units

Ask the children to use different measures to fill the same container. For example, fill a jug using cupfuls, spoonfuls, etc.

Measure
Workbook

Workbook Pages 7 and 8 *Capacity: non-standard units*

Ma 1/2 2/2d
ME/A
P/2 M/2a

Provide containers and non-standard measures so that the number of measures needed to fill each container is in the range 4 to 12 and is also different in each case.

Extension

The final activity on Page 7 is more difficult. The children could

- fill one bottle and use a funnel to pour into the other
- use a funnel to fill each bottle in cupfuls
- fill each bottle and pour to find how many times each fills the cup.

If either of the last two ways is used the children can write the number of cupfuls under each drawing on the page. If the containers are identified by coloured stickers the children could write 'The blue one holds more'.

Extension

The final activity on Page 8 is more difficult as no provision is made for writing the answers on the page. The children can however write the number of spoonfuls under each container. The children are left to decide on whether to fill with level or heaped spoonfuls if sand is being used.

VOLUME: NON-STANDARD UNITS
Introductory activities

Ma 1/2 2/2d
ME/A
P/2 M/2a

This section is concerned with filling the space inside boxes using either building bricks or books as non-standard units of volume.

At this level the children are simply finding which of two marked boxes 'holds more'.

1 Tidying toys

The idea of 'packing' can be introduced by asking children to tidy a collection of toys into boxes with lids or cartons with flaps for closing. Discussion should encourage statements such as

'The teddy does not go into this box.'
'All the toys go into this box.'
'This box holds more than this one.'

2 Packing shoes

Shoes can be packed into boxes to find which of the boxes holds most and, perhaps, which holds fewest shoes.

3 Packing boxes

Cereal packets or tea-bag boxes or chalk boxes all of the same size can be used to pack a large cardboard box. Different ways of packing the boxes should be discussed as well as the approximate nature of the answers.

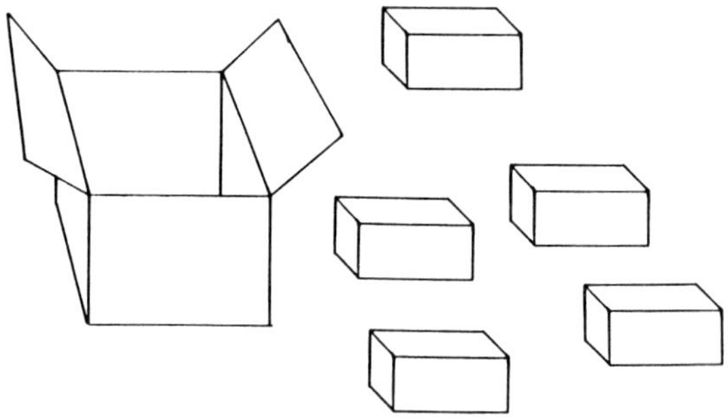

Ma 1/2 2/2d
ME/A
P/2 M/2a

Workbook Page 9 *Volume: non-standard units*

For the top of the page, the teacher should choose two boxes each capable of holding between 10 and 20 bricks. One box should have a blue circle on it, the other a red circle. For the bottom part of the page the teacher should choose two boxes each capable of holding between 8 and 20 books all of the same size. One box should have a green circle on it, the other a yellow circle.

4 Additional activity

The children might fill the same box using *different* non-standard units, such as chalk boxes, tea-bag boxes. This activity would help to establish the idea that the smaller the measuring unit, the more are needed.

Area

Ma 1/2 2/2d
ME/A PSE
P/2 M/2a

Overview

This section

- introduces the concept and language of area
- deals with comparison of areas by perception and by covering with non-standard units.

	Teacher's Notes	Measure Workbook
Concept of area: non-standard units	110	10 to 12
Problem solving		*12*

Key words and phrases

greater/smaller area   greatest/smallest area

Resources

Useful materials

- counters, squares, etc. for covering shapes

Assessment and Resources Pack

Assessment

Check-ups

Measure Check-up Page 3

Assessment in Context

'Treasure Island' context: Questions 1, 13, 14

Resources

Contexts

The 'Islands' context contains activities about non-standard units of area.

Problem Solving Activities

2 Shape puzzles although concerned with shape also deals with covering various areas.

Resource cards

Resource Cards 18 and *19*, (Area puzzles)

Teaching notes

AREA: CONCEPT OF AREA, NON-STANDARD UNITS
Introductory activities

Ma 1/2 2/2d	
ME/A	PSE
P/2	M/2a

1 Comparing shapes

Show the children two card shapes and discuss which one covers more of the table. Show how their 'surfaces' can be compared by placing one on top of the other. Repeat for other pairs of shapes.

'This shape has a greater surface. It has a greater area.'

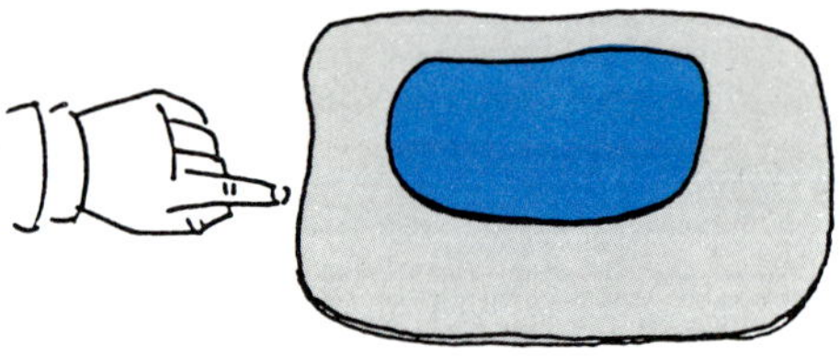

Running a hand across the surface helps to reinforce the concept of area.

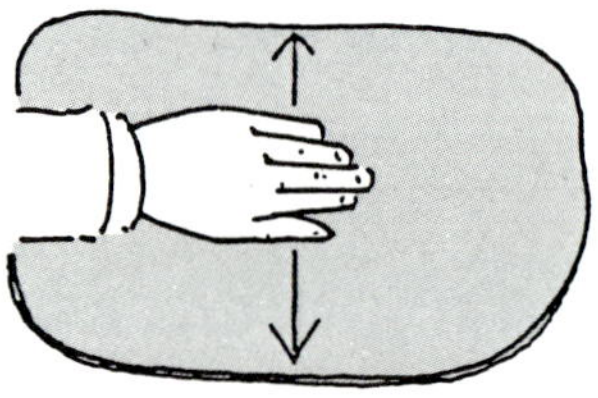

Many children will be able to tell a greater area by just *looking* at the shapes. Allow them to compare areas of leaves, circles, etc in this way to find which has the greater/ smaller area. The children might attempt Measure Workbook Page 10 at this point.

2 Fish

Ask each child to make two paper fish so that one has a greater area than the other.

Discuss with the group which of *all* the fish has the greatest area/smallest area.

Discuss the areas of two fish which are not similarly shaped and where it is difficult to decide, even when one is laid on top of the other, which has the greater area.

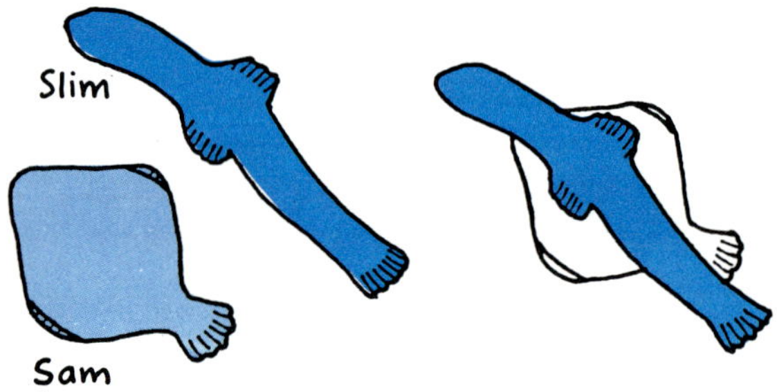

This leads to the idea of covering each fish with counters or squares in order to decide which has the greater area.

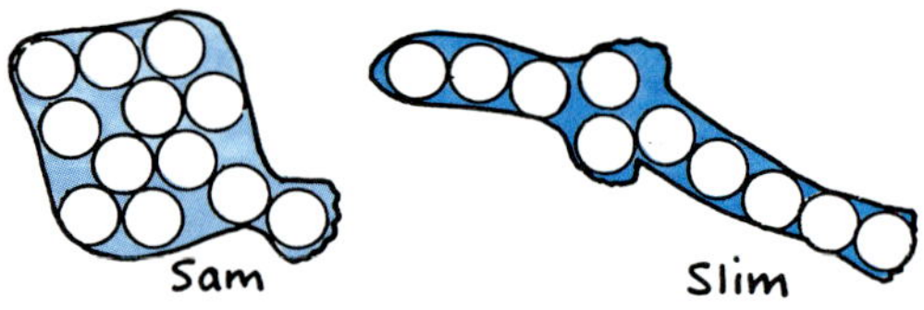

It takes 12 counters to cover Sam and 10 for Slim so Sam has a greater area than Slim. This work is related to Workbook Page 11.

3 Using squares

Introduce the idea of using squares for this kind of covering activity. Establish that squares cover surfaces/shapes without leaving gaps and can sometimes give a better measure of area. For example,

A has an area of about 15 squares whereas B has an area of about 18 squares. This relates to Workbook Page 12.

The children should have practice in using counters and squares to cover areas before they attempt Workbook Pages 11 and 12.

Workbook Pages 10 to 12 *Concept of area* *Non-standard units*

These pages check up on children's ability to compare areas of flat shapes by looking (Page 10) and by covering (Pages 11 and 12). Squares of 2 cm edge would be ideal for the work on Page 12. As far as possible children should be allowed to tackle the problem solving activity at the foot of Page 12 in their own way. Some may follow a trial-and-error procedure by drawing a flag and then covering it to see how many squares are needed while others may lay out the squares *first* and then draw round them to make the flag shape.

4 Resource cards

Resource Cards 18 and *19* (Area puzzles) can provide a useful additional activity, as they are closely related to the work on Measure Workbook page 12.

Measure
Workbook

Ma 1/2 2/2d
ME/A PSE
P/2 M/2a

Problem solving

Assessment and Resources Pack

Time

Ma 2/3e 2/2d
T/A,B
M/3b,2c

Overview

This section

- extends telling the time to half hours, from analogue and digital clocks
- introduces months of the year and days of the week.

	Teacher's Notes	Measure Workbook
Clockface work introducing half past	113	13, 14
Digital displays	115	15
Months of the year	116	16
Days of the week	117	17, 18

Key words and phrases

colour to match	half past	today
day after	o'clock	tomorrow
day before	time	yesterday

January, February, March, April, May, June, July, August, September, October, November, December
Sunday, Monday, Tuesday, Wednesday, Thursday, Friday, Saturday

Resources

Useful materials

- a large clock with geared hands
- small card clocks for individual children
- flashcards of key words and phrases, see above
- time flashcards, for example **half past 6**
- digital display flashcards, for example **6:30**
- calendar pictures and flashcards for the months of the year
- days of the week flashcards
- set of cards showing different clock times, for example 

Assessment and Resources Pack

Assessment

Check-ups

Measure Check-up Page 4

Assessment in Context

'At the fair' context: Question 5
'Treasure Island' context: Question 5

Resources

Contexts

'The street' context contains activities about o'clock and half past times, days and months.
The 'Islands' context has activities about o'clock and half past times, time sequences, and days of the week.

Resource cards

Resource Cards 20 to *23* (Opening and closing times) deal with hours and half hours.

Teaching notes

TIME: CLOCKFACE WORK INTRODUCING HALF PAST
Introductory activities

Ma 2/3e
T/A,B
M/3b

The o'clock times were introduced in the Measure Workbook of Heinemann Mathematics 1. Some suggestions for practical work to revise this and to introduce 'half past' are given below.

1 Introducing half past

The teacher could use a real clock or a large clock with geared hands and move the hands to a time such as 4 o'clock. The position of the hands could be discussed.

Starting at 4 o'clock, the hands can slowly be turned to 5 o'clock, pointing out that the long hand has moved 'all the way round' while the short hand has moved from 4 to 5. A real clock takes a long time to do this.

The hands can then be re-set to 4 o'clock and turned slowly round to **half-past 4,** pointing out that
'The long hand has gone **half way** round.'
'The hour hand is **half way** between 4 and 5.'

The clock can then be wound on to show the sequence of o'clocks and half pasts, and these can be read aloud by the children.

2 Making a clock

Large numeral cards for 1 to 12 can be placed in the correct order by children to form a floor clockface. One child then kneels at the centre and, by pointing, indicates the time. This can be repeated for other times and with other children.

There could be a discussion of times like 'just before . . .', 'just after . . .'.

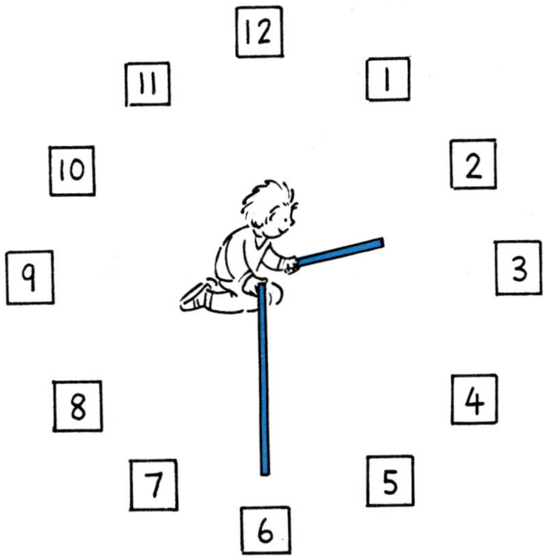

3 Important times

Clockface cards can be used by the children to show several familiar times and these can be displayed in sequence.

4 Feeding times

Use pictures of animals.

When the teacher gives the time for each animal to be fed, a clockface and/or a flashcard is placed alongside the picture. This activity is similar to the work on Pages 13 and 14 of the Measure Workbook.

5 Ordering times

Children can be asked to put times in the same day in order given a set of either clockface cards or a set of cards with written times. For example,

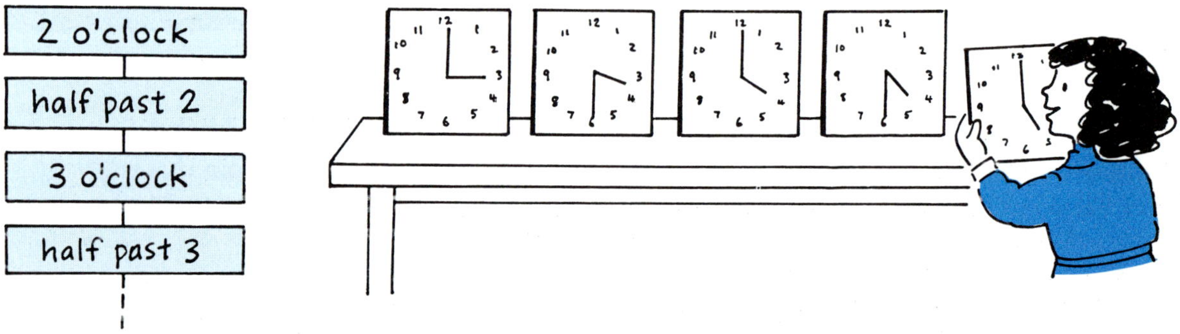

6 Setting a clock to a certain time

A geared clock could be used by the children to 'Set the clock to half past three' and so on.

Ma 2/3e
T/A,B
M/3b

Workbook Pages 13 and 14 *Time: half past*

Most of the times on these two pages are 'half pasts' but there are also two 'o'clocks'. The children have to be able to write times for themselves, i.e. half past 9, in the later examples.

Questions can be asked about the completed page. For example, 'Which animal did the children see at half past 9?' and so on.

TIME: DIGITAL DISPLAYS
Introductory activities

Measure
Workbook

Ma 2/3e
T/A,B
M/3b

1 Another way to show half past

From the work done in Heinemann Mathematics 1, the children should be able to read both a clockface and a digital display for the 'o'clock' times.

The teacher now has to establish that as there was a '**half way**' between four o'clock and five o'clock on the clockface, there is also a '**half way**' between four o'clock and five o'clock on the digital display. This is

2 Matching times

Use flashcards to give the children practice in matching 'o'clocks' and 'half pasts' on both kinds of clocks. For example,

3 The postbox

The class postbox could be used to show different digital times for the letters to be collected. For example, the children have to read the collection time and place a clockface showing this time next to the postbox.

Workbook Page 15 *Time: digital displays*

The children are asked to match clockface times, digital times and written times by colouring each set of three the same colour.

Ma 2/3e
T/A,B
M/3b

4 Additional activity

Resource Cards 20 to *23* (Opening and closing times) of the *Assessment and Resources Pack* provide games for the children in which reading the time is involved.

Assessment and Resources Pack

TIME: MONTHS AND DAYS
Introductory activities

Ma 2/2d
T/A,B
M/2c

Most of this work is oral and should be ongoing throughout the year.

1 Months and events

A wall chart might show pictures of typical events for a particular month. For example,

2 Months and weather

The months of the year can be associated with pictures of the weather and seasons. For example,

3 Months in order

A wall chart showing the sequence of the months and likely events which may occur can be on display.

A poster which shows the sequence of months in a circular display can also be completed by the children placing the flashcards in their correct order. The poster can then be used for discussion.

'Which month comes after June?'

'Which month is before January.'

'Which was last month?'

'Which is next month?'

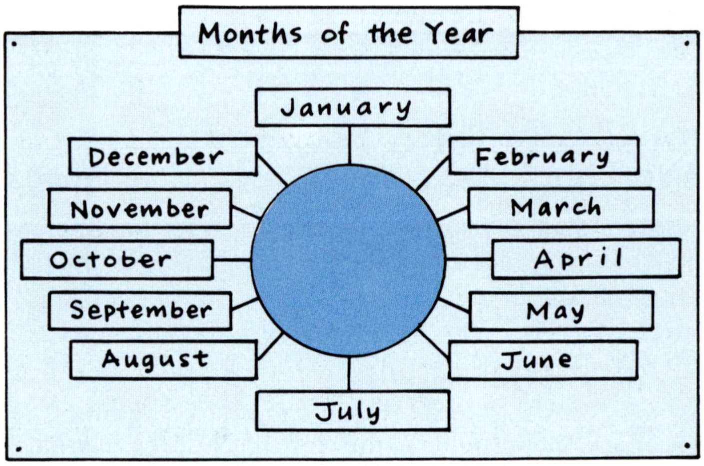

4 Months and days

Many teachers keep charts of various kinds which are changed or added to each day.

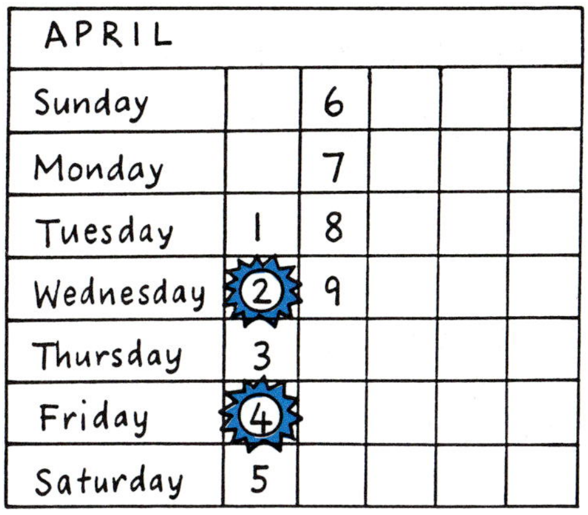

On the calendar, the birthdays of children in the class could be highlighted as they occur. For example, there were birthdays on Wednesday 2nd and Friday 4th April.

5 Birthday graph

A graph could be drawn by the children to show the birthday months of the class.

6 Days of the week

From a calendar, wall chart or diary, the children could answer questions like

'What day is tomorrow?'
'What day was yesterday?'
'What is the day before Monday?'
'What is the day after Saturday?' and so on.

Flashcards can also be placed in the correct order by the children.

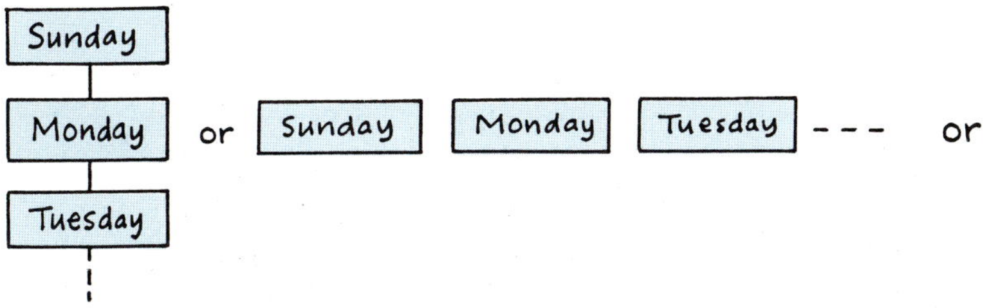

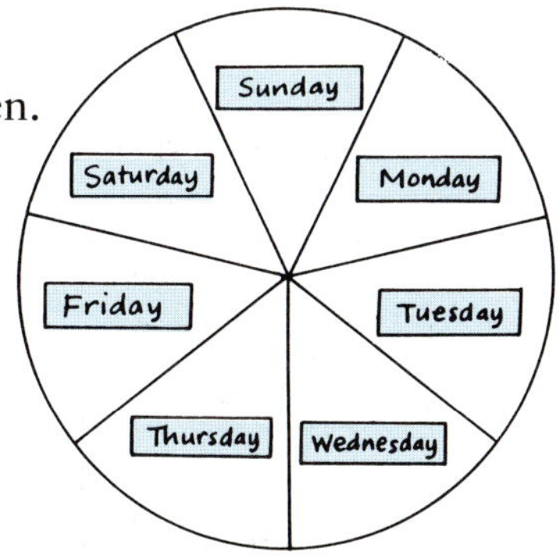

Workbook Page 16 *Time: months of the year*

Ma 2/2d
T/B
M/2c

On this page, the children have to associate familiar events with certain months of the year. While Christmas is clearly matched to December, some of the matchings will depend on the children's individual birthday months.

Workbook Pages 17 and 18 *Time: days of the week*

Ma 2/2d
T/A
M/2c

These two pages display the daily happenings for one week in the life of Tig. They should be discussed by the children as should the days when the happenings occur.

The children are then asked to match events to days and then to write days on which particular events took place. The children might be asked questions like

'What did Tig do on the day after she was riding her bicycle?'
'What was she doing on the day before Friday?'
'What was the day after the day she went swimming?'

Commonly used units: length, weight, capacity, time

Ma 4/2c
ME/B
M/2c

Overview

This section deals with some of the commonly used measure units which may well be part of the everyday experience of children. These include non-metric as well as metric units. The emphasis here is on recognising which units are associated with particular contexts. It is not suggested that the children measure with all of these units at this stage or try to develop full concepts of such units.

	Teacher's Notes	Measure Workbook
Commonly used units	119	19, 20

Key words and phrases

hour(s)	metre(s)	litre(s)	pound(s)
minute(s)	mile(s)	pint(s)	second(s)

Resources

Useful materials

Shop packages, price lists, advertisements, magazine and newspaper cuttings, pictures of road signs showing mileages, etc. . . . which contain references to the above units.

Assessment and Resources Pack

Assessment

Assessment in Context

'Treasure Island' context: Question 20

Teaching notes

COMMONLY USED UNITS
Introductory activities

Ma 2/2d
ME/B
M/2c

1 Shopping

In shops and supermarkets the children will see and hear about commodities which are bought and sold by the pound, pint, litre, metre, etc.

They will hear their parents say
'pint of milk'
'pound of cheese'
'two metres of ribbon'
and phrases like these should be familiar to the children.

Discussion with the children, helped by using wrappers, packages, price lists, pictures, etc. will give some meaning to these units.

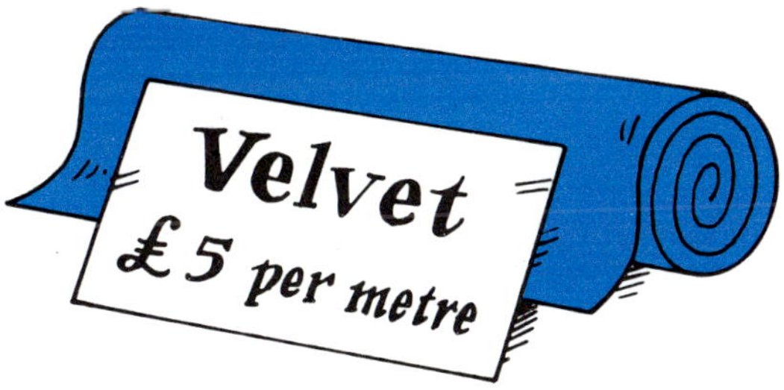

2 Advertisements, magazines, newspapers

These can be collected and used, as above, for discussion purposes. For example,

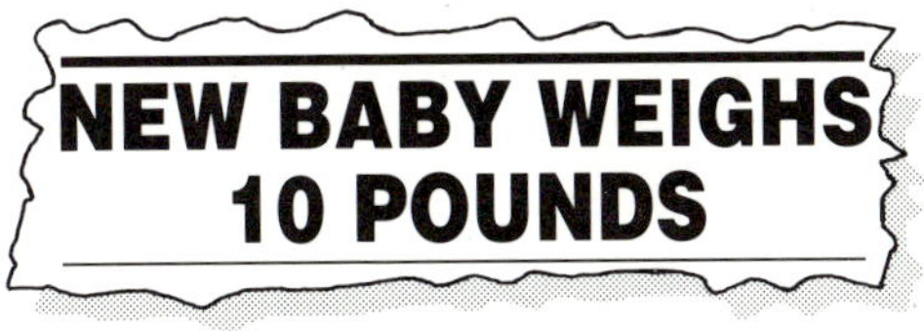

Workbook Pages 19 and 20 *Commonly used units*

Ma 2/2d
ME/B
M/2c

These pages show situations in which different units of measure are used. The children have to make a sensible choice from a given list of units. Their ability to do this will depend on their own experience and on earlier discussion of similar situations.

LENGTH 2
Group investigation

Measure Workbook Pages 21 and 22 provide an extra activity for a group of children. An important aspect of this work is the discussion which has to take place in order that the investigation can be satisfactorily carried out.

Ma 1/2 2/2d
ME/A PSE
P/2 M/2c

Workbook Pages 21 and 22 *Length investigation*

The first task is for the children to measure their own heights. The non-standard unit to be used is the length of one hand. The result, for **each** child, should be in the region of 9 hands.

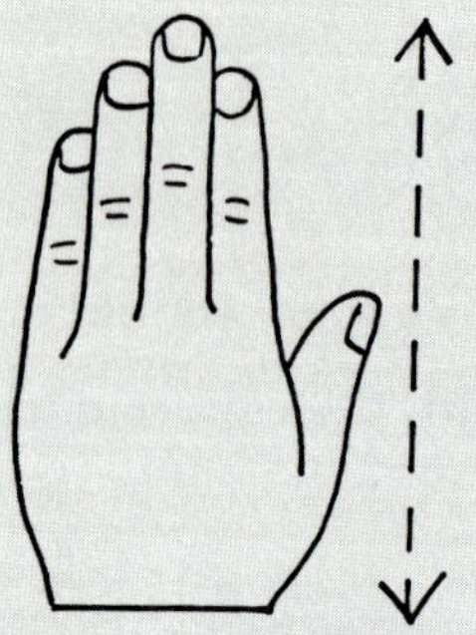

The teacher could then ask

'If I measured my height using **my** hands, how many hands high do you think I would be?'

The teacher could show that he/she is also about 9 of his/her hands high.

The second task is for the giant's hand to be cut out from Page 22, compared for size, and discussed by the children. In order to estimate the giant's height, **the children have to accept that his height, also, would probably be in the region of 9 or 10 of his hands.**

Using the giant's hand, the children can then show the appropriate height of the giant alongside the classroom door, with the teacher's help.
He is too big for most classroom doors.

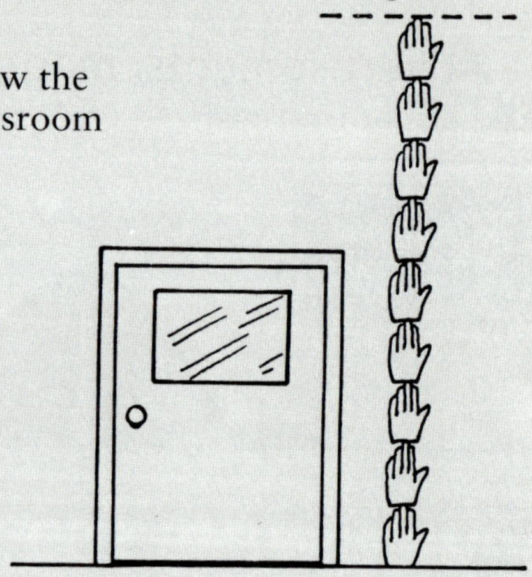

Shape Workbook

Ma 1/2 4/2ab 3/1a
RS/A,B,D PM/A,B PS/B PSE
P/2 A/1a S/2acd,3ab

Overview

The work in this Workbook divides naturally into four sections dealing with 3D shape and pattern, 2D shape and pattern, right angles and right-angle turns, and transformations.

An outline is given below but details of content, resources and language appear at the start of the teacher's notes for each section.

		Teacher's Notes	Shape Workbook	Shape Workcards
3D SHAPE AND PATTERN	**Recognising and naming cubes, cuboids, cylinders, cones, spheres and pyramids** **3D shape patterns**	123	1 to 4	1 to 6
2D SHAPE AND PATTERN	**Recognising and naming squares, rectangles, triangles, circles, pentagons and hexagons** **2D shape patterns** **Problem solving and investigation**	127	5 to 10	
RIGHT ANGLES	**Introducing right angles** **Right angles in shapes** **Right-angle turns**	133	11 to 14	
TRANSFORMATIONS	**Moving along, turning round and flipping over**	137	15	
	Extension		*6, 14, 15*	*5, 6*
	Problem solving		*4, 9*	*6*
	Investigation		*10*	

3D shape and pattern

Ma 1/2 4/2a 3/1a
RS/A,B PS/B
P/2 S/2a,3a A/1a

Overview

This section

- revises recognition and naming of cubes, cuboids, cylinders and cones
- introduces pyramids and spheres
- includes 3D shape pattern work.

	Teacher's Notes	Shape Workbook	Shape Workcards
3D shape models	124		1 to 6
3D shape names and patterns	125	1 to 4	1 to 6
Problem solving		*4*	*6*
Extension			*5, 6*

Key words and phrases

machine	cone	cuboid	pyramid	curved
pattern	cube	sphere	cylinder	flat

Resources

Useful materials

- cartons, tubes, tins and other junk material
- wooden or plastic cubes, cuboids, cylinders, cones, spheres, pyramids
- plasticine or other modelling material and small pieces of hardwood for patting plasticine
- coloured pencils

Assessment and Resources Pack

Assessment

Check-ups

Shape Check-up, Pages 1, 4

Assessment in Context

'At the fair' context: Questions 4, 10
'Treasure Island' context: Question 33

Resources

Contexts

There are several 3D shape activities in both 'The street' and 'Islands' contexts.

Teaching notes

3D SHAPE MODELS
Introductory activities

Ma 1/2 4/2a
RS/A,B
P/2 S/2a,3a

1 Sweet factory theme

Shape Cards 1 to 6 and Shape Workbook Pages 1 to 4 all relate to a theme about a sweet factory where the children create sweet-producing machines and the sweets themselves.

Discuss the theme with the children before introducing model making activities. The sweets involved are Sherbet Spheres, Chewy Cuboids, Crumbly Cones, Cool Cubes and Crunchy Cylinders.

2 Making machines

Look at Shape Cards 1 to 6 with the children and discuss the machines for making sweets and the different 3D shapes with which the machines can be built. The children should have met cubes, cuboids, cylinders and cones when using Heinemann Mathematics 1.

Two new shapes should be introduced and discussed. Spheres are 'round' and pyramids 'come to a point'.

It is likely that the pyramids will have square bases. The groups of children should realise that they need not follow exactly the pictures on Cards 1 to 4 but could create their own machines using cartons, cardboard tubes and other junk materials. Show them how to join shapes with glue or sticky tape. Some examples of the sweets themselves should be considered to decide what the machine might be like.

3 Making sweets

Discuss the different sweets which feature in the cards and how the children might make them with plasticine. It is worth spending some time on this. Let the children attempt to make the different 3D shapes and give help and suggestions as required.

- **Spheres** may be made by rolling soft plasticine between the palms to make a ball shape.
- **Cylinders** can be made by rolling with a small piece of hardboard. The circular end faces can be produced by pressing and patting.

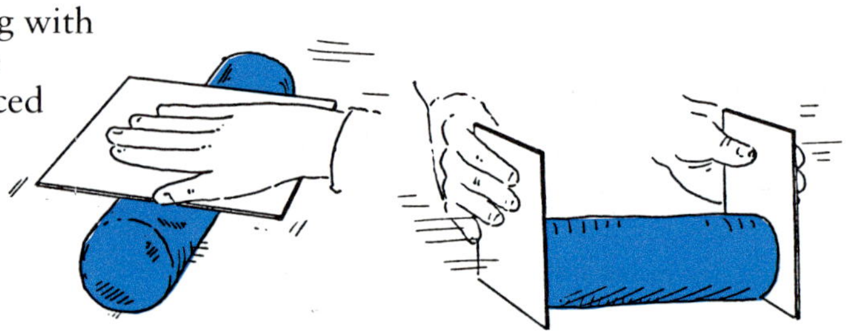

- A **cone** can be made with a little practice by rolling the plasticine between the hands to make the required pointed shape.

- A **cube** is made by starting with a plasticine ball and pressing with hardboard to make the flat faces.
- A **cuboid** is made similarly by starting with a lozenge-shaped piece of plasticine instead of a ball shape.

When it is felt that the children are well enough prepared they can tackle Shape Cards 5 and 6.

3D Shape Cards 1 to 6

Ma 1/2 4/2a
RS/A,B
P/2 S/2a,3a

These cards provide an opportunity for the children to apply the knowledge and skills acquired in the previous discussion and activity.

All the children's sweet machine models and sweets can be displayed together to create a group sweet factory.

The shapes used in the machines should be discussed and the machines labelled. There should be oral and some written reporting about the shapes, their flat and curved faces, how they were stuck together, etc. These shapes should include the pyramid with its square base and triangular faces and the sphere with its curved surface.

Extension/ Problem solving

There are extension activities at the end of each of Cards 5 and 6. On Card 5, there are various ways that the children might combine four spheres into one sweet. For example,

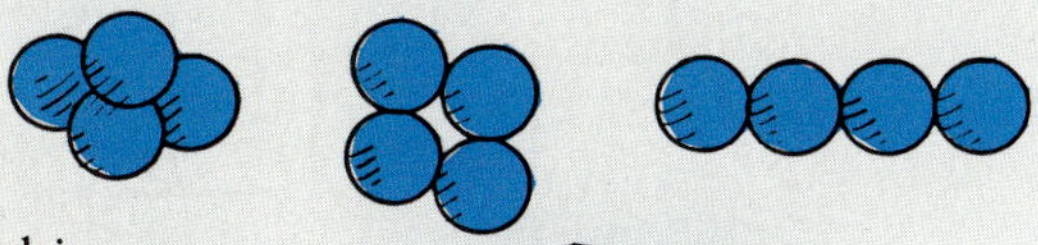

For Card 6 they should combine two cones of the same base size like this:

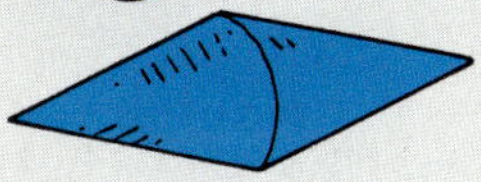

3D SHAPE NAMES AND PATTERNS
Introductory activities

Ma 1/2 4/2a 3/1a
RS/A,B PS/B
P/2 S/2a,3a A/1a

The children should have experience of model building and shape making activities such as those on Shape Cards 1 to 6 before they proceed to the next part of the work which relates to Workbook Pages 1 to 4. The early part of the workbook is concerned with recognition of 3D shapes, with knowing their names and with reading and writing these names. Here are two suggestions for practical preparatory work.

1 Lucky dip

Provide a bag containing a selection of 3D shapes. Each child takes a turn at feeling a shape in the bag, naming it and then withdrawing it for confirmation. The children should be encouraged to talk about the features of the shape which helped them to identify it – flat or curved faces. They should also be encouraged to name the shapes of faces.

2 Make a pattern

Ask each child in turn to place shapes in line according to a given pattern.

After practical activities like these the children can attempt Workbook Pages 1 to 4.

Ma 1/2 4/2a 3/1a
RS/A,B PS/B PSE
P/2 S/2a,3a A/1a

Problem solving

Workbook Pages 1 to 4 *3D shape names and pattern*

Supply empty cardboard boxes for holding the sweets referred to on Page 2.

These four pages continue the sweet factory theme introduced in Shape Cards 1 to 6. They provide a check-up on children's knowledge of the cuboid, cube, cylinder, cone, sphere and pyramid. The sweets referred to at the bottom of Page 2 may be shapes the children have made or they could be plastic or wooden ones.

On Page 4, the children should tick the correct name or colour the box for the name. It is important to verbalise such sequences to see what comes next, for example, red pyramid, yellow sphere, green cone, . . . red pyramid, yellow sphere, green cone, . . . *red pyramid* . . . In the last example the children could draw the next shape or describe it in words.

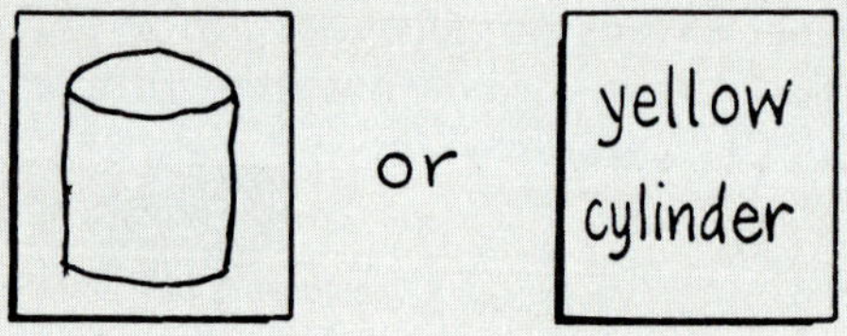

2D shape and pattern

Ma 1/2 4/2a 3/1a		
RS/A,B,D	PS/B	PSE
P/2	S/2a,3a	A/1a

Overview

This section

- involves recognising and naming squares, triangles, rectangles, circles
- provides work on pattern involving 2D shapes
- introduces pentagons and hexagons
- contains 2D shape problem solving and investigation.

Key words and phrases

square	circle	pentagon
rectangle	triangle	hexagon

Resources

Useful materials

- plastic squares, rectangles, triangles, circles, pentagons, hexagons
- coloured pencils

Assessment and Resources Pack

Assessment

Check-ups

Shape Check-up, Pages 2 and 3

Assessment in Context

'At the fair' context: Questions 6, 27, 28

'Treasure Island' context: Question 4

Resources

Contexts

'The street' and 'Islands' contexts contain many 2D shape and pattern examples.

Problem Solving Activities

2 Shape Puzzles

Resource Cards

Resource Cards 24 and *25* (Shape jig-saws)

Teaching notes

2D SHAPE NAMES AND PATTERNS
Introductory activities

Ma 1/2 4/2a 3/1a
RS/A PS/B
P/2 S/2a,3a A/1a

This section revises the shapes introduced in Heinemann Mathematics 1 – squares, rectangles, circles and triangles.

1 Sort them out

Provide the children with a selection of 2D shapes (circles, squares, rectangles and triangles) and a labelled sorting tray or large sheet of paper with four labelled areas.

Ask each child in turn to pick a shape and place it in the correct section. This activity relates to Workbook Page 5.

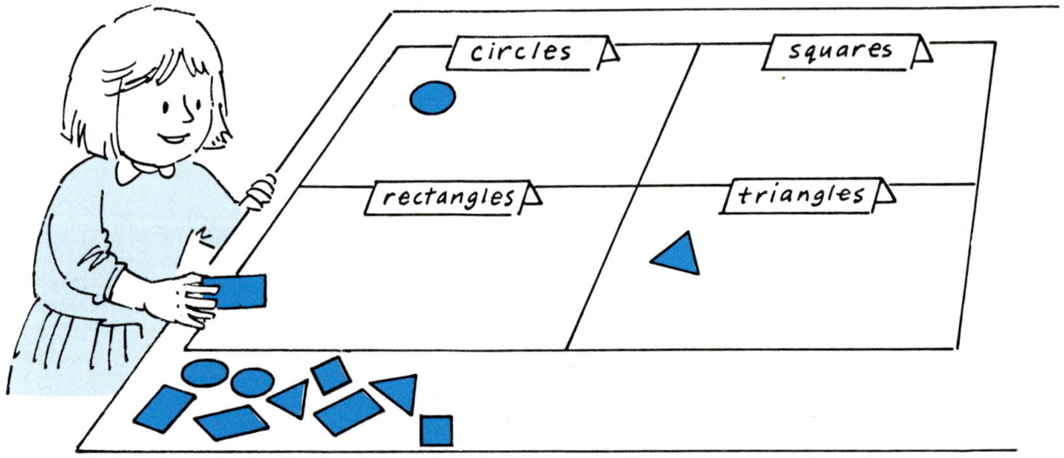

The shapes might then be sorted in other ways, for example,

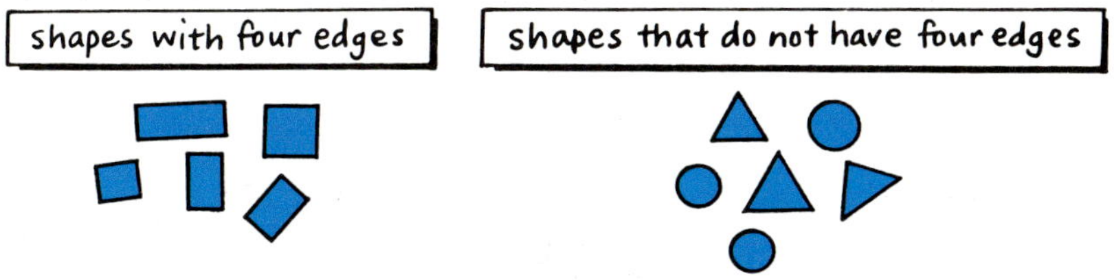

or

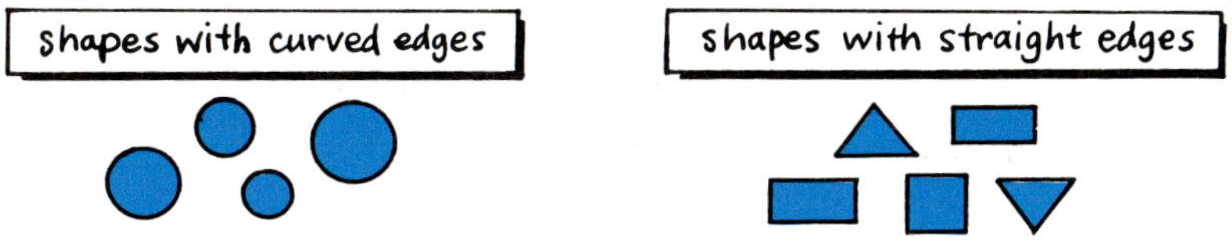

The children should choose criteria for sorting and then describe their work.

2 Snake pattern

Provide a large paper snake and ask a child to make a pattern of shapes along its length by placing shapes in a given sequence, for example, 'circle, triangle, triangle, . . . , circle, triangle, triangle, circle, . . . and so on.

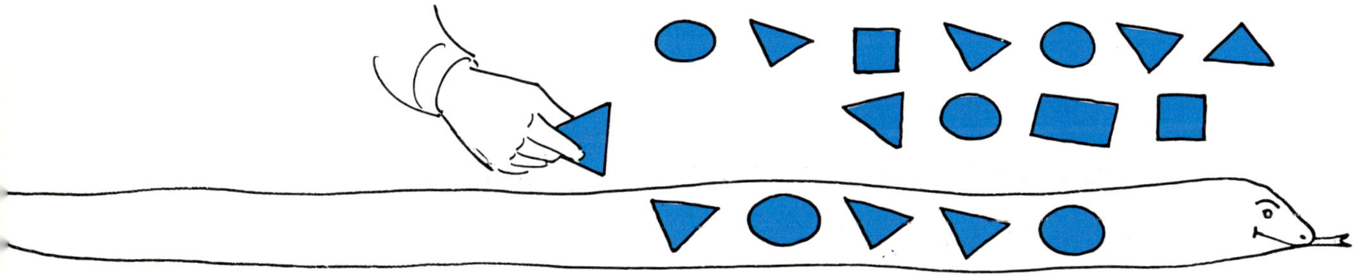

Repeat for other sequences.

3 Patch the clown

Provide the children with a poster-size outline of a clown. Ask them to draw or stick on the following patches:

3 more circles
4 more triangles
2 more squares
3 more rectangles.

They can then record how many shapes there are on the clown:

'There are ☐ circles
☐ triangles
☐ squares
☐ rectangles.'

Workbook Pages 5 and 6 *2D shape names and patterns*

Ma 1/2 4/2a
RS/A PS/B
P/2 S/2a,3a

These pages give practice in naming 2D shapes and in the kind of pattern work described above.

Extension

The extension activity at the foot of Page 6 requires children to make a paper caterpillar and draw their own pattern along its length. The shapes in the pattern could be coloured and the finished caterpillars used for a wall display.

2D SHAPES: PENTAGONS AND HEXAGONS
Introductory activities

Ma 4/2a
RS/A,D
S/2a,3a

1 Introducing the pentagon
Show the children a variety of card pentagons and ask them to count the five straight edges that each shape has.

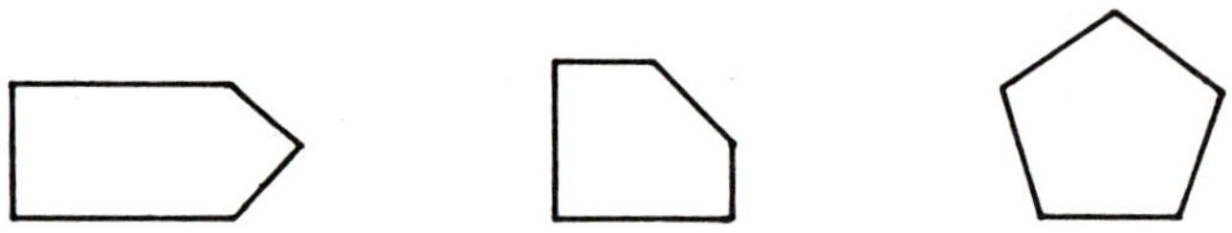

Pictures of objects in the environment can also be used.

Introduce the written word:

2 Find the pentagon
Card pentagons mixed with other shapes can be used to give the children practice in identifying and naming the new shape. A wall chart could also be used for this purpose. The children should count the five edges of each pentagon.

3 'I saw a pentagon'
Encourage children to look for pentagon shapes in the environment. This shape is not as commonly seen as the hexagon but there are plenty of house gables which are pentagonal in shape.

4 Drawing pentagons
Ask the children to draw some pentagons and to write the name.

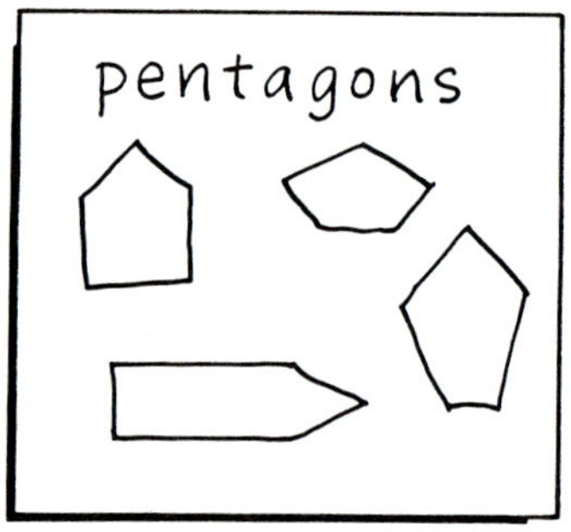

5 Introducing the hexagon

Activities similar to those described above should be carried out to familiarise children with the six-sided shape, the hexagon. This shape is more often seen in the environment, for example, biscuit tin lids, honey comb cells, hexagonal nuts and bolt heads, paving stones.

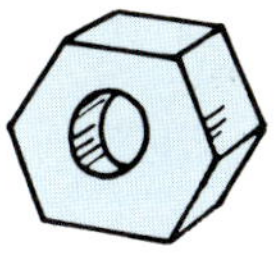

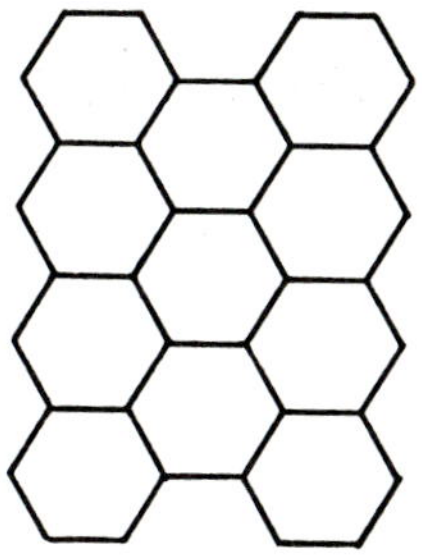

Ma 4/2a
RS/D
S/2a,3a

Workbook Pages 7 and 8 *2D shapes: pentagons and hexagons*

These pages provide practice in recognising pentagons and hexagons. Most children will do this by counting the number of edges. When the colouring on Page 8 is completed the pentagons form the letter 'P' and the hexagons the letter 'H'.

2D SHAPE
Additional activities

1 Three of a kind game *(for a group of 12 children)*

Ma 1/2a 4/2a
RS/A,B,D PSE
P/2 S/2a,3a

Twelve cardboard shapes are required: 3 squares, 3 triangles, 3 pentagons and 3 hexagons. Mix the shapes and give one to each child. Each child has to find the two other children in the group with the same shape. The first trio to form is the winning trio.

2 Shape snap game *(for 2 or 3 players)*

A set of cards is required, containing four each of the following shapes: triangle, square, rectangle, pentagon and hexagon.

The game is played according to the usual rules for 'Snap'.

3 Snap again *(for 2 players)*

Provide a set of red shape cards

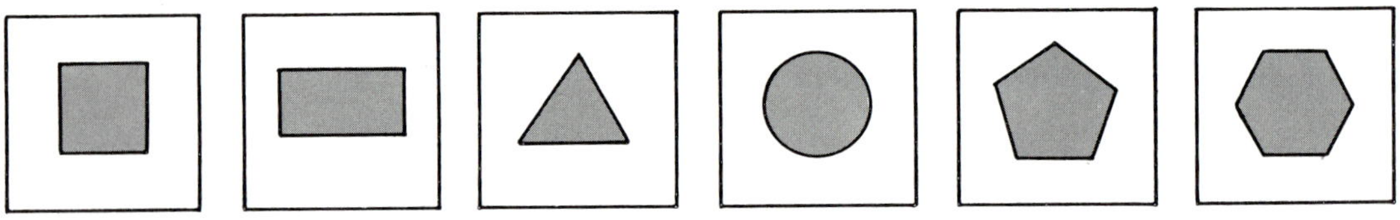

and a set of blue name cards.

One child starts with the red cards and the other with the blue cards. The usual 'Snap' rules apply.

Assessment and Resources Pack

4 Resource cards

Resource Cards 24 and 25 from the *Assessment and Resources Pack* give further experience of 2D shapes. They can be used by individual children or perhaps by two children in co-operation.

Ma 1/2 4/2a
RS/A,D PSE
P/2 S/2a,3a

Problem solving

Workbook Page 9 *Problem solving*

This page involves recognition of 2D shapes. The child has to visualise the placement of a shape in a hole so that the colour design is completed correctly. For example, the blue triangle can only go in the top left position and not in the bottom left position as there it would have to be partly blue and partly yellow.

Ma 1/2 4/2a
RS/B,D PSE
P/2 S/2a,3a

Investigation

Workbook Page 10 *Investigation*

This page also involves knowledge of 2D shapes. Possible solutions are

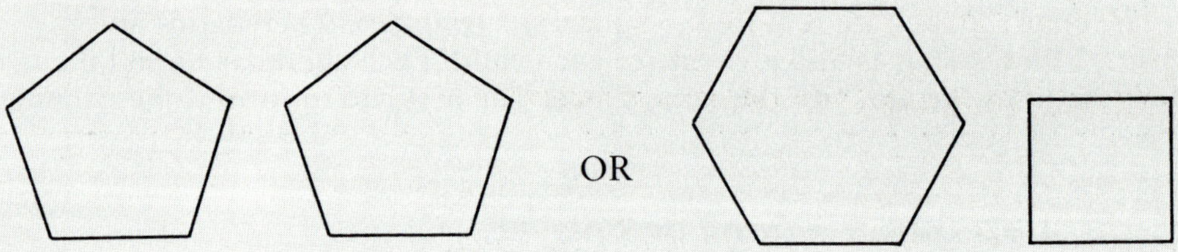

Right angles

Overview

This section introduces the right angle and right-angle turns.

	Teacher's Notes	Shape Workbook
Right angles	134	11, 12
Turning through right angles	135	13, 14
Extension		*14*

Key words and phrases

right angle	forward	back	start
turn left	turn right	finish	

Resources

Useful materials

- small card 'turtle' with direction arrow
- coloured pencils
- 2D and 3D shapes

Assessment and Resources Pack

Assessment

Check-ups

Shape Check-up, Page 3

Assessment in Context

'Treasure Island' context: Questions 18, 23

Resources

Contexts

'The street' and 'Islands' contexts contain one or two activities about turning through right angles.

Resource Cards

Resource Cards 26 to 28 (Find the gold)

Teaching notes

RIGHT ANGLES
Introductory activities

Ma 4/2a
A/B
S/3b

1 Spotting right angles

- Discuss right angles or 'square corners' with the children. Establish that a square has four square corners or right angles and so has a rectangle.

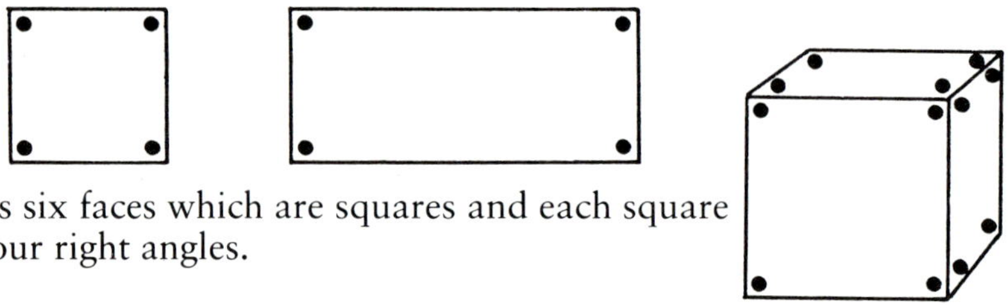

A cube has six faces which are squares and each square face has four right angles.

- The corners of the classroom windows and doors are normally right angles. Ask the children to spot other right angles in the room such as the corners of the chalk-board or a wall picture. They can also look for right angles in the world outside, for example, in bricks, paving slabs, etc.
- Other shapes may have right angles too, for example, triangles, pentagons and hexagons. Sometimes the right angle may be less obvious until the shape is turned round, for example in the triangle on the right.

2 Right angle tester

Show the children how to use a corner of a sheet of paper as a right angle tester.

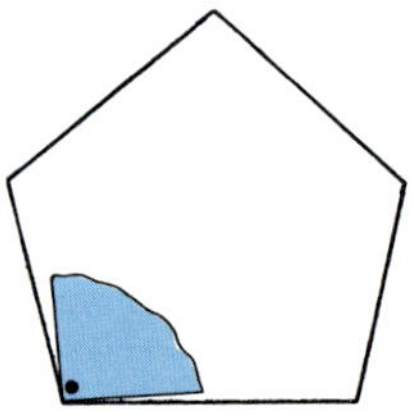

The children can then sort through a set of shapes to find their right angles, checking with the tester when necessary and then marking the right angles with a coloured blob.

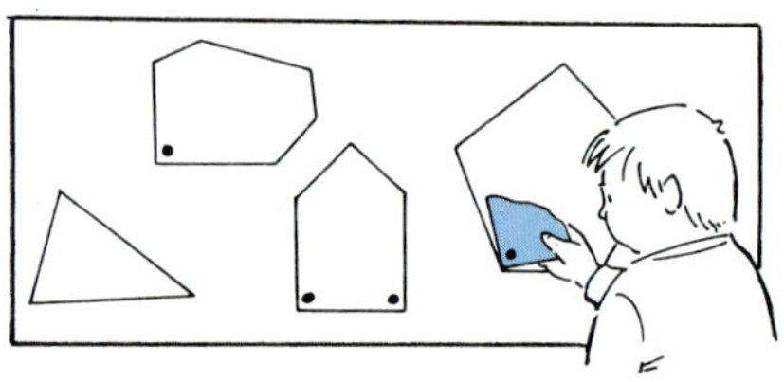

3 3D shapes

The right-angled corners of the faces of cubes and cuboids can be tested in a similar way. For example, ask the children to use a cereal box and mark the right angles with sticky circles after testing. Discuss the 6 faces which are rectangles. Each rectangle has four right angles.

Workbook Pages 11 and 12 *Right angles*

These pages give children further practice in spotting right angles. In cases of doubt a right-angle tester, as described above, could be used. The picture with its frame has 14 right angles and the shapes on Page 12 have 18 right angles altogether. The children are not likely to spot all of these.

Ma 4/2a
A/B
S/3b

TURNING THROUGH RIGHT ANGLES
Introductory activities

Ma 4/2b
PM/A,B
S/2c

The next section deals with turning through right angles and also involves moving forward and back. This work is related to the sort of activities which are often carried out using a floor turtle under the control of a microcomputer using LOGO. The instructions 'turn left' and 'turn right' are used here to denote *right*-angle turns which in a LOGO implementation would be 'LEFT 90' and 'RIGHT 90'.

1 Left and right

Discuss with a group of children who is to the right and who is to the left, of each child. Get them to practise turning 'left' and 'right' (through a right angle) at your instruction. The children might think of this as playing at soldiers.

Use a large space, perhaps with floor tiles or a grid marked in chalk, to allow the children to practise moving to instructions. For example,

'Forward 2.
Turn left.
Forward 3.
Back 1.
. . . and so on'.

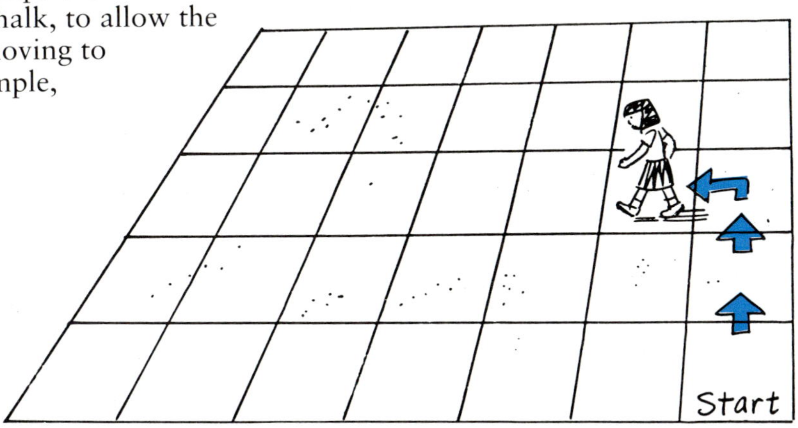

It is important that the children realise that when they 'turn left' they do not move forward or back until the next instruction.

2 Move the turtle

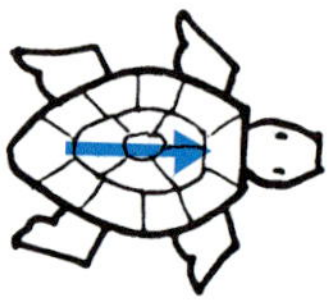

Prepare a grid on a large sheet of paper or the chalkboard. Use a turtle made from green card or another small object to move across the grid.
Instructions about moving forward and back and turning left or right can now be given which the children have to follow by moving the turtle. A piece of chalk used as a turtle has the advantage of leaving a trail. 'Forward' must be understood to mean 'in the direction the turtle is facing'.

The use of LOGO and a floor turtle would, of course, be a good way of doing work of this kind.

3 Find a way

Draw objects on a wall grid to represent houses, trees, animals, etc. Ask a child to describe the moves required to go say from the tree to the horse (forward 2, turn left, forward 1).

Ask another child to describe *different* moves to go from the tree to the horse (for example, turn left, forward 1, turn right, forward 2) and so on.

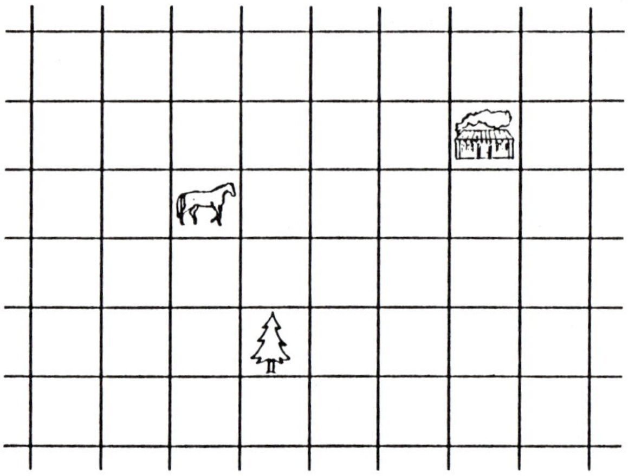

Ma 4/2b
PM/A,B
S/2c

Workbook Pages 13 and 14 *Right-angle turns*

In spite of having done the activities discussed in the foregoing notes, children may find this page difficult. To help them succeed with the page the following suggestions are made.

- Give each child a small card square or counter with an arrow marked on it. The child can use this to move across the page.

- Discuss the scenario with the child, pointing out the various land marks – house, well, pond, etc.
- Talk through one of the journeys with them as they use their card arrow. Check their moves step by step until you are satisfied that they understand how to follow the instructions for the journey between the red start and finish stones.
- Finally, ask them to try the other journeys.

Transformations

Ma 4/2b

Overview

This section provides an introduction to ideas involving moving along, turning round and flipping over 2D shapes.

	Teacher's Notes	Shape Workbook
TRANSFORMATIONS **Moving along, turning round, flipping over**	138	15
Extension		*15*

Key words and phrases

moved along   turned round   flipped over

Resources

Useful materials

- envelopes, picture cards with blank backs

Assessment and Resources Pack

Resources

Problem Solving Activities

2 Shape puzzles

Resource Cards

Resource Cards 24 and *25* (Shape jigsaws).

Teaching notes

TRANSFORMATIONS
Introduction

Ma 4/2b
S/2d

This unit introduces recognition of three different types of movement:
moving along in a straight line (translation)
turning movement (rotation)
flip movement (reflection).
These transformations are described below.

1 Moving along

A flat object such as a workcard may be moved to another position *without flipping it over or turning it round*. For example, a card may be moved from the start position on the wall say to any of the other 3 positions shown. No turning round or flipping over of the card is involved.

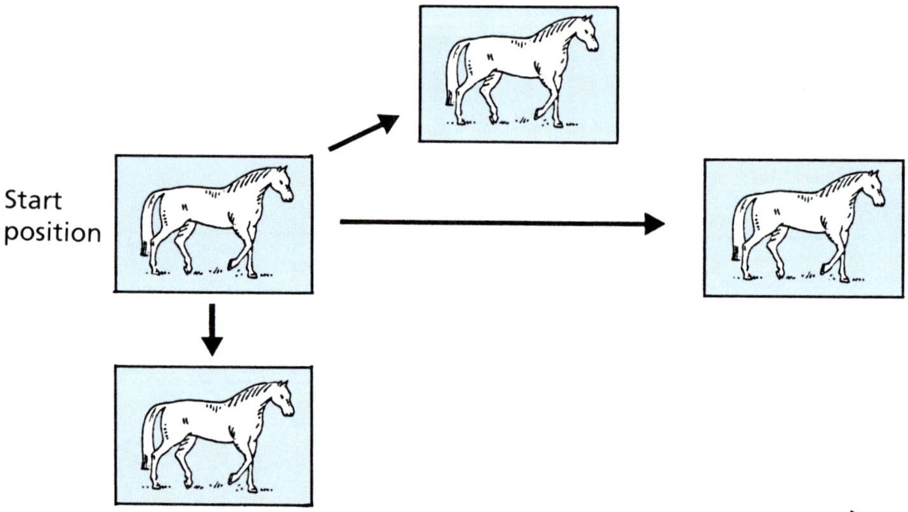

2 Turning round

The same card may be turned round or rotated to a new position as shown here. *It is not moved along or flipped over.*

The original start position is indicated by the dotted line.

3 Flipping over

This time the card is turned *over* so that it is in its original position but with the blank back showing instead of the front. *It is not moved along or turned round.*

Before flipping over

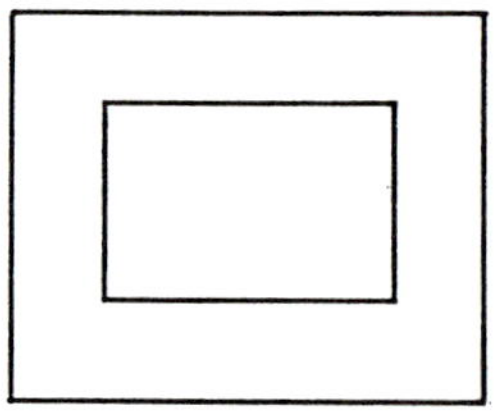

After flipping over

TRANSFORMATIONS
Introductory activities

Shape
Workbook

1 Moving, turning and flipping a picture card

Ma 4/2b
S/2d

Use a card with a picture on the front and a blank back. Ask the children to move it in a straight line along the wall or chalkboard from its starting position without turning it round or flipping it over. Discuss what has happened to the card.

Repeat for 'turning round' and 'flipping over' movements of the card.

Spend sufficient time on these activities until the children can distinguish between the movements and can demonstrate them using pictures or shapes. Some children, perhaps the more able, might then attempt Workbook Page 15.

Workbook Page 15 *2D shape: transformations*

Ma 4/2b
S/2d

Extension

The children might work in pairs or as a small group using a real envelope with a stamp and address to help them understand the movements illustrated.

Anita has moved the envelope along, Jill has turned it round and Tom has flipped it over.

Handling data
Workbook

Ma 1/2 4/2a 5/1a,2a
C/A,B O/A,B D/A,B I/B

Handling data Workbook

Overview

This section

- presents data in pictorial form to be organised in a table and then displayed as a simple block graph
- extends work on simple relationships and mapping diagrams
- presents tasks where information has to be collected, tabulated, displayed and then interpreted
- discusses ideas of events which are impossible, certain or uncertain to happen.

		Teacher's Notes	Handling data Workbook
BLOCK GRAPHS	**Drawing graphs from given data**	141	1, 2
	Drawing graphs from data which can be organised according to different criteria	142	3, 4
	Horizontal display	143	5, 6
RELATIONSHIPS	**Mapping diagrams**	144	7, 8
COLLECTING AND INTERPRETING DATA	**Data collection**		
	Organisation of data using tick charts	145	
	Frequency tables	148	9 to 13
	Displaying and interpreting data	149	
CARROLL DIAGRAMS	**Two-attribute sorting**	150	14
PROBABILITY	**Impossible, certain, uncertain**	152	15
	Extension		*5, 6, 10, 11*
	Problem solving		*11*
	Investigation		*9, 10*

Key words and phrases

block graphs	impossible	uncertain
is coloured	certain	bingo

Resources

Useful materials

- squared paper
- coloured pencils
- selection of 2D and 3D shapes, cubes
- SPMG Infant Picture 9: The play park

Assessment and Resources Pack

Handling data
Workbook

Assessment

Check-ups

Check-up for the Handling data Workbook

Assessment in Context

'At the fair' context: Questions 9, 14, 23, 24
'Treasure Island' context: Questions 28, 29, 30

Resources

Contexts

'The street' and 'Islands' contexts have several activities related to handling data.

Problem Solving Activities

13 Fruit

Resource cards

The following cards contain pictures for attribute sorting:
Resource Cards 29 and *30* (Pets)
Resource Cards 31 and *32* (Pirates)

Teaching Notes

BLOCK GRAPHS
Introductory activities

Ma 1/2 5/2a			
C/A,B	O/A,B	D/A,B	I/B
P/2	D/2c		

Simple block graphs were introduced in Heinemann Mathematics 1, Workbook 4 (Pages 13 to 15). Ideas for collecting information and drawing graphs are given below.

1 Which party drink?

Ask the children which of three drinks is their choice for a party. The information could be collected either by a show of hands which are counted or by each child writing his/her choice on a piece of paper and then sorting the pieces into three piles. The choices are then entered into a table. For example,

Drink	How many?
orange	8
lemonade	6
coke	11

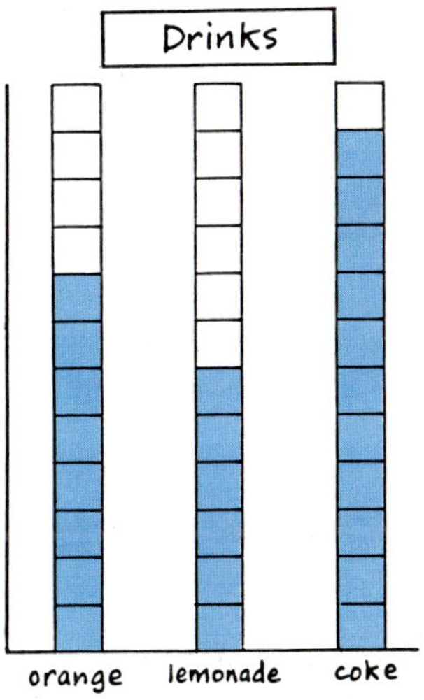

The data can then be displayed as a block graph drawn on squared paper. The blocks can either be coloured using pencil or paint or by using sticky squares of different colours.

Similar graphs could be drawn for other favourite choices:
kinds of crisps
sweets
party games

2 The playpark

Pictures, charts and posters can often be used as sources of data which can then be organised into three or four categories and represented graphically.

Using a picture like SPMG Infant Picture 9: The playpark, the children could count, for example, the numbers of children who are playing at the slide, the seesaw and the pool.

The data could then be displayed as a simple block graph.

	How many?
slide	9
see-saw	2
Pool	7

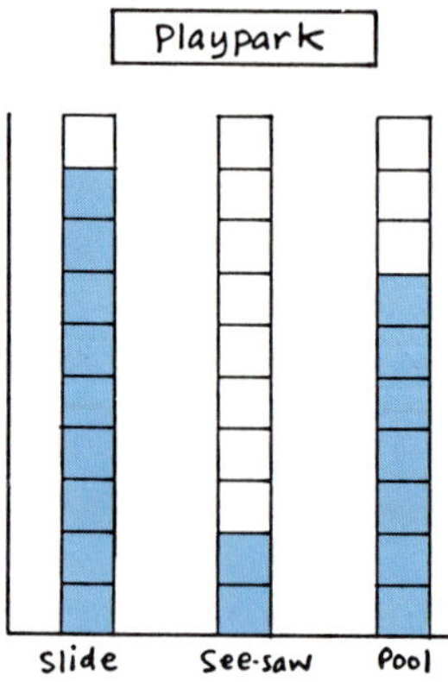

After actitivies like those above the children might attempt Pages 1 and 2 of the Handling data Workbook.

3 Birds

The children should also have the opportunity of choosing different criteria for organising the same data.

Give each child a square of paper or card. Ask the child to draw a bird with either a *long* beak or a *short* beak and then colour it blue, green or red.

The collection of birds can then be sorted into sets according to the criteria chosen by the children. Two graphs can now be drawn.

blue	5
green	7
red	4

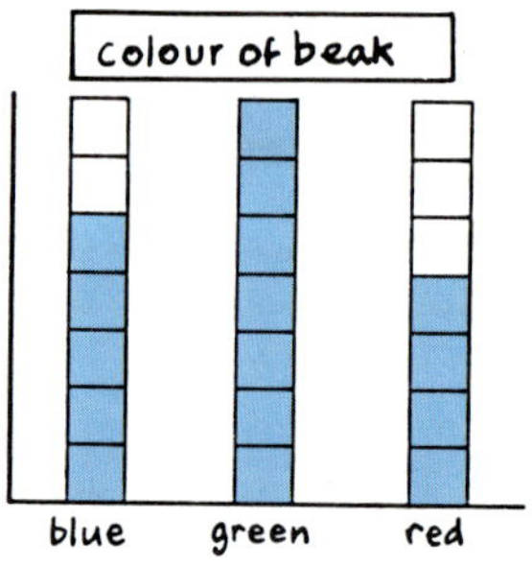

long beaks	9
short beaks	7

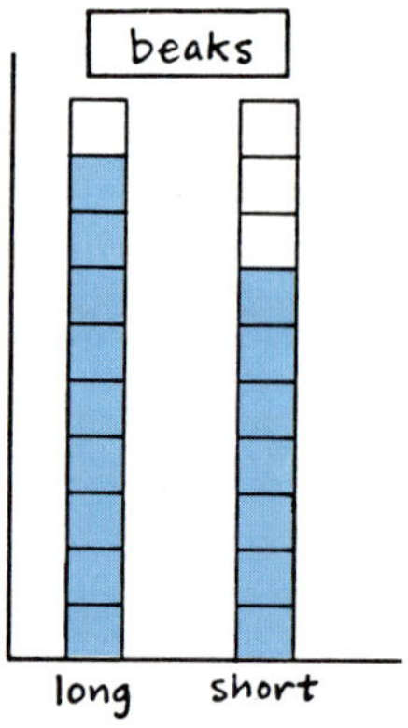

This type of activity is associated with Pages 3 and 4 of the Handling data Workbook where the children choose their own criteria.

4 My monster

The children should also have experience of horizontal block graphs. The activity below can also be used to provide opportunities to choose criteria for organising the data.

On a square piece of paper or card, each child in the class draws a monster with

- 1 eye or 2 eyes or 3 eyes
- 2 legs or 4 legs
- squares or triangles or circles.

The collection of monster pictures can then be sorted into sets, counted and displayed in a graph. The children can choose how to classify the data and make up a table. For example:

1 eye	7
2 eyes	2
3 eyes	8

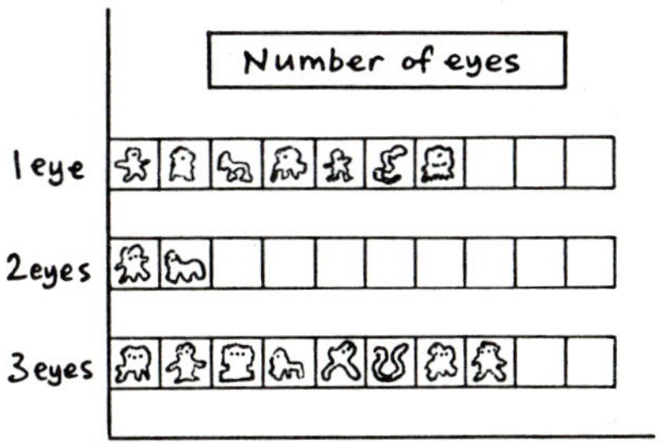

Other criteria for sorting are monsters with 2 or 4 legs
or monsters with circles or squares or triangles.

This activity is a useful preparation for Workbook Page 6 where a horizontal display is involved.

Workbook Pages 1 and 2 *Constructing a block graph*

Ma 5/2a
O/A,B C/B D/B
D/2c

From the picture of an obstacle course on Page 1 the children count the three types of obstacles and enter data in the table provided on Page 2. They may find it helpful to tick each item in the drawing as it is counted. The children then colour a number of squares on the graph to match the number of cones, sticks and balls.

Workbook Pages 3 and 4 *Choosing criteria Classifying/recording/processing data*

Ma 5/2a
O/A,B C/B D/B
D/2a

From the picture of birds on Page 3 the children, after inspection and discussion, sort the picture contents into three sets of their own **choice**.
Possible choices are

- birds in air (flying), birds on land, birds on water
- swans, ducks, hens

The table on Page 4 can then be completed, the graph coloured, and an appropriate title inserted. The discussion which follows should include how the birds were sorted and which category had most/least, etc.

Workbook Pages 5 and 6 *Recording/displaying data*

Ma 4/2a 5/2a
D/A,B C/B O/B I/B
S/2a,3a D/2a

Extension

This is extension work which not all pupils should attempt. The children should identify the shapes in the drawing of 'Big Eyes' on Page 5. They may find it helpful to label each shape, for example,

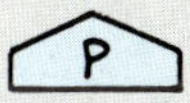

for pentagon, 

for triangle, and so on

or to tick each shape as it is counted.
There are 4 triangles, 3 rectangles, 5 pentagons and 4 hexagons in 'Big Eyes'.

Once the data has been entered in the table on Page 6, it is represented by colouring the horizontal display. The children are then asked to write something about their graph.

RELATIONSHIPS
Introductory activities

Ma 5/1a
D/B
D/1c

This section consolidates and extends work on simple relationships and mapping diagrams first introduced in Heinemann Mathematics 1, Workbook 4.

1 Snacks

Ask four children to show what they have brought for today's snack. Using a prepared diagram, ask individual children to draw lines to show what, for example, Jack has brought. Repeat for the other three children.

The opposite process can be used where a diagram like the one below is used as a set of instructions to distribute prepared items to children.
'What did Tom bring?' and so on.

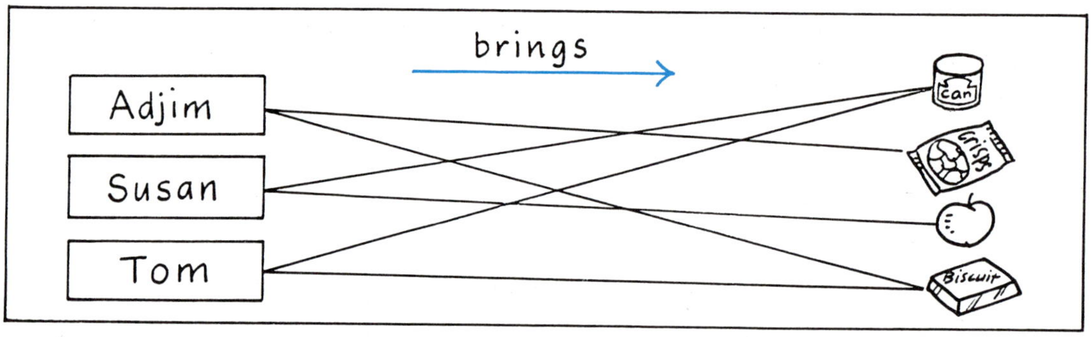

2 At the party

This activity involves coloured balloons and hats. Use a diagram like the one below and ask each of the three children to choose a hat and a balloon, from a prepared box, to match what the diagram shows.

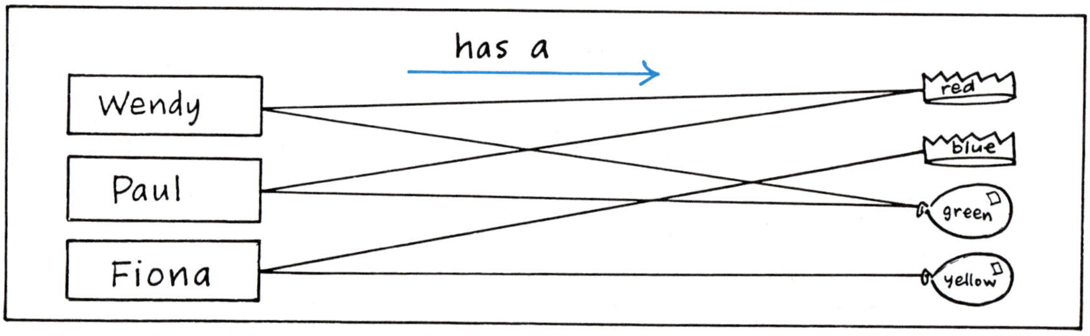

The other children should check that each has chosen correctly.

Handling data
Workbook

Ma 5/1a
D/B
D/1c

Workbook Pages 7 and 8 *Relationships*

Discuss the double page picnic scene to ensure that the children know that Kay, Sam, Lyn and Amir are at the picnic and that each has brought some of the four items – a roll, a can of orange, an apple and crisps. The children then complete the mapping diagram on Page 7 by drawing lines.

The children then have to colour the shirts as shown in the mapping diagram on Page 8. Some of the shirts have two colours which the children can show in different ways, for example

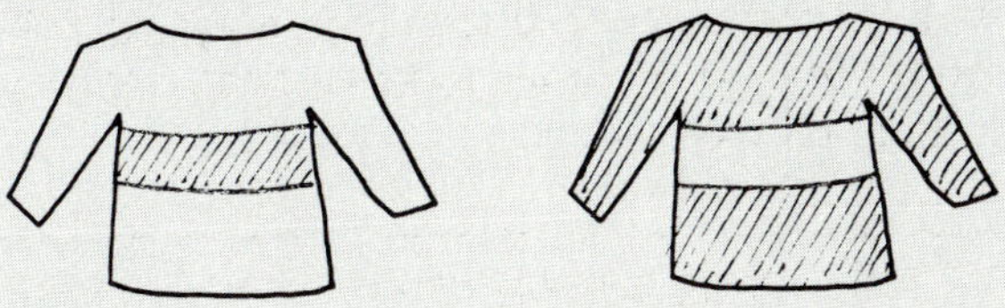

There are different possible correct colourings for Kay, Sam and Amir.

COLLECTING AND INTERPRETING DATA
Introductory activities

Ma 5/2a			
C/B	O/B	D/B	I/B
D/2c			

The activities in this section of the work give the children the opportunity to collect and organise data from a variety of first-hand and secondary sources, for example, the children themselves, everyday objects in the children's immediate environment and pictures. Some suggestions for introducing the ideas are given below.

As children become familiar with the techniques of gathering data using tick charts, etc., they should be encouraged to discuss the format of collection sheets and eventually design their own.

1 Who am I?

Ask the children to paint a picture of themselves and then tell a story about it.

Flashcards can be made for each of the attributes, for example, blue eyes | brown hair | red jumper

Pictures and flashcards can then be displayed.

Encourage the children to talk about the pictures and interpret them by trying to guess who each picture shows.

2 Jumpers

Ask the children to complete a prepared sheet about the jumper they are wearing. For example,

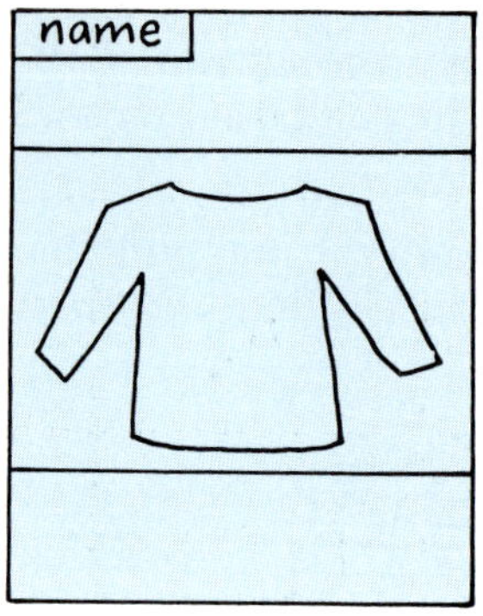

Each child could

- put his/her name in the top box
- colour the jumper to match the one he/she is wearing
- ✓ the bottom box if the jumper has stripes
- ✗ the bottom box if it does not have stripes.

These sheets could then be collected and displayed as a wall chart.

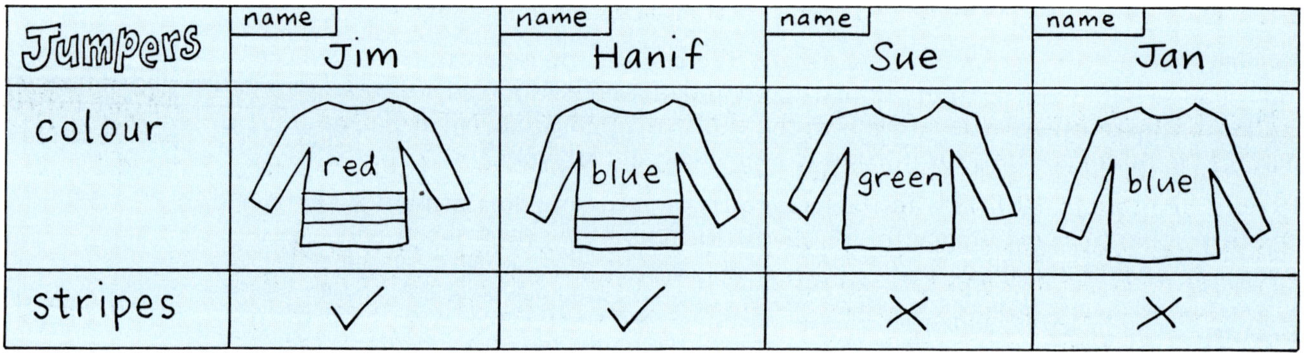

It is important that the children discuss their findings with each other and with the teacher.

For example,
 'Who wears a blue jumper?'
 'Who wears a green jumper?'
 'Who wears a red jumper with stripes?'
 'Who wears a blue jumper without stripes?'
 'How many people have a jumper with stripes?' . . . and so on.

Often the responses to questions such as these may be given orally. However, on occasions the teacher may wish to record the responses on card and display them beside the chart.
At times the teacher may wish the children to record some of the responses themselves.

Shoes with or without laces can be used instead of jumpers.

3 Do you like?

Ask a group of children to find out how many people like ice-cream and/or jelly or any other suitable food items.

One important feature of this task is that it asks the children to collect the information from other children and to record the information as they go.

The children record their classmates' responses to each question by drawing a 'smiling' face or a cross.

It is important that the children discuss their findings with each other and with the teacher. For example,

'How many people like ice-cream?'
'How many do not like ice-cream?'
'How many like jelly?'
'Who does not like jelly?'
'Who likes ice-cream but does not like jelly?'

Answers may be given orally or recorded on cards displayed beside the wallchart.

Workbook Pages 9 and 10 *Collecting and interpreting data*

Ma 5/2a
C/B O/B D/B I/B
D/2c

Before the children tackle the activities on these pages it is essential that they have completed some of the introductory activities.

Investigation

On Pages 9 and 10, the children are collecting information about the colour of eyes, hair, shoes and socks for a group of up to eight children. The information is recorded by **colouring** in pictures in the workbook. Before the children start this activity it is important that they talk to each other and to the teacher about the nature of the task. Again, discussion is essential before the children tackle the written questions about interpreting the information.

Investigation/Extension

At the bottom of Page 10 the children are asked to find out about the colour of schoolbags in the class. The children should be encouraged to devise a chart on which to collect the information and to discuss their findings once the chart is completed.

ADDITIONAL ACTIVITIES
Collecting and interpreting data

Ma 5/2a
C/B O/B D/B I/B
D/2c

With each activity, it is essential that the children discuss their findings with each other and with the teacher. Some children should be encouraged to design their own data collection sheets.

1 Resource cards

Assessment and Resources Pack

The pirates on *Resource Cards 31* and *32* of the *Assessment and Resources Pack* can be used to provide another source from which to collect and record information. For example, they can find out which pirates have hats and/or parrots.

2 Ourselves

A number of activities related to the children and their immediate environment can be explored.

Our lunchboxes

Find out about the size and colour of lunch boxes in the class.

Games we play

Find out about favourite playground games.

Where we live

Find out about where people in the class live.

INTERPRETING DATA AND FREQUENCY TABLES
Introductory activities

Ma 5/2a
C/B O/B I/B
D/2c

Ideally the activities suggested below should be tackled by pairs of children and their results discussed by larger groups.

1 Counters

Provide a bag containing an assortment of coloured counters (about twenty) and a cardboard recording sheet for each child. For example,

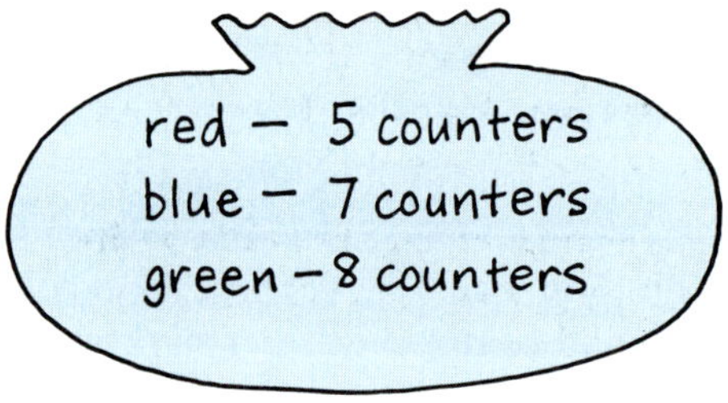

counters

red		
blue		
green		

Ask two children to take it in turns to remove a counter from the bag and to place it on the record sheet.

Once all of the counters have been removed from the bag the children can record how many of each colour they have. For example,

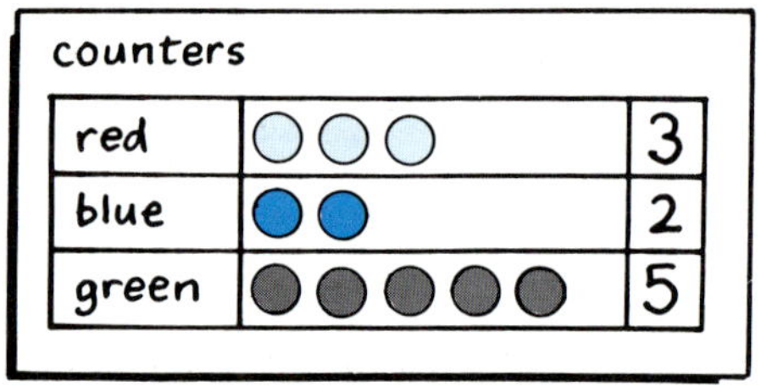

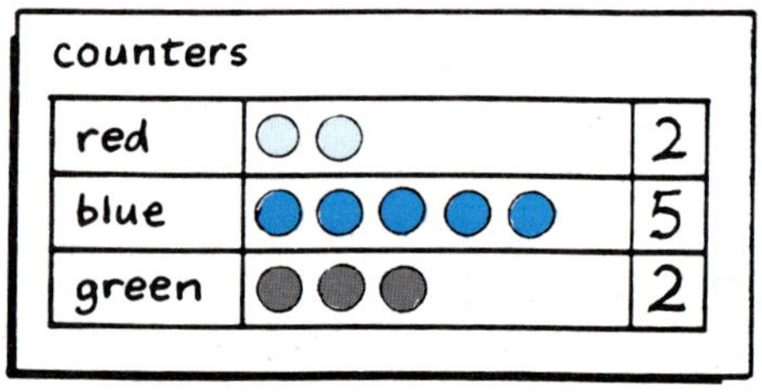

This activity could be repeated using a similar sheet to the one above but where the children place a tick (✓) on the sheet instead of the counter, for example,

shapes

red	✓✓✓	3
blue	✓✓	2
green	✓✓✓✓✓	5

This activity relates to Page 12 of the Handling data Workbook.

2 Shapes

Boxes of 2D or 3D shapes can be used in a similar way. A child takes out shapes one at a time and records on a tick chart or frequency chart.

shapes

cuboids	✓✓✓✓	
spheres	✓	
cylinders	✓✓✓✓✓✓✓	

Some children may be able to predict, before the box is empty, whether there are likely to be more cylinders than spheres in the bag. This activity relates to Handling data Workbook, Page 13.

Handling data
Workbook

Workbook Pages 11, 12 and 13 *Interpreting data* *Completing a frequency table*

On Page 11 the children are asked to interpret a graph showing the number of cubes picked out of a bag by two children.

At the foot of this page the children are shown the cubes that **one** of the children picked out of the bag and have to refer back to the graph to work out which cubes the other child picked. This is a difficult, problem solving activity.

The work on Pages 12 and 13 relates directly to the introductory activities. On both pages the children are selecting an object from a bag and using a tick sheet to record their findings. A graph is then drawn to show their results. For Page 12, prepare a bag containing, say, 8 red, 5 blue and 6 green cubes. For Page 13 the bag should contain, say, 6 cubes, 2 cones, 5 spheres, 4 pyramids.

Although there are no questions in the workbook it is important that the children discuss the results of their activities with each other and with the teacher.

Ma 5/2a
C/B O/B D/B I/B
D/2c

Extension/
Problem solving

FREQUENCY TABLES
Additional activities

For each activity, it is important to discuss the format of the recording sheet the children will use to collect the information and also their findings once the information has been organised and displayed.

Ma 5/2a
C/B O/B D/B I/B
D/2c

1 School Lunches

Ask the children to find out which type of lunch each child in the class is having today.

school lunches date ____________

home	✓✓✓	3
packed	✓✓✓✓✓	5
hot	✓✓✓✓	4
snack	✓✓✓✓✓✓✓✓	8

2 Pets

Ask the children to find out what the most popular pet in the class is. Each child should select only *one* pet.

3 Hobbies

Frequency tables can be used to collect information about the children's hobbies. Graphs can then be drawn to show the result of the survey.

Carroll diagrams

The Carroll diagram is named after Lewis Carroll of 'Alice in Wonderland' fame. The diagram is a special way of recording a sorting involving two attributes, for example, curly hair and glasses.

The Carroll diagram below shows the information about curly hair and glasses like this:

	curly hair	not curly hair
glasses	Tom	Shareen
no glasses	Paula Mary	Jack

CARROLL DIAGRAMS
Introductory activities

Ma 5/2a
D/B
D/2d

1 Sorting ourselves

Try to choose two attributes so that at least one child possesses both. Pick attributes appropriate for the group of children. These could be simply 'girls' and 'red hair'. Draw a blank Carroll diagram on the chalkboard or provide a wall chart suitably labelled and ask the children to say which names should go in each box. The result might be

	girl	not a girl
red hair	Maureen	Robert
not red hair	Jane Shani Alice	Jim Sam Winston

Repeat this discussion and activity by asking the children to suggest two different attributes belonging to members of the group.

As a variation on this activity, chalk a large Carroll diagram on the floor, complete with labels and ask the children to stand in the appropriate boxes on the diagram.

2 Sorting toys

Provide a four-compartment sorting tray (or large sheet of paper divided into four areas) and a selection of toy vehicles. Ask the children to choose two attributes and sort the toys accordingly. This might result in

3 Resource cards

Assessment and Resources Pack

A selection of the sixteen pirate pictures from *Resource Cards 31* and *32* in the *Assessment and Resources Pack* may be used. The children can choose any two attributes, for example, hats and hooks. Draw and label a blank Carroll diagram. Ask the children to discuss which pirate should be placed in each compartment on the diagram and to place the cards accordingly. For the six cards Jake, Tom, Ben, Jim, Pug and Liz, the result would be

The children should be asked to explain *why* they put a pirate in a particular box.

This activity should be repeated for other selections of pirate cards and for different attributes.

Later, the children could write the names of the pirates in the appropriate boxes on the diagram. When the teacher feels that they have had sufficient practice the children could try Workbook Page 14.

Workbook Page 14 *Carroll diagram*

Ma 5/2 a
D/B
D/2d

Assessment and Resources Pack

This page is related to the activity about pirates described in Activity 3 above. It provides a check-up on children's understanding of Carroll diagrams. Again, children should be asked to explain why a pirate has been included in a particular section of the diagram. Other pirates from *Resource Cards 31* and *32* can be used to extend the activity.

PROBABILITY
Introductory activities

Ma 5/2b
D/2ef

1 Certain, impossible and uncertain

Discuss events within the experience of the children and try to establish whether each event is certain, impossible or uncertain. The discussion should be kept at the fun level as far as possible and deal with events which might appeal to the interests of young children. The discussion might involve statements like the following where the children have to respond by saying one of the words 'certain', 'uncertain' or 'impossible':

'Tom will be a boy tomorrow.' (certain)
'Jean will be an old lady tomorrow.' (impossible)
'Mary will wear her wellies tomorrow.' (uncertain)
'Jim's dog will read him a bed-time story tonight.' (impossible)
'Paul will be absent from school next week.' (uncertain)
'The elephant at the zoo will learn to flap its ears and fly.' (impossible)

After sufficient discussion along these lines the children should be asked to complete Workbook Page 15.

Ma 5/2b
D/2ef

Workbook Page 15 *Probability*

The events on this page should be discussed as a group before one of the word 'boxes' for impossible, uncertain, or certain is ticked or coloured in. Only the second statement 'It will rain tomorrow' is intended to be uncertain.

Index